Qualitative Interpretation
Analysis in Psychology

Qualitative Interpretation and Analysis in Psychology

Carla Willig

 Open University Press

Open University Press
McGraw-Hill Education
McGraw-Hill House
Shoppenhangers Road
Maidenhead
Berkshire
England
SL6 2QL

email: enquiries@openup.co.uk
world wide web: www.openup.co.uk

and Two Penn Plaza, New York, NY 10121-2289, USA

First published 2012

A catalogue record of this book is available from the British Library

ISBN-13: 9780335241415 (pb)
ISBN-10: 0335241417
e-ISBN-13: 9780335241439

Library of Congress Cataloging-in-Publication Data
CIP data has been applied for

Typeset by Aptara Inc., India
Printed in the UK by Bell and Bain Ltd, Glasgow

Fictitious names of companies, products, people, characters and/or data that may be used herein (in case studies or in examples) are not intended to represent any real individual, company, product or event.

MIX
Paper from
responsible sources
FSC
www.fsc.org   FSC® C007785

The **McGraw·Hill** Companies

Praise for *Qualitative Interpretation and Analysis in Psychology* by Carla Willig

"This new book by Carla Willig closes a gap in qualitative research in psychology and beyond. It focuses on the process of understanding in qualitative data analysis by taking the perspective of interpretation: What links our understanding with social and psychological phenomena in qualitative research? With its broad coverage of the literature and its clear style of writing it will be most helpful for anyone applying qualitative research to psychological phenomena."

Uwe Flick, Alice Salomon University, Berlin and Vienna Universities

"In this work Carla Willig takes on one of the most pressing challenges in qualitative inquiry: how are we to confront multiplicity in interpretation? I began reading with great curiosity; I came away feeling that this is the best treatment of this complex subject I have yet encountered. Combining conceptual sophistication, the skill of clarity, and a welcome sense of balance, Willig illuminates and enriches. Her discussion on the ethics of interpretation sets the book apart. Now I clamor to join the discussions demanded by this fascinating work."

Kenneth Gergen, Senior Research Professor, Swarthmore College, USA

"Carla Willig's balanced and insightful text goes to the heart of what is stake in debates over qualitative analysis: the act of interpretation itself. Beginning with the idea that the researcher must recognise both the responsibility and privilege of research, Willig clearly demonstrates how interpretation is actually performed and how to negotiate the epistemological and practical issues that are involved. Opposing the tendency for the researcher to disappear in the act of 'doing analysis', this book offers a distinctively human and affective vision of interpretative work. There is much here for both dedicated qualitative researchers and curious empiricists of every stripe. Students of psychology, read on: you have nothing to lose but your prejudices."

Steven Brown, Professor of Social and Organisational Psychology,
University of Leicester, UK

"At last! This is the book that qualitative researchers in psychology have required for some time, and it fills a significant gap for the field. Willig provides a brilliantly written comprehensive account of the importance and value of interpretation in qualitative research, covering theory, ethics and debate around interpretation, and including detailed practical applications that reveal the complexities and complications involved in interpretative analytic work. This text exposes the necessity of reaching for interpretation in qualitative data analysis, and is essential reading for qualitative researchers, whatever their level of expertise, both within and beyond psychology."

Kerry Chamberlain, Professor of Social and Health Psychology,
Massey University, New Zealand

Contents

Boxes and interview extracts

Acknowledgements

Writing this book has been an enjoyable and stimulating experience. This is in no small part due to many interesting and thought-provoking conversations with friends and colleagues about what it means to make meaning. I have also benefited enormously from supervising research students on the doctorate programme in Counselling Psychology at City University London whose creative engagement with their qualitative data has been inspiring. Perhaps most importantly, therapeutic encounters with clients over the last ten years have led me to grapple with the challenge of making meaning and to decide to work through my relationship with interpretation (a work still very much in progress!). There are, therefore, many people who have had a profound impact on my thinking and whose contribution to the reflections presented in this book I want to acknowledge here. As always, it is impossible to identify all of them by name, and there are also those whose identity needs to be protected in the interest of confidentiality.

Having said this, I do want to take this opportunity to thank a number of individuals for the support, encouragement, and inspiration they have provided without which writing this book would not have been as enjoyable as it has been. It is also likely that the finished product would have been weaker as a result although, of course, I take full responsibility for my interpretation of the ideas presented here.

First, I would like to acknowledge Pete Green whose lively interest in my engagement with all things interpretative has been a great help, and who drew my attention to the importance of translation as a form of interpretation. Thanks also to Pete for the use of his extensive library, which allowed me to read widely and well beyond the disciplines of psychology and qualitative research methodology. It meant that writing the book never turned into a predictable chore – a 'job to be done' – instead remaining a journey of discovery throughout. Clinical supervision sessions with Ernesto Spinelli helped me to think through the implications of looking at the world in different ways, and never to forget that there are always more ways of looking at experience than I could ever imagine. Thanks also to members of the 'Being and Nothingness' Reading Group (Angela Frampton, Malcolm Freeman, John Joyce, Ryan Kemp, Cyrus Moola, Clare Morgan, and Jonathan Smith) for making it possible to continue a conversation for $2\frac{1}{2}$ years and not get bored with it, and for putting interpretation into practice in a way that was both enjoyable and stimulating.

I want to acknowledge the importance of my conversations with Susan Strauss, whose ability to practise a hermeneutics of empathy is inspiring, and Sue Berger, who has shown me that it is possible to combine a commitment to theory with the ability to fully respect alternative realities. I would like also to thank Cristina

Boserman and David Harper for many stimulating and intriguing conversations about the meaning of experience.

I was very lucky to have had the support and encouragement of Jacqui Farrants, Head of the Department of Psychology at City University while I was working on this book. I could not have wished for a more supportive manager.

Thanks also to Monika Lee who, as editor at McGraw-Hill, supported this book project from the start. Monika's confidence in me and her commitment to this project have been much appreciated.

I am also grateful to my research assistant Margarita Bojtschuk for her extensive literature searches and transcription work.

I am indebted to Stephen Frosh, Chris Griffin, and Jonathan Smith for accepting my invitation to talk to me about their views on interpretation and for allowing me to tape record and reproduce the conversations in the appendices to this book. The conversations were a valuable experience for me, enjoyable and inspiring, and I feel that I have learned an enormous amount from them.

I would like also to acknowledge the generosity of the research participants in the extreme sport study who shared their experiences with me and whose accounts provide data that are used to demonstrate qualitative interpretation in Part 2 of this book.

Finally, thank you Bertie and Freddy for allowing me to catch glimpses of the world through feline eyes and for reminding me that there are experiential realities far removed from my own.

Part 1

Theory and concepts: what is 'interpretation'?

1   Introduction

Vignette 1: Tango

Andrew and Marie are dancing a tango. The music has started but Andrew and Marie are not moving yet. Poised, they are waiting for the gentle opening sequence of the track to come to an end before they take their first steps. When they do, they move slowly, taking a step only on every fourth beat. Their embrace is close and Marie's head is resting on Andrew's shoulder. Around them, other couples are moving across the dance floor, some of them whirling past, marking every beat of the music with a step. Andrew and Marie are dancing in slow motion, as though they were drawing imaginary lines on the floor with their feet. Their dance expresses a certain languid dreaminess and it speaks to the violin arrangement of the music; in fact, it is as though they are dancing only to the violin and none of the other instruments. It seems as though they are in a world of their own, shared only with one another and the sound of the violin.

Vignette 2: Crime Detection

In 'The Blue Carbuncle', world-famous detective Sherlock Holmes demonstrates his skills of deduction by analysing the clues provided by a hat that had been left behind at the scene of a crime. The hat is an old, battered, black felt hat with red silk lining that has become rather discoloured. There is a piercing on the brim for a hat-securer (an elastic band used to keep the hat in place) but the elastic is now missing. The hat is cracked and dusty. Discoloured patches on it have been smeared with ink to disguise them. While his assistant Dr Watson fails to deduce anything of interest from the evidence presented by the hat, Holmes concludes that the owner must be someone who had been well-off but who has now fallen upon hard times (the hat is of very good quality but had not been replaced when the fashion changed several years ago), someone who had foresight and good sense but is now less fastidious (the hat-securer cannot be bought in shops so must have been specially ordered; however, it had not been replaced once it had broken), someone who although clearly having lost his former place in the world has not entirely lost self-respect (the discoloured patches on the hat have been covered up with ink), and someone whose wife has ceased to love him (the hat had not been brushed for weeks). In addition, grey hairs left inside the hat together with the smell of lime-cream and marks of moisture due to excessive perspiration lead Holmes to conclude that the hat's owner was middle-aged and not in good physical condition. Dr Watson is amazed at how much Holmes is able to deduce from what appears to be an ordinary old hat; however, he admits that Holmes' reasoning is entirely plausible and that the insights gained from it are valid.

Vignette 3: Psychotherapy

A psychotherapist-in-training is talking to her clinical supervisor about a client whose behaviour has changed recently. Previously always on time and very reliable, the client has now started to arrive late for most sessions and occasionally also misses sessions without giving notice. The psychotherapist-in-training is puzzled by this and is finding it difficult to decide how to respond to the client's behaviour. She has taken this dilemma to supervision in the hope of gaining some clarity and, ideally, to formulate a plan of action. Together, the trainee and the supervisor think about what the client's behaviour may mean and what the client may be trying to communicate by suddenly being unreliable. The supervisor asks the trainee whether the client might be testing her – might he be trying to find out whether she will still care for him, even when he is no longer 'the good client'? Is he trying to test their relationship – does he want to know whether it is strong enough to cope with him 'behaving badly'? The trainee says that this is possible. She also wonders whether the client's behaviour might be a response to her having cancelled a couple of sessions recently due to her being on jury service. Perhaps the client felt let down? Perhaps her absence reminded him that there are other sometimes more important things in her life than him? Perhaps he felt the need to ensure that he did not become too dependent on his therapy sessions and perhaps one way of doing so was to make them (appear) less important by being late for them and occasionally forgetting them altogether? The supervisor and the trainee agree that the trainee will check out what the lateness and the absences mean to the client as soon as the opportunity presents itself.

Vignette 4: Dating

Lou and Sam have been out for a meal followed by a few drinks in a bar. This was their first date and they have both enjoyed their evening together very much. Both of them are reluctant to end the evening and so they have stayed in the bar for a long time. It is getting late and neither of them is sure about how to, or indeed whether to, say goodbye. Having sat in front of their empty glasses for a while, the atmosphere is beginning to become somewhat tense. Finally, Sam suggests that they walk home together as both their flats are in the same part of town. Relieved, Lou agrees and the two set off, once more talking animatedly. When they are approaching the street where Lou lives, he decides to invite Sam in for a cup of coffee. Sam is pleased as this confirms that Lou is indeed interested in deepening their relationship; at the same time, though, Sam wonders whether the offer of a 'cup of coffee' is really an invitation to spend the night with Lou. Although Sam is attracted to Lou, he is not sure that he is ready to have sex with him. Sam is keen to avoid any misunderstandings at this stage of their relationship and so he decides to play it safe and de-cline the invitation to have coffee, suggesting instead that they meet again the next day.

The four vignettes presented above describe scenarios that are concerned with very different activities. Tango dancing, crime detection, psychotherapy, and dating re-quire different skills, they generate different emotions, and they involve different kinds of relationships. And yet, they all have something in common, something without which none of them could proceed, something that makes them mean-ingful and that gives them direction and purpose. This something is the act of interpretation.

Interpretation, in its most basic sense, refers to the construction of meaning. Interpretation is concerned with elucidation, explanation, and understanding. Interpretation is required to gain access to the meaning and significance of some-thing that presents itself – whether this is a piece of music, a client's behaviour, a lover's question, or a hat. Interpretation is what happens when we (try to) answer the question 'what does it mean?'.

Often we interpret without being aware of it. We give meaning to what happens around us so quickly and with so little conscious thought or deliberation that it appears as though there is no 'gap' between what presents itself and what we make of it. In such a situation, it is 'obvious' what something means and we are not aware of any alternative meanings. Andrew and Marie's response to the music in the tango vignette is an example of this. At other times, interpretation is a much more conscious activity. This happens when we are dealing with situations whose meaning is ambiguous or uncertain, where we need to actively work out what is going on. An extreme example of deliberate interpretation as a form of problem-solving is presented in the crime detection vignette. In general, deliberate interpretation takes place when we are motivated to understand what is going on (for example, when we want to know what something means so as to decide how to respond to it, as in the dating vignette) and when we are struggling to make sense of something (for example, when we are surprised by what is happening, as in the psychotherapy vignette). So while interpretation occurs all the time, it becomes an issue when we encounter a situation that is important to us but which we are not sure that we fully understand and whose meaning is uncertain. Interpretation, therefore, means looking for answers to questions we have about the situation.

This book is about deliberate interpretation. It is concerned with the process and outcome of interpretation in qualitative research in psychology where the phenomenon whose meaning we are uncertain about is our data. Interpretation is the challenge at the heart of qualitative research. Without interpretation, we cannot make sense of our data. This is because qualitative research itself is primarily concerned with meaning. Through qualitative research, we aim to better understand how people make sense of their experiences and what people's actions mean, both to themselves and to others (i.e. what they express, symbolize or communicate). We aim to find out more about the quality and texture of people's experiences and about how people do things, their social and psychological practices. To achieve these aims, the qualitative researcher needs to ask questions about the data and to make connections between different components and aspects of the data. And this means that the researcher is making meaning; or, to put it another way, is making the data meaningful and, therefore, adding meaning to the data. This book aims to provide guidance in relation to the conceptual, practical, and ethical dimensions of interpretative practice in qualitative psychology.

Overview of the book

The remainder of this chapter explores the notion of 'interpretation' in more detail. It provides some historical background to the practice of interpretation and it introduces different approaches to interpretation. The relationship between 'data analysis' and 'interpretation' is clarified and the relevance of interpretation to contemporary qualitative psychology is established. The chapter concludes with a discussion of some of the ethical challenges associated with interpretative activity.

Chapter 2 reviews the use of interpretation in qualitative psychology. The chapter reviews a range of orientations to the practice of interpretation, including psychoanalytic, phenomenological, and discursive orientations. It explores historical reasons behind the avoidance of the term 'interpretation' in qualitative research and reflects on qualitative psychologists' preference for describing their interpretative activities as 'data analysis'. The 'turn to interpretation' in recent years and the emergence of the 'psychosocial' approach to qualitative psychology are also introduced.

Chapter 3 returns to the topic of ethics in interpretation. It reflects on the social, political, and psychological consequences of interpretation for those whose experiences and actions are being interpreted. The chapter introduces the notion of 'interpretative violence' and what happens when meanings are imposed on people. This chapter is concerned with interpretative power and its potential and actual abuses. It raises questions about who 'owns' interpretations and who has the right to produce them and use them. It also discusses the role of ethical considerations in the evaluation of qualitative research.

Chapter 4 examines the relationship between language and interpretation. The chapter raises questions about the relationship between the process of meaning-making and the use of language. As such, it foregrounds the intimate connection between language and interpretation, and it examines their interdependence.

Chapters 5, 6, 7, and 8 are concerned with the application of the ideas and concepts introduced in Chapters 1–4. Chapter 5 introduces a dataset that will be interpreted in three different ways in Chapters 6, 7, and 8 respectively. The aim of these chapters is to demonstrate how the same interview extracts can be read in quite different ways when different interpretative perspectives are adopted. These chapters are also concerned with the theoretical, ethical, and practical implications of such different readings. Thus, Chapters 6–8 illustrate the dilemmas, challenges, and opportunities inherent in the process of interpretation.

Chapter 9 reflects on the challenge of interpretation in qualitative research in the light of what has been discussed in Chapters 1–8. It reviews and appraises the types of insight that can be generated on the basis of different orientations to interpretation, and it provides guidance regarding the use of criteria for evaluating interpretative research. The chapter argues that interpretation is both a responsibility and a privilege, and it encourages ethical interpretative practice.

The book concludes with transcribed conversations with well-known and highly experienced qualitative researchers (Professors Stephen Frosh, Christine Griffin, and Jonathan A. Smith) about the meaning and practice of interpretation in qualitative research.

Origins of 'interpretation'

Interpretation as a formal, purposeful, and self-conscious activity first emerged in the culture of late classical antiquity. Originally, interpretation was concerned with making sense of difficult and/or obscure documents, usually mythical or religious writings such as biblical texts. Sontag (1994: 6) describes this early approach to interpretation as 'respectful' in that it was motivated by a desire to 'reconcile the ancient texts to "modern" demands'. Here, interpretation was about making sure that ancient texts that had been revered and held sacred for a long time continued to play their traditional role within a culture despite the fact that their literal meaning did not make any obvious sense to a contemporary audience. Post-mythic consciousness and the emergence of scientific enlightenment meant that these texts did not speak for themselves any more; instead, they needed to be interpreted to reveal their deeper, often symbolic, meaning in order to stay relevant. Sontag (1994: 6) gives the example of the biblical story of the exodus from Egypt, the wandering in the desert for forty years, and the entry into the promised land, which was interpreted by Philo of Alexandria as an allegory of the individual soul's journey through emancipation, tribulations, and final deliverance. Schmidt (2006: 4) points out that the act of interpretation is based on 'the principle of charity or good will' because any interpretation is based on the assumption that, however nonsensical or obscure a text may appear to be, on some level 'what is written does make sense'. Since ancient times, the art of interpretation, or 'hermeneutics' (see Schmidt, 2006, for an excellent introduction), was practised in a range of disciplines including the interpretation of the law (legal hermeneutics), interpretation of the Bible (biblical hermeneutics), and interpretation of the classics (philological hermeneutics). Later, with the writings of Friedrich Schleiermacher (1768–1834) and Wilhelm Dilthey (1833–1911), interpretation as a generalized human endeavour ('universal hermeneutics') emerged as a concern suggesting that interpretation happens whenever we try to understand spoken or written language or, indeed, any human acts.

With the idea that interpretation is ubiquitous and that all understanding requires interpretation came the desire to better understand what we are doing when we are interpreting something. How do we give meaning to a text, an action, a social phenomenon? What procedures do we follow when we try to make sense of something? What procedures should we follow? Are there better and worse interpretations? Are some of them 'true' and others 'false'? These questions continue to be debated and we shall return to them throughout this book. For now, however, I review different approaches to interpretation that have emerged over the last two hundred years or so and that continue to influence the work of those who make interpretation their profession (such as qualitative researchers and psychotherapists).

Approaches to interpretation

Interpretation aims to find meaning in (written or spoken) accounts or other forms of human expression. Within the context of this book, we are concerned in particular with accounts of experience that take the form of written texts. Interpretation is a response to the question 'what does it mean?', and it is concerned with generating a deeper and/or fuller understanding of the meaning(s) contained within the material (or phenomenon) that presents itself. So what sorts of meanings might be distilled from a text (or other phenomenon) through the act of interpretation?

Depending on what we are looking for and depending on which aspects of the material we choose to focus our attention on, an interpretation could generate any of the following:

- A better understanding of the author's intended meaning (i.e. a clearer sense of what the author was trying to express through the material).
- A better understanding of the author's unconscious (i.e. unintended) communication (i.e. an understanding of what may have motivated the author to say what she[1] said even though she may not be aware of this motivation herself).

---

[1] The use of 'she' throughout the book is standing in for 'he or she'.

- A better understanding of the social, political, historical, cultural, and/or economic context that made it possible (or indeed necessary) for the author to express what she expressed.
- A better understanding of the social and/or psychological functions of what is being expressed (i.e. an insight into what is being achieved, in relation to other people or the self, by what is being expressed).
- A better understanding of what the text may tell us about the nature and quality of a more general concept such as 'human existence', 'social progress', or 'human psychology'

Interpretations are generated when we ask questions both of and about the material we are trying to understand. We can ask 'what did the author want to tell us?' or we can ask 'what did the author try to conceal?'; we can ask 'what must have been the (social, political, economic) conditions that led the author to produce the text at that particular time?' or we can ask 'what was the author really trying to achieve by producing the text?', or even 'what is this text telling us about what it means to be human?'

Robert Louis Stevenson's well-known story of 'The Strange Case of Dr Jekyll and Mr Hyde' (Stevenson, 2004) provides an excellent example of a text that has stimulated an enormous amount of interpretative activity since it was first published in 1886. A number of very different interpretations have been offered, each one of them approaching the text from a different angle, asking different questions of the text. The tale itself tells the story of a double-life led by a respectable and kindly medical doctor (Dr Jekyll) who finally loses control over his 'dark side' (which manifests in the identity of the violent and impulsive Mr Hyde) and commits a murder. The story was initially interpreted as a moral allegory about the struggle between what is good (Dr Jekyll) and what is base (Mr Hyde) in human beings, and a warning about what can happen when we yield to the latter. However, some contemporary reviewers saw in Stevenson's story a psychological study of something akin to what we would now describe as bipolar disorder, with its starkly contrasting moods and conduct. Later interpretations read 'Jekyll and Hyde' as a Freudian tale about the struggle between the ego (Dr Jekyll) and the id (Mr Hyde), whereby the narrative documents a progressive breaking down of the ego's defences against instinctive forces. Such a reading invokes a story about sexual repression and its consequences. Another interpretation of the story sees in it the workings of substance-addiction, which begins with the addict's belief in his ability to choose his moments of escape through inebriation (initially, Dr Jekyll believes that he can let go of the Mr Hyde persona whenever he wants to) and ends with an acknowledgement of defeat when the addict realizes that he has lost control of his actions (as the story progresses, Dr Jekyll loses the ability to control the timing of his transformations into Mr Hyde). Yet another reading of the text invokes the double-life (and accompanying emotional turmoil) of a Victorian homosexual who divides his existence into a socially acceptable, respectable public persona (Dr Jekyll) and a hidden and 'unspeakable' (because socially unacceptable) 'alter ego' (Mr Hyde). Finally, reflecting Victorian anxieties about a modern city life that brings different social classes into close contact with one another, the story has also been read as a tale that seeks to expose the hypocrisy of the middle classes (as represented by Dr Jekyll) who are not, in fact, so very different from those whose lifestyle they publicly disavow (as represented by Mr Hyde) and try to keep at bay through processes of labelling (e.g. as 'deviant' or 'criminal') and exclusion (from polite society, from clubs, from the professions). There are also other more technical (e.g. linguistic and structural) interpretations of the story (see Dury, 2004, for a comprehensive review of the various interpretations of 'Jekyll and Hyde').

The fact that very different interpretations of the same text can be generated as a result of asking different questions of and about the text suggests that every interpretation is underpinned by assumptions that the interpreter makes about what is important and what is worth paying attention to as well as what can be known about and through the text. In other words, the type of interpretation we generate depends upon the epistemological position we adopt before we start the process of interpretation. It is also shaped by the interpreter's ethical and perhaps also political commitments in that the questions we ask about a text tend to be informed by our wider projects, be they personal, intellectual, social, or political in nature (see Willig, 2012 for a fuller discussion of the epistemological bases of qualitative research in psychology).

For example, if we are concerned about the effects of the socio-economic and cultural conditions within which a particular social groups finds itself, we will likely want to know how these conditions may have shaped the text we are about to interpret (e.g. what is possible for members of the social group to say about their experience and how do they say it?) and also what the text can tell us about those conditions themselves (i.e. what can the text tell us about how members of this social group live their lives?). Alternatively, if we are interested in the psychological mechanisms that underpin people's accounts of their experience, we may want to know what the text can tell us about the workings of defence mechanisms (e.g. what is *not* talked about in the text?) or other manoeuvres designed to protect the author of the text (e.g. what impression is the text trying to create and what is done to achieve this?).

The process of interpretation can generate quite different types of accounts and, therefore, different types of knowledge, ranging from (apparently) straight-forward 'translations' of a surface meaning into a deeper, 'true' meaning (e.g. such as the claim that the tale of Dr Jekyll and Mr Hyde 'is really about' repressed homosexuality) to an elaboration of meanings that adds texture to the original account without replacing it with something more 'true' (e.g. an exploration of how the 'split' between Jekyll and Hyde is invoked through the repeated motif of the mirror). Broadly speaking, there are two rather different orientations to the interpretative task. These have been characterized as interpretation driven by 'suspicion' and interpretation driven by 'empathy', respectively (Ricoeur, 1970; see also Langdridge, 2007, for a clear account of the difference between these two). We shall look at each of these in turn before reflecting on their relationship with one another.

'Suspicious' interpretation

Here, interpretation aims to 'get to the truth of the matter'. It is akin to detective work where clues are interpreted to find out what 'really happened'. Appearances are not taken at face value (hence the reference to 'suspicion') and instead are used as cues that point to a more significant, latent meaning. Take the crime detection vignette on page 3. Sherlock Holmes interprets the hat's various characteristics in a way that reveals crucial information about the hat's owner. It is not the hat's characteristics in themselves that are important; it is what they point to, and what they can therefore tell us about the hat's owner, that really matters. 'Suspicious' interpretation aims to unmask that which presents itself, to bring out latent meaning which is contained within but which is not immediately obvious or which is actually obscured by appearances. Psychoanalysis (in its original 'classical' Freudian form) is a good example of the use of 'suspicious' interpretation. Indeed, within the psychoanalytic tradition, interpretation is defined as the 'procedure which, by means of analytic investigation, brings out the latent meaning in what the subject says and does' (Laplanche and Pontalis, 1983: 227). The metaphor of the psychoanalyst as a detective (whose job it is to discover a secret) or an archaeologist (whose job it is to dig up precious material from deep below the surface), both of which were used by Freud himself, illustrates this conceptualization of interpretative activity. The power of this approach to interpretation is that it can render apparently trivial (e.g. the clues in a criminal case) or irrational (e.g. a patient's neurotic symptoms) manifestations meaningful by going beneath the surface, following their traces right back to their origin and, therefore, discovering their 'true' meaning. For example, in 'The Interpretation of Dreams', Freud describes the following case, which illustrates the neatness of solutions arrived at through this type of interpretation (and which, incidentally and no doubt unintentionally, also invokes the connection between psychoanalysis and crime detection):

> On another occasion I had an opportunity of obtaining a deep insight into the unconscious mind of a young man whose life was made almost impossible by an obsessional neurosis. He was unable to go out into the street because he was tortured by the fear that he would kill everyone he met. He spent his days in preparing his alibi in case he might be charged with one of the murders committed in the town. It is unnecessary to add that he was a man of equally high morals and education. The analysis (which, incidentally, led to his recovery) showed that the basis of his distressing obsession was an impulse to murder his somewhat over-severe father. The impulse, to his astonishment, had been consciously expressed when he was seven years old, but it had, of course, originated much earlier in his childhood. After his father's painful illness and death, the patient's obsessional self-reproaches appeared – he was in his thirty-first year at the time – taking the shape of a phobia transferred onto strangers. A person, he felt, who was capable of wanting to push his own father over the precipice

from the top of a mountain was not to be trusted to respect the lives of those less closely related to him; he was quite right to shut himself up in his room

(Freud, 1976: 361–2)

'Suspicious' interpretation tends to be theory-driven. To extract (or, it could be argued, construct) deeper meaning from an account, it is necessary to have access to a theoretical formulation that provides concepts with which to interrogate the text. In a sense, the theory provides the lens though which the text is read. For instance, in the example above, Freud's interpretation of the young man's obsession is based upon the application of the notion of the unconscious and the mechanism of repression of unacceptable wishes. It also invokes the idea that adult experience is shaped by psychic material originating in childhood. A theory-driven interpretation offers a reading that is informed by a set of given concepts whose usefulness and validity are being presupposed. The theoretical orientation of a 'suspicious' interpretation is usually made explicit upfront, for example by referring to it in the title of the work whereby an author may offer a 'psychoanalytic interpretation of a client's fear of flying' or an 'existential interpretation of experiences of ageing'. One criticism of 'suspicious' interpretations is that they make the data fit the theory, which means that they can never constitute a genuine test of the theory (e.g. Popper, 1945). However, it could be argued that testing the validity of theories is not the aim of interpretation. We shall return to the purpose and usages of interpretation in empirical research in the final chapter of this book.

'Suspicious' interpretations are also explanatory in that the ultimate aim of the interpretation is to generate an account that can explain the manifestation (be it a text, a symptom, a behaviour or a wider phenomenon) by referring to its underlying meaning. Applying theoretical concepts to the material in question to make sense of what, at first sight, appears trivial, irrational, or meaningless is a way of explaining it. 'Suspicious' interpretations provide explanations of why something presents itself in just the way that it does. To return to the example from 'The Interpretation of Dreams', Freud explains the young man's obsessional neurosis by tracing it back to the man's early life when his experience of his over-severe father led him to fantasize about murdering him. The symptom associated with his obsessional neurosis – the fear of having murdered someone – is interpreted as being a displaced (and therefore disguised) version of his suppressed desire to murder his father, which dates back to his early childhood. The interpretation of the symptom, therefore, also provides an explanation of it.

A 'suspicious' approach to interpretation is based on the assumption that all is not what it seems, that what presents itself (in the form of accounts and behaviours, for example) needs to be de-coded before it becomes intelligible and that, to do this, the interpreter needs to make use of good theories or at the very least apply powerful explanatory concepts to the material. Such an approach to interpretation presupposes that the phenomena we encounter (be they accounts, behaviours, symptoms, social practices, historical events, or whatever) are merely the surface level manifestations of underlying processes and structures that generate them. What we encounter, that is to say what appears before us, is not the whole story. In fact, it is only the tip of the iceberg; real understanding can only be gained by looking underneath to find out 'what is really going on'. According to Ricoeur (1996: 152), this approach to interpretation aims 'at demystifying a symbolism by unmasking the unavowed forces that are concealed within it'.

One consequence of this approach to interpretation is that the interpreter occupies the role of the expert who is capable of generating a superior understanding of the phenomenon under investigation. The interpreter who has access to the theories required to de-code what presents itself is in a position to gain a better understanding of the account, behaviour or experience than the person who is actually at the centre of it (e.g. the analytic patient, the research participant, the social actor). From this point of view, to experience something or to enact something is not the same as understanding it. That is to say, the patient who experiences a neurotic symptom does not necessarily understand its meaning and origin; the worker who goes on strike does not necessarily understand their role in the class struggle; the disaffected teenager does not necessarily understand their rebelliousness as a manifestation of a moment of life-stage transition, and so on.

'Empathic' interpretation

This approach to interpretation seeks to elaborate and amplify the meaning that is contained within the material that presents itself. Here, the interpreter stays with (rather than digs below) what presents itself and focuses on what is manifest (as opposed to that which is hidden). The interpreter attempts to illuminate that which presents itself by paying special attention to its features and qualities, by making connections between them and by noticing patterns and relationships. Looking at the material from different angles, zooming in and out, foregrounding different parts of the whole as well as moving between a focus on parts and a focus on the whole, are all ways in which this type of interpretation seeks to increase understanding. The aim here is to 'complete the picture' rather than to 'boil things down' to their underlying meaning.

'Empathic' interpretation requires the interpreter to enter the phenomenon, to get inside it and to try to understand it 'from within' (hence the reference to 'empathy'). This type of interpretation refrains (as much as possible) from importing ideas and concepts from outside of the material that is being interpreted. 'Empathic' interpretations are very much grounded in the data. The aim is to amplify meaning rather than to explain what something 'is really about'. So, for example, while a 'suspicious' interpretation of a person's fear of flying may suggest that this particular fear is 'really' a manifestation of a more generalized, unacknowledged death anxiety, an 'empathic' interpretation would stay with the experience of a fear of flying and unpack exactly how this presents itself, what form it takes, what kind of physiological changes are associated with it, when it is particularly bad and when it is relatively mild, how the person talks about it and to whom, and so on and so forth. As a result of this process of elaboration of meanings, further light is shed on the phenomenon, and its nature and quality are clarified. As a result, understanding of the phenomenon and what it means to the person who experiences it are increased. 'Empathic' interpretations do not set out to explain why something occurs or to identify a causal mechanism underpinning the phenomenon. It may be that, as a result of conducting an 'empathic' interpretation, meanings emerge that make the phenomenon more recognizable to the interpreter. For example, the elaboration of meanings around the fear of flying may generate a connection between the fear of flying and the destinations of the flights (e.g. the person may feel more anxious when flying to their country of origin than when flying to a holiday destination). However, an 'empathic' interpretation would not then reduce the fear of flying to a fear of returning home by translating the one meaning into the other. 'Empathic' interpretation is about staying with and amplifying meaning rather than de-coding and translating it from one set of concepts into another.

All this does not mean, however, that 'empathic' interpretation only works with what is explicit in the material that is being interpreted. In other words, there is a difference between conducting an 'empathic' interpretation and simply describing or summarizing what presents itself. After all, interpretation is concerned with clarification, elucidation, and understanding. It does seek to add something to the material that is being interpreted, even if that something is implicit in the material itself rather than being brought to bear on it from the outside. For example, an 'empathic' interpretation may involve the elucidation of an absence. Take the example of a client who starts her counselling session by emphasizing that 'every cloud has a silver lining', and proceeds to tell the counsellor about the various coping strategies she is using to 'stay positive'. Here, the client has not actually mentioned, explicitly, why she feels the need to 'stay positive' and, by implication, that she is struggling with feeling low. The client's distress has only shown itself indirectly through her disclaimers and assurances. Interpretation as amplification of meaning requires that attention be paid to the absent term (the low mood) to which the coping strategies are a response. As such, it does require that we move beyond that which is foregrounded by the client, the manifest content which in this case is the positivity, and that meaning is added. However, interpretation as amplification of meaning does not replace the manifest content with another, more 'real' or 'true' meaning but rather it sheds further light on that which is foregrounded by illuminating the background against which it is set. It is a question of pointing to parts of the picture (perhaps less obvious, somewhat obscured ones) as opposed to introducing entirely new ideas or concepts into it.

This means that, in contrast to 'suspicious' interpretations, 'empathic' interpretations are potentially accessible to anyone, including those who are having the experiences that are being interpreted. Although 'empathic' interpretation is not easy and is a skill that needs to be developed and practised, it does not require familiarity with existing theories. Also, 'empathic' interpretation benefits from being carried out collaboratively, for example when a client and a psychotherapist work together to gain a better understanding of the client's thoughts, feelings, and actions. This approach to interpretation does not construct an opposition between the one who interprets (the expert) and that which is being interpreted (e.g. the research participant's or the client's words); rather, 'empathic' interpretation seeks to generate shared understanding by helping the interpreter to enter the world of the other (e.g. the research participant, the client) and, by doing so, helping the other to notice aspects of their experience that they have not noticed before. It follows that this approach to interpretation 'aims at a re-collection of meaning in its richest, most elevated, most spiritual diversity' (Ricoeur, 1996: 152).

The relationship between 'suspicion' and 'empathy'

The characterizations of the two approaches to interpretation provided above suggest that they are distinct, even opposing, approaches that have little in common. However, this is not necessarily the case and in this section I reflect on the relationship between 'suspicious' and 'empathic' interpretations.

As we have seen, according to Ricoeur, the two approaches to interpretation produce different kinds of knowledge concerned with understanding (generated through 'empathy') and explanation (generated through 'suspicion'), respectively. However, Ricoeur (1996) is quick to point out that neither of the two interpretative positions on its own can generate satisfactory insight and that a combination of the two is required. This is because neither 'a reduction of understanding to empathy' nor 'a reduction of explanation to an abstract combinatory system' will do, as the former is based upon the 'romantic illusion of a direct link of congeniality between ... the author and the reader', while the latter presupposes the 'positivist illusion of a textual objectivity closed in upon itself'; instead, Ricoeur argues, what is required is 'a dialectic of understanding and explanation' (Ricoeur, 1996: 153–4). Indeed, Ricoeur (1996: 154) goes as far as 'to define interpretation by this very dialectic of understanding and explanation'.

Ricoeur's position is the product of his intensive engagement with the extensive literature in philosophical hermeneutics that has been grappling with the question of what constitutes a 'good interpretation' for a very long time. Philosophers such as Schleiermacher, Dilthey, Husserl, Heidegger, and Gadamer, among others, have sought to clarify the meaning and nature of interpretation, and its relationship with and place within the human condition. The challenge that all of these philosophers have faced is to find a way of accepting the subjective nature of the process of attributing meaning to something while acknowledging that interpretations are more than idiosyncratic flights of fancy on the part of the interpreter, that they generate a kind of knowledge which is meaningful and which has some validity in its own right and not just by virtue of its relationship with the interpreter. Solutions offered to this problem range from Husserl's attempt to develop a method that would allow the meaning of things to show themselves uncontaminated by the interpreter's presuppositions and expectations to Heidegger's turn to ontology whereby what is of interest is the role of meaning-making in human beings rather than the truth value of the products of this activity. In between these two positions, others have tried to specify just how much distance, how much of a reflexive gap, there can (or indeed needs to) be between the subject (i.e. the interpreter) and the object (i.e. the material to be interpreted) of the interpretation for some kind of knowledge to be produced. The challenge at the heart of interpretation is that to make sense of something, to understand something, we need to adopt a perspective from which to view it and we need to have a relationship with it and ask questions about it. However, this standpoint inevitably shapes how something is seen and, therefore, what can be known about it, thus removing the possibility of an 'objective' or 'neutral' view. This paradoxical dynamic is reflected in the 'hermeneutic circle', which describes how parts of a whole can only be understood on the basis of an understanding of the whole, while the whole itself can only be grasped on the basis of an understanding of the parts. For example, when we read or hear a sentence, we make sense of the meaning of individual words in the light of the meaning of the entire sentence (e.g. there is no way of knowing which meaning to attribute to the word 'blind' without having access to the context in which it is used, e.g. 'Please, draw the blind' versus 'She has been blind from birth'). At the same time, however, if we did not know the meaning of individual words in the first place, we would not be able to develop an understanding of the meaning of the whole sentence. Thus, the hermeneutic circle points to an interdependency between the parts and the whole, with neither of them taking precedence.

Prior knowledge and what we bring with us to the interpretative event play an important role in the process of making sense of something. Indeed, it could be argued that an interpretation tells us more about the interpreter than it does about the material that has been interpreted. However, Gadamer (1991; see also Schmidt, 2006, chapter 5) proposes that, for any understanding to take place, there needs to be a fusion of the interpreter's and the text's horizons so that in the encounter between the interpreter and the text new insight can be generated. It is the combination of the old (in the form of the interpreter's presuppositions and assumptions which are informed by tradition and received wisdom) and the new (in the form of the text) that makes understanding possible. Ricoeur (1991: 74; see also Schmidt, 2006, chapter 7) makes a related point when he says that 'the text . . . belongs neither to its author nor to its reader'. Rather, the appropriation of the text by the interpreter requires that they enter the world of the text and make it their own by taking up possibilities inherent within it. However, it is one thing to say that interpretation requires that the interpreter and the text adapt to one another and that both of them are changed by the encounter, but it is quite another thing to claim that the product of this assimilation is valid knowledge. This raises the question of how we evaluate an interpretation. As one would expect, hermeneutic philosophers' views on this question diverge radically, ranging from the position that the application of a correct methodology can generate valid interpretations (Ricoeur) to the view that interpretative truth is an experiential event that occurs when an interpretation's (always partial) truth shines forth and convinces those who encounter it, suggesting that agreement indicates the validity (or truth) of the interpretation (Gadamer). Other views include the position that there is no interpretative 'truth', since meaning itself is the product of a process of discursive construction that relies upon a de-centred system of signifiers which only acquire meaning in relation to one another but which do not signify anything 'real' that exists outside of the system of signifiers (Derrida).

It is clear, then, that how we go about generating interpretations and how we evaluate other people's interpretations depends to a large extent on our views about the nature and purpose of the act of interpretation. Anyone who engages with interpretation as a conscious and purposeful activity needs to think about the epistemological (and, after Heidegger, also the ontological) status of interpretation and to adopt a position in relation to the questions raised above. This is important because it helps us to clarify our relationship with the insights generated by our (and others') interpretations and to use them responsibly and ethically. Different interpretative positions and their applications will be discussed throughout this book, hopefully facilitating the reader's understanding of the range of positions and their uses.

So far, we have established that to interpret something, to make sense of something, we need to be close enough to it to be able to find meaning in it, while at the same time we need to be distant enough to be able to reflect on it and evaluate it. Interpretation is more than experiential immersion in something but, at the same time, to interpret something we need to be affected by it in some way. Philosophical hermeneutics as a discipline has been concerned with providing greater insight into this complex process and has tried to determine what exactly is involved in 'understanding'. While this book is not about philosophical hermeneutics as such, and while a review of the various highly complex and often technical theories of interpretation on offer within the discipline is beyond the scope of this book, it is important to acknowledge that the approaches to interpretation taken by qualitative psychologists have certainly been influenced by this literature.

Interpretation in qualitative psychology

Explicit discussions about interpretation in qualitative psychology are a relatively recent development. I have argued elsewhere (see Willig and Stainton-Rogers, 2008a, chapter 1) that until quite recently there had been a tendency among qualitative researchers to avoid a direct engagement with interpretation. It is interesting to note that the vast majority of published qualitative studies in psychology present 'qualitative analyses' of data but do not use the word 'interpretation' in their accounts. This raises the question of the relationship between 'data analysis' and 'interpretation' to which we shall return. This tendency to sidestep interpretation could be the result of an implicit adherence to a positivist epistemology in much qualitative research, as proposed by Alvesson and Skoldberg (2002), which requires that the subjective element in such research is minimized and an appearance of objectivity is created. This is often done by taking the data at face value (that is, by attributing realist status to it; see Willig, 2012) and analysing it by systematically categorizing participants' statements into a hierarchy of themes that are then presented as the 'findings' of the study. Here, interpretation does not (appear to) enter the picture until the very end when links are made between the 'findings' of the study and relevant literature and theories in the field.

Of course, it could be argued that 'analysis' and 'interpretation' are not, in fact, very different activities. Indeed, dictionary definitions of 'interpretation' include the synonym 'analysis' (among others, such as 'elucidation', 'clarification', 'understanding', and 'explanation'). Qualitative data analysis requires that we do something to (or with) the data to generate a better understanding of what the data tell us. Data analysis is required precisely because the data does not speak for itself. Unlike artistic productions such as poems, novels, or plays, where it is the audience who are invited to interpret the material, qualitative research seeks to present its audience with something that goes beyond simply reproducing the data it has collected. Qualitative analysis claims to 'add value' through the process of analysis (whichever particular method of analysis is used) by extracting, clarifying, elaborating, and/or explaining the meaning(s) contained within the data. As such, data analysis always involves interpretation. Even thematic analysis, which has been described as a 'foundational method for qualitative analysis' in that it provides 'core skills that will be useful for conducting many other forms of qualitative analysis' (Braun and Clarke, 2006: 78), can only proceed with the description and organization of the data on the basis of a set of assumptions about the purpose and, therefore, the focus of the analysis.

In recent years, qualitative researchers have begun to talk about interpretation much more explicitly, and they have described different ways in which interpretation can enter qualitative data analysis. Some researchers (e.g. Crossley, 2004; Hollway and Jefferson, 2005) have drawn on established psychological theories to shed light on the deeper meanings contained within research participants' accounts. Here, a 'hermeneutics of suspicion' is applied to the data to generate insights about the participants' unconscious motivations and the deeper psychological dynamics that drive their overt behaviours and that inform verbal accounts of their experience.

Other researchers (e.g. Eatough and Smith, 2008; Frosh and Young, 2008) advocate a binocular approach where both 'bottom-up', descriptive analyses (which stay with participants' accounts) and 'top-down', theory-driven interpretations (which import concepts and perspectives into the analysis) have a place in the analysis. Here, researchers sometimes talk about 'levels of interpretation', ranging from an empathic-descriptive level, where the researcher tries to capture meaning from the point of view of the participant, to a critical-hermeneutic level, where the researcher builds an alternative narrative that offers a deeper understanding of the phenomenon of interest and that draws on pre-existing theoretical perspectives (see, for example, Eatough and Smith, 2008; Larkin et al., 2006). Indeed, Eatough and Smith (2008: 191) argue that such a 'dual reading' – involving both a reading stimulated by and grounded in the participant's own experience and sense-making, as well as a deeper hermeneutic interpretation that may be different from the one the participant may offer – 'is indeed the hallmark of a good inter-pretative phenomenological analysis'.

Ethical challenges

To interpret another person's experience means claiming to have access to (some of) its underlying meaning. During the act of interpretation, the interpreter moves beyond the surface meaning of a description or representation and asks: 'What does it mean?' As a result, the act of interpretation always involves a degree of appropriation; the interpreter processes what she or he sees, hears and/or reads, digests it, metabolizes it, and generates something new. Whether this happens in collaboration with the person whose experience is being interpreted (as would be expected in a more 'empathic' reading) or whether it is done from the top down (as would occur during a 'suspicious' reading), something is added to the original material and (part of) that something comes from the interpreter. This means that the interpreter has the power to shape what comes to be known (by the research participant, by the counselling client, by a wider audience) about the person's experience. However, power always carries the risk of being abused and there are circumstances in which the experiences of some (usually less powerful) people are misrepresented by other (usually more powerful) people. For example, much has been written about the power issues raised by psychoanalytic practice where the analyst's expert status together with the patient's distressed and often vulnerable condition can lead to the imposition of meanings upon the patient's experience, meanings that can be unhelpful, inaccurate or even damaging (for reviews, see Frosh, 1997; Lomas, 1987). For example, a patient's assertion that she is feeling better and is thinking about ending therapy can be interpreted as a 'flight into health' and as a form of resistance to the therapeutic process. At a more overtly political level, the imposition of meanings by ruling elites with the aim of silencing those who challenge their power is another example. Here, polit-ical protest can be interpreted as an expression of mental disturbance leading to the incarceration of political dissidents in asylums, as happened in Soviet Russia and still happens in some parts of the world today. Similarly, socially undesirable behaviours or behaviours that challenge social norms can, through interpretation, be converted into symptoms of mental ill health and then treated accordingly. Historical examples of this include pathologizing interpretations of female sexual-ity leading to medical interventions such as clitoridectomy, still widely practised in the USA at the beginning of the twentieth century, and of homosexual desire leading to electroshock treatment and re-conditioning schedules for gay men, still widely used in the second half of the twentieth century. It is clear that interpre-tation can be (ab)used to control, oppress, or manipulate others. This means that interpretation raises ethical questions, including questions about ownership (who 'owns' the interpretation). Does the interpretation belong to those who have gen-erated it or to those whose words and actions have been interpreted? We need to think about the status of the interpretation – what does it tell us about? Does it tell us something about the nature of the experience that has been interpreted or does it tell us something about those who have produced the interpretation, or perhaps both? We also need to think about the effects of the interpretation – what are its consequences for those who have produced it and for those at the receiving end of it? Once in circulation, does the interpretation change the lives of the people involved in them, and, if so, does it improve them or make them worse? Does it change power relations between people or does it reinforce existing relations?

The ethical challenges associated with interpretation in qualitative psychology are particularly acute where researchers are seeking to generate 'suspicious' interpretations, particularly those that participants themselves would not recognize or agree with. These challenges will be discussed in greater detail in Chapter 3.

Box 1   Hermeneutics in Action: 'Take Care of Yourself' by Sophie Calle

The French artist Sophie Calle demonstrates the power of interpretation through an exhibition first shown at the Venice Biennale in 2007 (see Calle, 2007). The exhibition, entitled 'Take Care of Yourself', consists of a display of 107 interpretations – some written, some spoken, and some enacted through song or dance – of one and the same short text. The original text was a 600 word long email message from Calle's boyfriend in which he ended their relationship. In the email he explained that he had decided to end their relationship because, even though he still loved her, he was unable to remain sexually faithful to her. He refers to various 'rules' and 'conditions' that Calle had 'laid down' at the beginning of their relationship, which meant that he could no longer continue with the relationship. The email ends with the words 'Take care of yourself'.

Calle's response to receiving the mail was to send a copy of it to 107 women inviting them to make sense of (that is, interpret) the message. Calle selected women representing a wide range of professions and backgrounds, including a criminologist, a social worker, psychoanalysts of various persuasions, a nursery school teacher, a stylistic analyst, a poet, a moral philosopher, a prisoner, a forensic psychologist, a novelist, a probation officer, a clown, two actresses, and an opera singer. She also invited her mother and a friend's young daughter to shed light on the message. The interpretations offered varied widely, ranging from the prisoner's view that 'this letter is a wonderful token of trust, respect and love' to the forensic psychologist's assessment that 'this letter, if authentic, was apparently written by a manipulator, a seducer, whose relationships with others are based on domination and ascendancy'. Different readings foreground different aspects of the text; some examine in detail the linguistic style and structure of the email, whereas others place it in its historical context. Some approach the text as evidence of personal and psychological characteristics on the part of its author, Calle's ex-boyfriend, while others document their own emotional responses to the email. Some use the content of the message to construct a poem, a short story, or a fairy tale. Calle's mother offers some very personal advice to her daughter, concluding that 'beautiful, famous and intelligent as you are, you'll soon find someone better', while a friend criticizes her for soliciting interpretations in the first place, suggesting that 'the choir you have formed around this letter is the choir of death'.

Reading the email and looking at the 107 interpretations is a compelling experience. It brings home the power of interpretation and meaning-making, demonstrating vividly just how much meaning can be contained within (or, perhaps better, found within or constructed from) a relatively brief text. It also demonstrates the creative potential of the various (personal, theoretical, artistic) frameworks brought to bear on the text by the 107 participants.

Based on Willig, C. (2009a) Reflections on 'interpretation', inspired by Sophie Calle's 'Take care of yourself', *Qualitative Methods in Psychology Newsletter*, 7 (May): 12–14.

2 Interpretation in qualitative research

Qualitative research is concerned with meaning. It aims to shed light on how people make sense of experiences and what their behaviours mean to themselves and to others. Qualitative research is concerned with the quality and texture of human experience and with the ways in which people construct and communicate meaning in social contexts. Such research does not work with pre-defined variables and it is not concerned with establishing cause–effect relationships. Instead, it aims to understand what is going on, for people and between people, as they live their lives. The objective of qualitative research is to describe, to understand, and sometimes also to explain but never to predict (see Willig, 2008a, chapter 1; Willig, 2012). It would appear, then, that qualitative research and interpretation share a concern with making sense, with finding meaning, with understanding. As such, one would expect qualitative research in psychology to have a close and productive relationship with interpretation. However, this is not the case. The relationship between qualitative research in psychology and interpretation has been an uneasy one. It is only recently that this has begun to change. This chapter reviews the ways in which qualitative psychologists have engaged with interpretation, their covert and overt uses of interpretation, their resistance to it and their struggle with the ethical implications of producing interpretations. The chapter reviews a range of orientations to the use of interpretation in qualitative psychology, including those adopted by psychoanalytic, phenomenological, and discourse analytic research approaches. It discusses the 'turn to interpretation', which has emerged in recent years (see also Willig and Stainton Rogers, 2008b), and introduces the 'psychosocial' approach to qualitative psychology, which has grown out of this. The chapter anticipates the fuller discussion of the ethical challenges associated with interpretation presented in Chapter 3 by reviewing some of the debates about the politics of interpretation that have taken place between qualitative psychologists in recent years.

Qualitative psychologists' reluctance to 'interpret' data

In the early days of qualitative psychology, researchers found themselves in a position of having to justify their choice of methodology and to defend its validity as a psychological research method. In those days, qualitative methods were not yet recognized as a legitimate way of conducting psychological research. Studies using qualitative methods were not published in psychology journals, qualitative methods were not taught on psychology courses, and those who insisted on using such methods were spending much of their time in discussions about the validity (or otherwise) of their chosen approach to research. This climate meant that qualitative psychologists felt the need to assert the legitimacy and validity of their research. Being confronted with the charge that qualitative research was not scientific as it was not using the hypothetico-deductive model of research that dominated psychology at that time, qualitative psychologists felt the need to demonstrate that their research, too, was methodical, rigorous, and replicable and that, therefore, it was on a par with quantitative psychology. At the time, it seemed important to differentiate qualitative psychology from other forms of interpretative enquiry associated with the humanities. Although qualitative psychologists had critiqued the notion of 'science' and 'scientific research' and had challenged what this had come to represent in the form of positivistic research that uncritically reproduced established categories of meaning and ways of understanding human behaviour (e.g. Gergen, 1973, 1989; Gilligan, 1982), most qualitative researchers still tried to ensure that their own research met (at least some of) the standards associated with rigorous (if not 'scientific') research. Indeed, Alvesson and Skoldberg (2002) suggest that until recently much qualitative research has implicitly adhered to a positivistic epistemology. This has meant that its presentation has tended to mirror the structure of quantitative research reports (i.e. introduction, literature review, methodology, results, discussion). It has also meant taking data at face value and not moving beyond the careful and systematic categorization of the data into 'themes' that were hierarchically organized and then presented as 'findings'. Within this framework, interpretation is not an acknowledged part of the process of analysing data and anything resembling explicit interpretation 'does not enter the picture until the very end, when the "findings" are reflected upon in the discussion section of the report' (Willig and Stainton Rogers, 2008b: 8).

As discussed in Chapter 1, qualitative researchers have preferred the term 'analysis' to 'interpretation' even though the two activities are closely related. The term 'analysis' invokes a sober, clear-headed, and systematic activity carried out by someone who is meticulous and accurate, and who pays attention to detail. It tends to be used to describe demanding and exacting activities such as 'political analysis', 'economic analysis', or 'financial analysis'. It is, of course, also associated with the testing of compounds and biochemical analyses in the laboratory. A successful 'analysis' can be expected to provide answers to important questions, answers that can direct future activities and interventions in the real world. By contrast, 'interpretation' is associated with the arts, with creativity, and with the imagination. We 'interpret' literature – novels and poems – and we talk about the ways in which a performer – an opera singer, a pianist, an actor – has 'interpreted' their material. 'Interpretation' is stimulating, it is interesting, and it can be illuminating; however, it is not seen as something that provides us with factual knowledge, the kind of knowledge, for example, that allows us to build houses and develop medical treatments. In addition, 'analysis' is associated with science, whereas 'interpretation' is associated with arts and humanities. Smith (2007) echoes this concern by claiming 'scientific' status for qualitative analysis when he endorses Duke's (1977) portrayal of hermeneutic activity while distancing himself from Duke's (1977) characterization of it as 'an art'. Having cited Duke's (1977) description of the process of hermeneutic enquiry, Smith (2007: 7–8) writes: 'I think that this is a beautiful and pithy passage. The only thing I would take issue with or problematize is the notion that this "makes it an art". I do not disagree with that but would say that, for me, the qualities invoked can also be described as making it a "science"!'

I, too, have felt the need to take issue with a characterization of qualitative research that suggests that there is no need for method in generating interpretations. Forshaw (2007) argued that since qualitative research had 'turned its back on truth', there was no need to be concerned with method. Instead, he suggested, qualitative researchers ought to 'adopt the relatively "loose" approach taken by those who write about literature' (Forshaw, 2007: 479) and not worry about the validity of their interpretations. He proposed that even 'superficial' readings can yield something of value and that perhaps we would be better off accepting that our interpretations are driven by creativity and invention, that they can be interesting and stimulating but nothing more than that. My response (Willig, 2007a) to this argument was that although qualitative analysis cannot, and does not aim to, uncover 'the truth', the process of developing an interpretation involves a cyclical process of critical reflection that involves systematic questioning of the researcher's own emerging interpretations; it is not the product of his or her unmediated associations and reactions to the data. I suggested that there is a difference between interpretation as practised in qualitative analysis, and a simple, subjective reaction to a text. So, one reason why qualitative researchers feel reluctant to openly embrace the language of interpretation may well be their desire to distance themselves from an association with the arts and to fend off accusations of their research being no more than intuition and, therefore, as lacking in validity.

There is a second reason why qualitative researchers have been wary of interpretation. Qualitative psychology emerged from a critique of positivist research that was based upon the assumption that 'the external world itself determines absolutely the one and only correct view that can be taken of it, independent of the process or circumstances of viewing' (Kirk and Miller, 1986: 14). Qualitative psychology grew out of an understanding that the psychological knowledge which had been accumulated over the years was not simply a reflection of reality, an objective assessment of how people tick, but rather an edifice of theoretical and empirical work that was grounded in a particular tradition of pre-existing knowledge and expectations and which reflected, rather than challenged, basic assumptions about people that circulated in society at a particular time (see Gergen, 1973). For example, feminist scholars pointed out that, until the 1970s, the vast majority of studies using human participants had been carried out using male undergraduate students. It was assumed that this group of people (predominantly young, white men from middle-class backgrounds living in the USA) constituted the prototypical 'human subject' of psychology, and findings from these studies were generalized to the human population as a whole. As a result, these men set the standard (regarding intellectual performance, moral development, communication skills, etc.) against which the performance of other members of society was measured – and, more often than not, found to be wanting. Critics of this 'male-as-the-norm' approach (e.g. Gilligan, 1982) argued that qualitative research was needed to identify which dimensions of experience and behaviour were actually relevant to the other social groups and to develop bespoke models of their functioning based upon these. Positivist psychology's claim to have obtained an objective, unmediated picture of the reality of human experience and behaviour was seen as a way of legitimizing and perpetuating an unequal society. Critics argued that what became known as the 'God trick' (Haraway, 1988), involving the use of elaborate procedures designed to eliminate bias (standardized instructions for research participants, minimization of contact between researchers and participants, blind or double-blind procedures for data collection and analysis, and so on), was a way of maintaining the illusion that the researcher was not implicated in their research, and that the researcher's own standpoint (i.e. the way they look at the world, the questions they are asking, the variables they select as being of interest) did not shape the research and the insights (the 'knowledge') that emerged from it.

Qualitative psychology's roots in the critique of positivist psychology and its investment in the idea that qualitative research is there to 'give voice' to those who had been excluded from traditional psychological research (i.e. women, ethnic minorities, the elderly, those who are in one way of another 'socially excluded') mean that qualitative psychologists are highly sensitive to the dangers associated with the imposition of meaning and of pre-conceived theoretical formulations upon research participants' experience. Qualitative psychologists have been wary of interpretation because interpretation carries the risk of silencing the voices of those we are researching as we overlay them with our own voices, with our theories, with our narratives.

The critique of psychoanalysis

Psychoanalysis, which probably constitutes the most well-known application of interpretation in psychology, has been at the receiving end of much criticism, precisely because of its tendency to read accounts through a particular theoretical lens. As such, psychoanalysis is a prime example of what Ricoeur (1970: 32) has described as 'interpretation as exercise of suspicion'. Here, interpretation is akin to a process of translation. The interpreter has access to a code that enables him or her to translate the account from a language that cannot be understood by ordinary people, including the person who produced the account. This is a language of symbols, substitutions, and displacements of meaning. The interpreter translates these into a language that is familiar and which talks of wishes, desires, and intentions. Through translation, then, the true meaning of the account is disclosed. Here, interpretation is 'understood as a demystification, as a reduction of illusion' (Ricoeur, 1970: 27). This approach implies that the content of human consciousness can be 'false' and that we need to view with suspicion our own thoughts and feelings as they present themselves to us in consciousness. It also implies that there is a correct reading, a true translation, which requires interpretative work in order to be obtained and which not everyone is able to access. It therefore invokes the notion of a 'science of meaning, irreducible to the immediate consciousness of meaning' (Ricoeur, 1970: 34). This, in turn, means that experts, those trained in the correct method of deciphering the contents of consciousness, are required to carry out the labour of interpretation and that it is they, not the person whose experience is examined, who have the last word in establishing its true meaning. Similarly, the psychoanalytic notion of 'resistance' means that the patient's rejection of the analyst's interpretation can be read as a manifestation of the patient's unconscious attempts to sabotage treatment and, therefore, as confirmation of the accuracy of the analyst's original interpretation. It has been argued that within this system there is no real space for the patient to assert his or her own view of what is going on and that, as Spinelli (1994: 199) puts it, 'the therapeutic relationship that is based on analytic interpretations fosters the client's dependence on the therapist and comes to resemble a relationship such as might be seen between parent and child'. This is a relationship where, it could be argued, ultimately 'mum/dad knows best'.

The critique of psychoanalysis and its identification of the ethical problems associated with the (ab)use of power on the part of the analyst resonates with the concerns about interpretation which have led to qualitative psychologists' reluctance to interpret. Although interpretation has been talked about much more openly among qualitative psychologists in recent years and its explicit use has become much more legitimate, ethical concerns about its implications for the power relations between researcher and participant continue to be expressed. Two debates published in the *British Journal of Social Psychology* provide an excellent illustration of the nature and range of the arguments deployed both for and against (certain types of) interpretation in qualitative psychology in recent years. The next section will review these debates in more detail.

Interpreting beyond the data: a debate about validity and ethics

Hollway and Jefferson (2005) published an analysis of two semi-structured interviews with a man called Vince who was experiencing health problems and a difficult situation regarding his employment. In their analysis, Hollway and Jefferson (2005: 147) drew on psychodynamic theory to identify what they call 'psychic defences' to help us understand why Vince developed health problems at a particular point in time. The interviews were conducted as part of a research project into the fear of crime, which meant that Vince was not aware of the fact that the researchers were going to analyse the interviews psychodynamically. Hollway and Jefferson (2005: 150) point out that, in their analysis of Vince's account, 'the workings of powerful unconscious conflicts' are of central importance. This means that the researchers assumed that Vince himself did not have access to information about what motivated his actions and choices and, therefore, that they could not take Vince's account 'at face value'. Hollway and Jefferson (2005: 151) explain that '[D]rawing as we did on a psychoanalytic theorization of anxiety, it was not appropriate to rely on interviewees' conscious self-knowledge of [their internal] states'.

Hollway and Jefferson (2005) approached the interview texts as a form of evidence about Vince's life, which, once interpreted, could provide insights into its conflicts and motivations. To generate their interpretations, they paid particular attention to non-verbal information such as changes in emotional tone, long pauses, avoidances, and sequencing and/or juxtaposing of particular topics.

Let us look at Hollway and Jefferson's (2005) analysis of the interviews before engaging with Spears' (2005) and Wetherell's (2005) critique of their approach.

Vince, a hard-working, active man in his forties who was married with three children, had developed depression and anxiety leading him to take an extended period of sick leave. Vince himself explains his illness as being the result of the stress and anxiety he had been experiencing over the course of the previous three years as a result of the threat of losing his job. Vince had been involved in a court case about an insurance claim, which, if the outcome should be unfavourable, would have led to him losing his job. This was because Vince, a long-distance lorry driver, had parked his employer's van with its keys inside and it had been stolen. In the event, after three years the case came to court and Vince's employer won the case, which meant that Vince could keep his job. However, the resolution of the court case did not ease the pressure on Vince and he became ill. Hollway and Jefferson (2005: 153) argue that logically once the court case had been resolved favourably, the pressure could be expected to go, so '[T]his alerts us to the possibility that Vince's own explanation is insufficient, in which case we need to go behind it and re-examine his psychosocial reality'. Such an examination involves looking at the discourses Vince draws on to construct meaning around his experiences (e.g. constructions of masculinity as involving the ability to provide for a family) as well as the biographical significations that help us to understand his investment in a particular type of identity (i.e. that of an honest, hard-working, and responsible family man). Hollway and Jefferson (2005) propose that Vince's dis-identification with his father, whom he describes in very negative terms as a heavy-drinking, selfish waster, and his identification with his hard-working and long-suffering mother mean that Vince is committed to an identity that is built around hard work, support for his family, reliability, and honesty. At the same time, Vince's relationship with his boss shows elements of idealization, leading Hollway and Jefferson (2005) to propose that it was the boss's role as an ideal father figure in Vince's life that made the boss's betrayal (including the threats to sack Vince should the insurance claim fail, as well as blackmailing Vince into lying to the insurance company about where exactly he had parked the van) so much more emotionally charged. When Vince says that, at the end of the court case (Hollway and Jefferson, 2005: 159),

> I thought well, at least it's over and done wi' you know, the pressure will go. But it never did. So I carried on working for a few months and er, like I say, eventually I just cut off.

Hollway and Jefferson conclude that 'it is not only his job but his boss that Vince is cutting off from' (p. 159). As such, they argue, their analysis of Vince's account helps us understand why Vince (really) got sick when he did and that it is able to do this by going beyond, or perhaps better below, Vince's own surface level account of his motivations. Ultimately, they propose, Vince's illness is a way of allowing Vince to 'cut off' from his job and from his boss without compromising his identity as a hard-working and responsible family man. Vince's conflict between wanting to leave and needing to stay is resolved through an illness which he experiences as 'forcing him' to stay away from work. Hollway and Jefferson (2005: 161) summarize their interpretation as follows:

> By becoming too sick to work, Vince achieves a resolution, not through thought but through the body. This resolution is an elegant one. On the one hand he has not chosen to quit his job. He and others can honestly say that he would be working if he could. His intentions remain unimpeach-able. On the other hand, his collapse has achieved that desired-and-feared situation: he does not have to go to work. This resolution is also impressive in that he can hold on to the possibility of his job in the future (it will be held open for 2 years). Unfortunately since a return to work would pre-cipitate the conflict that his sickness resolves, we fear that Vince's illness will remain with him as long as there is any risk that, by getting better, he would feel obliged to return to his job. If, as we have argued, his sickness is the resolution, then it will have to continue. Clearly the cost of this resolution is huge.

In their commentaries on Hollway and Jefferson's paper, both Spears (2005) and Wetherell (2005) challenge the psychodynamic interpretation presented by questioning the evidence provided in support of it. Spears (2005: 167) wonders whether Vince's 'unconscious conflict' identified by Hollway and Jefferson is per-haps a conscious one instead, a conflict between 'dissonant selves' (or different sides of his identity) that makes it difficult for Vince to talk about some of the is-sues. Perhaps Vince is struggling to reconcile his own personal private knowledge and what amounts to a public confession to an audience (i.e. the interviewer as well as himself) in a way that does not leave him feeling (too) exposed? Spears (2005: 167) acknowledges that the analysis provides evidence of 'deep emotional conflicts' but feels that 'the warrant of a psychodynamic interpretation that has to be uncovered within Vince rather than one that is involved at the boundary of dialogue (disclosure, confession) is less obvious'.

Wetherell's (2005) critique of the paper also challenges Hollway and Jefferson's (2005) focus on the inner workings of Vince's troubled and conflicted psyche; instead, she suggests that Vince's account can be understood in the light of the discursive context within which it was produced. She points out that Vince's predicament is indeed awful and that 'Vince's task of making sense and finding a set of identity positions which are persuasive and acceptable to himself and to his audience is an exceedingly difficult one' (Wetherell, 2005: 171). Wetherell (2005) argues that Vince's account tells us much more about the kinds of identities which are problematic or troubled in our society, about the discursive resources available to account for one's actions, and the attributional work Vince's circumstances demand of him, than it does about Vince's psyche. Wetherell (2005: 171) argues that, in Hollway and Jefferson's (2005) analysis, '[T]he listener and the audience are erased, and thus the micro-social, interpersonal, and relational basis for Vince's account' are obliterated. Wetherell (2005) also expresses concerns about the ethical dimension of conducting the type of analysis presented by Hollway and Jefferson (2005) because it 'individualises' and 'psychologises' the participant's words, taking them out of their discursive context. It also constructs a version of the participant's personality that he may not recognize and/or agree with. Wetherell (2005: 169) writes, '[F]or ethical reasons ... one hopes that Vince will never have to engage with this analysis of himself as a timid man choosing illness to avoid confrontation with a bullying boss'.

'Offending the Other': pathologizing through interpretation?

The second debate about the value and legitimacy of interpretation in qualitative research revolves around an article by Crossley (2004), in which she presents an analysis of autobiographical and fictional narratives written by gay men across three different periods of gay history (pre-AIDS, during AIDS, and 'post'-AIDS). In the article, Crossley (2004: 225) argues that contemporary behaviours such as 'barebacking' (i.e. unprotected anal intercourse) are 'embedded in a "cultural psyche" that the individual gay man may not even be consciously aware of'. Crossley (2004) takes a similar stance to Hollway and Jefferson (2005) in that she argues that qualitative researchers should not take participants' accounts at face value because people's actions are often motivated by unconscious forces. She questions the value of interview-based and ethnographic research with gay men, as she believes that within such contexts participants tend to account for their actions by drawing on available cultural repertoires rather than revealing their underlying psychological motivations. Crossley (2004: 227) describes how she detected what she calls 'an increasingly hostile and sceptical stance' towards health promotion efforts among her interviewees in earlier research into gay men and safer sex (see Crossley, 2001) and how this led her to develop 'an understanding of gay men's unsafe sexual practices as a kind of symbolic act of rebellion and transgression which they are not *necessarily* consciously aware of' (italics in original). In the analysis presented in her article, Crossley (2004: 228) 'draws upon selected texts as a means of illustrating the way in which contemporary "unsafe" sexual practices (such as "barebacking") constitute a continuation and repetition of psychological conflicts and responses which have prevailed over three different historical periods: (1) pre-AIDS; (2) during AIDS; and (3) "post"-AIDS'.

Crossley (2004) concludes that the theme of gay male sexual practices as 'transgression' and 'resistance' recurs throughout the texts she has analysed. She hypothesizes that it is this which motivates unsafe sexual practices among gay men today 'whether or not individual gay men are consciously aware of this motivation' (Crossley, 2004: 237). Crossley (2004) also draws on the Kleinian concept of 'splitting', whereby when faced with anxiety people divide other people and experiences into those that are 'all good' and those that are 'all bad'. This is referred to as the 'paranoid-schizoid position'. According to Crossley (2004), contemporary gay men's behaviour is characterized by this 'paranoid-schizoid position' when they uncritically embrace and celebrate unsafe sexual practices. Crossley (2004) stresses that in her view desire is culturally produced and shaped (as opposed to being a purely biological innate drive) and that gay men's unconscious desire to transgress and resist sexual restrictions, their 'resistance habitus' as Crossley (2004: 236) calls it, is a product of their cultural history, a history of oppression and stigmatization. Nevertheless, Crossley (2004) argues, by encouraging reflection on personal histories and their connections with the social and historical context of gay history, a deeper understanding of the meaning of unsafe sexual practices can be obtained and, as a result, reappraisal of risky practices and alternative choices become possible.

Crossley's (2004) paper has been criticized for producing a 'suspicious' interpretation which draws on culturally dominant stereotypes of gay men (as being hedonistic, promiscuous, morally irresponsible, and interested in sex rather than relationships) and which reduces rather than increases a real understanding of the experiences of gay men (Barker et al., 2007; Flowers and Langdridge, 2007). Barker et al. (2007) point out that Crossley selected texts to support her argument, which limits the generalizability of the interpretation. Her use of commercial autobiography and fictional accounts is also criticized, as such texts do not necessarily represent the everyday experiences of gay men, especially since fictional accounts are likely to contain a large amount of fantasy material that is less likely to feature condom use or safe sex practices. Barker et al. (2007) question the meaningfulness of attempting to identify one generalizable psychological explanation for a sexual practice that may be engaged with in different ways for different reasons by different individuals and communities. Reading the texts through a psychoanalytic lens means that alternative explanations for the behaviour under scrutiny are excluded. As a result, Barker et al. (2007: 669) note that, '[T]he psychoanalytic conclusions in this paper risk depicting gay men as pathological'. Furthermore, Barker et al. (2007: 672) take issue with the ethical stance in Crossley's writing, which, they argue, 'is in danger of infringing the dignity of the gay men she writes about'.

Regarding the approach to interpretation adopted by Crossley (2004), Barker at al. (2007: 673) write:

> We suggest caution before rejecting a 'hermeneutics of meaning recollection' entirely in favour of a 'hermeneutics of suspicion', especially when writing about communities and practices that are easily stigmatized.

They go on to remind the reader of the fact that psychoanalysis has a long history of pathologizing gay men and lesbians, and point out that a perpetuation of stereotypical representations of gay men as transgressional and dysfunctional is likely to further fuel prejudice against them.

Flowers and Langdridge (2007) also take issue with Crossley's (2004) interpretation. In their discussion of Crossley's paper, they express concern about 'suspicious' social psychological research on 'the Other'; that is to say, on those who belong to communities or traditions that are different from those the researcher him- or herself belongs to. Flowers and Langdridge (2007) draw attention to the way in which Crossley (2004) dismisses the voices of gay men themselves (for example, by attributing interviewees' accounts to their 'unthinking' use of a cultural repertoire), preferring to foreground her own construction of what it means to practise 'gay sex', including 'sweeping claims about the culture of the "Other"'(Flowers and Langdridge, 2007: 683). Flowers and Langdridge (2007) also comment on the way in which Crossley (2004) fails to differentiate between the texts she has analysed and the subjectivities of those the texts refer to, blurring the distinction between the two and assuming that the one (the text) is a direct reflection of the other (gay men's subjectivities). Such a lack of awareness of the genre, status, and function of the texts means that it is easy for the analyst to impose her own subjectivity onto them and to conclude that she understands their 'true' meaning. Flowers and Langdridge (2007) criticize Crossley for failing to reflect upon her own standpoint and perspective and to trace their effect upon her analysis. The result is an interpretation that constructs gay men as pathological and deviant. They conclude:

> This is why it becomes vitally important to recognize our position, our tradition and subject it to critique before engaging in a critical suspicious analysis of the 'other', particularly if the 'other' is from a different tradition.
>
> (Flowers and Langdridge, 2007: 688)

These debates demonstrate that qualitative psychologists are keenly aware of the ethical challenges associated with interpretative activities and that at least for some qualitative psychologists interpretation can go too far. For them, the risk of misrepresenting participants' experiences by imposing theory-driven meanings upon the data is too great, and to avoid this risk they counsel against the application of a 'suspicious' approach to interpretation, preferring a purely 'empathic' approach instead. However, those who are willing to risk generating 'suspicious' interpretations argue that there is value in digging beneath participants' accounts of their experiences and that to refuse to do so would mean giving up the opportunity to gain a deeper understanding of what motivates people, especially at an unconscious level. They point out that taking people's accounts at face value means assuming that people are transparent to themselves and others and that there is no depth and no mystery to their experiences.

Both of these positions will be revisited throughout the remainder of this book and their implications for research practice will be explored more fully in Part 2. In the remainder of this chapter, we will review a range of orientations to the use of interpretation and their application through psychoanalytic, phenomenological, and discourse analytic approaches to qualitative research. The chapter ends with a discussion of the emergence of a 'psychosocial' approach to qualitative psychology.

The psychoanalytic case study

The psychoanalytic case study is probably the most obviously interpretative method of analysis we are going to review. Indeed, the psychoanalytic case study is all about interpretation, in that it offers a particular reading of a client's clinical material and presentation – a reading that aims to make sense of something (a symptom, an unexplained behaviour, an irrational preference or dislike) that has failed to make sense before. A psychoanalytic case study applies concepts and perspectives informed by psychoanalytic theory to solve what appears to be a riddle, to unravel a mystery. It translates surface level manifestations such as unreflected descriptions of experience and non-verbal expressions of emotions into their underlying, deeper meaning and, as a result, transforms a collection of puzzling phenomena into a meaningful account of a client's psychological dynamic, including their developmental history, unconscious desires, and defence mechanisms. Through the case study, psychological mechanisms such as distortions, substitutions, condensation, and displacements of meaning are identified and exposed as the psyche's ways of disguising the true significance of the client's experience, a significance that is not normally accessible to the client's own conscious mind. A successful psychoanalytic case study is, therefore, a tribute to the analyst's interpretative skills and ability. It is also satisfying to read in that it seems to offer a clear solution to a problem.

The brief case study from Freud's *Interpretation of Dreams* (1976: 361–2) cited in Chapter 1 (see pages 11–12) provides an illustration of the neatness of solutions that can be generated through this method. Here, the psychoanalytic case study is akin to a detective's 'case' (e.g. Agatha Christie's 'The Case of the Missing Will'), which requires detailed analysis to be solved. Indeed, Freud himself compared the work of the psychoanalyst to that of the detective:

> In both we are concerned with a secret, with something hidden . . . In the case of the criminal it is a secret which he knows and hides from you, whereas in the case of the hysteric it is a secret which he himself does not know either, which is hidden even from himself . . . In this one respect, therefore, the difference between the criminal and the hysteric is

fundamental. The task of the therapist, however, is the same as that of the examining magistrate. We have to uncover the hidden psychic material; and in order to do this we have invented a number of detective devices.

(Freud, 1906, in Summerscale, 2008: 103–4)

In terms of its approach to interpretation, therefore, the psychoanalytic case study is committed to 'suspicious' interpretations. As demonstrated through the discussion of the (controversial) studies by Hollway and Jefferson (2005) and Crossley (2004) earlier in this chapter, a psychoanalytic approach to qualitative data analysis presupposes that research participants 'may not know why they experience or feel things in the way that they do' and 'are motivated, largely unconsciously, to disguise the meaning of at least some of their feelings and actions' (Hollway and Jefferson, 2000: 26). For Freud, the psychoanalytical interview was 'a procedure for the investigation of mental processes which are almost inaccessible in any other way' (Freud, 1923/1964: 235, in Kvale, 2003: 22). To facilitate access to such processes and to minimize participants' opportunities to manipulate their responses, the psychoanalytic interview employs indirect questions that do not identify the actual focus of the study. Participants are also unaware of the theoretical orientation of the researchers, their underlying research question(s), and their hypotheses. In the analysis of the data, the participants' words are not (necessarily) taken at face value and attention is paid also to what is not said and to what participants appear to want (or do not want) to come across as saying. The psychoanalytic case study researcher is alert to any evidence, both verbal and nonverbal, that points to unconscious defences and motivations that may be at work in the participant. This means that the psychoanalytic case study's approach to interpretation positions the analyst as the expert who (potentially) has superior skills in accessing the 'true' meaning of the participants' experience. As Kvale (2003: 30) points out, psychoanalytical research involves 'a general style of research, which puts a strong emphasis on the training, theory and culture of the interviewer'. Another important feature of this type of research is the use of the relationship between the researcher and the participant whereby the researcher's own experience of the participant's material and style of presentation provide further data to be interpreted. Transference, which may be defined as a process during which a client's (or a research participant's) 'feelings, attitudes and behaviours which belong rightfully in earlier significant relationships' (Gelso and Hayes, 1998: 11, cited in Grant and Crawley, 2002: 4) are projected onto the interaction with the researcher or therapist in the here-and-now, and countertransference, which involves the therapist's (or researcher's) emotional response to that transference, both provide rich material for psychoanalytic interpretation. For example, a participant may respond to the interviewer's searching questions about her experience by repeatedly stating she does not believe that the interviewer is really interested in her experience. The interviewer may eventually begin to feel irritated and bored by the participant's stance, feeling pressurized into providing continuous reassurance. This dynamic between the researcher and the participant provides material for further exploration, perhaps leading the researcher to understand that the participant is projecting assumptions originating in her unsatisfactory relation-ship with her father onto him and that he, the researcher, is experiencing strong feelings of rejection in response to the participant's neediness and insecurity, thus repeating a pattern of relating that is familiar to the participant.

There is, of course, a difference between psychoanalytic research that is con-ducted purely in the service of knowledge production, and psychoanalytic case studies that are a by-product of clinical work. Kvale (2003: 37) cautions against a 'simple transferral of therapeutic techniques to research situations'. He reminds us that therapeutic sessions are primarily concerned with helping the client to change, whereas research interviews, even when they are psychoanalytically in-formed, are concerned only with knowledge production. This means that different ethical standards apply. In the therapeutic situation, the therapist and the client have contracted to work together to help the client make changes to their life. Their relationship is one that is based on trust, confidentiality, and collaboration. The client is aware that the therapeutic experience may well involve painful and challenging experiences and they accept this as a necessary part of the process of change. Any emotional turbulence experienced by the client will be contained and worked through within the context of the ongoing therapy. The therapist and the client meet at specified times, at regular intervals, over an extended pe-riod of time. The relationship (ideally) continues until both client and therapist agree that they wish it to end. The ending is usually anticipated well in advance and it is worked towards during the final phase of the therapy. By contrast, the relationship between a researcher and a participant is normally short-lived, in-volving either one or a small number of meetings. The research participant has agreed to talk to the researcher about some aspects of their experience; however, they have not agreed to undergo a process of change facilitated by an intense emotional engagement with another person. Furthermore, while the therapeutic relationship provides the client with an opportunity to engage in a dialogue with the therapist, and to question and challenge the therapist's interpretations as they emerge within the context of particular sessions, the research participant has less opportunity to object to the researcher's interpretations, as these will not emerge until after the interview has been analysed. The research relationship is clearly not as containing as the therapeutic relationship and it does not offer the same emo-tional safety. This is why Kvale (2003: 32) argues that although researchers 'have much to learn about modes of questioning and the interpretation of meaning from the psychoanalytical interview', some of the 'key aspects of the psychoanalytical interview . . . are ethically out of bounds for the academic research interview'.

Kvale (2003) identifies two distinct ways in which psychoanalytic research can be conducted. First, therapists who work with clients can reflect on this work and write up case studies retrospectively, in much the same way that Freud himself did. While this approach allows the therapist-researcher to make use of the full range of psychoanalytic tools and strategies, it means that complete confidentiality needs to be ensured in any publications arising from the work. This can be difficult when the client's material is in any way unusual or easily identifiable. Second, researchers can use psychoanalytic interviews and psychoanalytic strategies for interpretation and apply them to data obtained from research participants. In this case, it is important to ensure that participants are protected from some of the emotional challenges associated with psychoanalytic psychotherapy. In particular, where the researcher makes interpretations of a participant's material that transcend the participant's own self-understanding, Kvale (2003) argues that it may be unethical to confront the participant with them, as the participant has not asked for or consented to such a confrontation. However, it could also be argued that even to publish such interpretations stretches ethical boundaries (see, for example, Flowers and Langdridge, 2007, as discussed above).

Phenomenological research

The relationship between phenomenological research and interpretation is complex. This is because there are varieties of phenomenological research, some of which are more willing to openly embrace interpretative activity than others. In addition, there are disagreements among phenomenological researchers about the extent to which it is possible to avoid interpretation altogether. Some (e.g. Giorgi, 1992; Giorgi and Giorgi, 2008) distinguish between descriptive and interpretative phenomenology, arguing that these are distinct approaches based on different epistemological perspectives. Others (e.g. Eatough and Smith, 2008) propose that there are merely different levels of interpretation that a phenomenological researcher can engage with. These range from those that are more 'empathic' to those that are more 'suspicious'; however, some level of interpretation is inevitably involved in the analysis. Some of these differences between approaches revolve around disagreements about the extent to which description constitutes a form of interpretation in and of itself. Hermeneutic phenomenology, as for instance formulated and practised in Heidegger's philosophical analysis of what it means to be human (Heidegger, 1962), is based on the assumption that there is no stance that we can take which is not, in some way, already invested in the world, which is not shaped by our intentions and projects in the world. According to this view, our experiences and perceptions of the world are mediated by our relationship with the world and, therefore, it is not possible simply to 'describe' objects and events in their pure form. From a hermeneutic phenomenological point of view, there is no such thing as a 'pure form' (or indeed 'essence') because what presents itself to us, the phenomena that appear in our consciousness, take the form that they do precisely because of our relationship with them. In other words, they only become possible through us. For example, my perception of my cat as being small is only possible because I am much bigger than her. Without me (or something else) to be compared with, phenomenologically speaking, the cat has no size. In addition, once we attempt to capture the phenomena of lived experience in language, further interpretation takes place as our choice of terminology and sentence structure add further meaning and significance. From this point of view, language cannot simply 'describe' what is being perceived or experienced; instead, language constructs a particular version of it and this version is shaped by the intentionality of the author. Van Manen (1990) and Packer and Addison (1989, in Giorgi and Giorgi, 2008) present detailed discussions of what is involved in a hermeneutic approach to phenomenological research.

Despite these differences, however, I would argue that it is possible to identify some shared perspectives among phenomenological researchers and to delineate a common orientation to interpretation. In the remainder of this section, then, I shall focus on commonalities among phenomenological approaches to qualitative research in order to define and characterize what may be descried as a phenomenological approach to interpretation (however, for further information about the differences between 'descriptive' and 'interpretative' phenomenology, see Cohen and Omery, 1994; Finlay, 2009; Lopez and Willis, 2004).

All forms of phenomenological research are committed to staying very close to the text that is being analysed, ensuring that it is the participant's account (rather than the researcher's theoretical framework or their hypotheses) which drives the interpretation. The participant's account is not just the point of departure but also the foundation of the interpretation, and it is constantly revisited throughout the analysis. In phenomenological research, it is the participant's account that 'is privileged as the source for the interpretative activity which occurs' (Eatough and Smith, 2008: 190). Hermeneutic analysis does not mean importing a particular theoretical framework into the data and reading the data through its lens. Instead, a hermeneutic approach merely argues that it is impossible to enter a text without adopting some provisional perspective on it, without posing some initial questions about it, and without making some preliminary assumptions about its possible meaning(s). A phenomenological analysis (even a hermeneutically inspired one), however, will always subject its initial understanding of the material to sustained questioning and review, allowing the emerging understanding of the text itself to challenge the researcher's own preliminary assumptions about it. Thus, while the phenomenological researcher accepts that it may have been necessary to adopt a provisional perspective on the text to find a 'way in' to the data, they also accept that once the text has been entered, this initial perspective may prove to be inadequate to making sense of the account and it will then be the account itself that will continue to challenge and shape the researcher's interpretation of it.

The process of interpretation in phenomenological analysis is driven by the interplay between understanding and not-understanding. As Cohn (2005: 221) puts it: 'If we wish to understand it, a message needs to have an aspect that is familiar so that we can engage with it. But it also has an aspect which needs to be explored, "interpreted"'. Phenomenology is based on the assumption that in their appearance phenomena always both reveal as well as conceal part of themselves. This is similar to the idea that language is always a medium for both revelation as well as obfuscation, of clarification and mystification (see Sullivan, 2010: 14). This means that interpretation is of necessity a cyclical process, which requires the interpreter to move continuously through positions of knowing and not-knowing, which are adopted and then abandoned again throughout the analysis. It also means that there is no clear end point at which the analysis is complete and a full understanding has been achieved. Phenomenological analysis is potentially interminable because new meaning will continue to emerge as the researcher engages with the text. In addition, no one interpretation of the data can be described as 'the correct one'. Phenomenological interpretation seeks to amplify meaning by shedding light on various dimensions of the phenomenon under investigation; it does not seek to find out 'the truth' about it. As Cohn (2005: 221) writes:

> We need . . . to remember that the process of revealing the unknown part of a phenomenon does not replace a deceptive manifest utterance or symptom with the reality of a true meaning which invalidates what we have seen so far. On the contrary, the perceived phenomenon gains clarity, richness and meaningfulness whenever a new aspect of its totality is discovered.

Phenomenological analysis requires the researcher to be highly reflexive throughout the process of analysis and to attempt to be(come) aware of, and reflect upon, the ways in which his or her own assumptions, standpoint, and investment in the research shape the emerging understanding of the material. More descriptive approaches to phenomenological research would aim to identify and then 'bracket' any preconceptions and assumptions before embarking upon analysis (see Giorgi, 1992), whereas more interpretative approaches would acknowledge that some of the researcher's preconceptions and assumptions only emerge as they engage with and attempt to understand the text (see Smith, 2007). Again, this is a way of using a process of 'un-knowing' to increase understanding. It is also a way of acknowledging that any phenomenological interpretation of an account will be 'a blend of the meanings articulated by both participant and researcher within the focus of the study' (Lopez and Willis, 2004: 730). This means that the phenomenological researcher will change or transform the account as well as be changed or transformed by it. Interpretation in phenomenological research is not (only) something the researcher 'does to' the text; the text, too, exercises its effect upon the researcher, changing their way of thinking, feeling, and looking at the world. Phenomenological interpretation is, therefore, always intersubjective.

Phenomenological researchers vary in the extent to which they are prepared to transform a participant's account. Those who subscribe to a more descriptive approach would be reluctant to present an analysis that the participant may not recognize, seeking instead to extract and capture core concepts and essences that structure the account. Ideally and if done well, the participant ought to recognize the validity of such an analysis and, indeed, would be expected to find it helpful and illuminating precisely because it provides an accurate, concise, and integrated version of what the participant him- or herself has said. There are, however, exceptions to this and some descriptive phenomenologists such as Giorgi (2008, cited in Finlay, 2009) would not endorse this position, arguing instead that research participants are not in a position to validate a phenomenological analysis of their experiences. By contrast, a more interpretative (hermeneutic) phenomenological reading would be looking for meanings contained within the account that may not be apparent to the participant him- or herself. As Lopez and Willis (2004: 728) put it, '[T]he focus of a hermeneutic inquiry is on what humans experience rather than what they consciously know'. This means that the results of such an analysis may well be surprising or even challenging to the participant who generated the account in the first place. This is because the researcher may have made connections between parts and aspects of the data that the participant has not considered, and she or he may pay attention to features and details of presentation (use of past or present tense, repetitions, incomplete sentences, metaphors, terminology, and so on) that the participant is either not aware of or takes for granted. However, even a hermeneutic analysis would seek to stay with the data and find meaning only in what presents itself, rather than moving beyond the data by importing formal pre-existing theory into the data, transforming its meaning into something entirely different. Where theory is deployed, it is used to focus the inquiry and to establish a frame of reference from within which to begin the process of interrogating the data. As already mentioned, the researcher's interaction with the material will then shape the way in which, or indeed whether, such a framework will be used. Smith (2004) presents a helpful discussion of the differences between hermeneutic interpretations and those driven by formal theories such as psychoanalysis (see also Smith et al., 2009, chapter 5).

Discourse analysis

Discourse analysts are interested in the ways in which language constructs particular versions of experiences or events through people's accounts of them. They conduct detailed examinations of the choice of terminology, grammatical constructions, repetitions, use of metaphors and other rhetorical features that characterize a (spoken or written) text to demonstrate exactly how the text achieves its effects. Discourse analytic research can take different forms. The most well-known versions of discourse analysis are discursive psychology (e.g. Edwards, 2004; Wiggins and Potter, 2008) and Foucauldian discourse analysis (e.g. Kendall and Wickham, 1999; Parker, 1992) (see also Willig, 2008a, for a detailed discussion and comparison of these two versions). However, there are others; indeed, Wetherell (2001) identifies as many as six distinct ways of conducting discourse analytic research. However, all varieties of discourse analysis share a conceptualization of language as constructive and performative. Here, language does not reflect what happens elsewhere (e.g. thoughts and feelings inside a person or objective events that take place in the social world). Instead, language is seen as the medium that actually brings events and experiences into being by constructing them in a particular way, for particular purposes, in particular social contexts. From this point of view, language is not a means to an end and it is not a way of accessing what is really of interest to the researcher (such as participants' subjective experiences and their inner worlds, or the social processes they are involved in); instead, it is language itself that is of interest to the researcher. Discourse analytic research is driven by research questions about the capacities and characteristics of language rather than by questions about the participants and their experiences. For example, discourse analysts might want to know what kinds of discourses are used in the construction of illness talk or what kinds of subject positions participants take up when they talk about their attempts to give up smoking. Some versions of discourse analysis (e.g. Foucauldian discourse analysis) are more concerned with the availability of discursive repertoires and the social, cultural, and historical contexts within which particular ways of talking emerge. Other approaches (e.g. discursive psychology) focus on the specific ways in which discursive resources are actually deployed by participants within particular conversations. All forms of discourse analysis, however, are interested in the effects of discourse and in how particular ways of constructing meaning through language enable or prevent, empower, or constrain action.

Discourse analysts do not tend to describe their work as 'interpretation'. They are not interested in any hidden meanings that may be discovered within a text and they are not concerned with foregrounding and amplifying unacknowledged aspects of a text's meaning and significance. Rather, discourse analysts are concerned with how meaning is produced through language in the first place. This means that the analytic work focuses on the deconstruction rather than amplification of meaning. Meaning is removed, stripped away, if you will, rather than added through the process of analysis. And yet, I would argue that there is interpretation in discourse analysis. This is because discourse analysis is based on a particular understanding of the role of language. It presupposes a particular interpretation of the meaning of language itself, of its function and its position in human experience and action. In discourse analytic research, therefore, interpretation enters the picture at a very early stage, before any actual analysis of data has been conducted. Interpretation sets the scene for the analysis, it shapes the choice of methodology, and it informs the questions that the researcher asks of the text. It determines the 'status of the text' in that it dictates what the text is taken to represent and what it can tell us about; namely, information about the way in which language is used to construct a particular version of reality within a particular context. Discourse analysts, therefore, do not take participants' accounts at face value; instead, they subject them to an analysis driven by a particular theory of language and they generate insights about the function of discourse that those who produced the accounts are unlikely to be aware of or indeed recognize. In this sense, it could be argued that far from refraining from interpretative activity, discourse analysis could be described as adopting a 'suspicious' approach to interpretation.

For example, in her analysis of a married couple's account of their experience of life since the wife was diagnosed with ME (also known as chronic fatigue syndrome), Horton-Salway (2001) approaches the data from a discursive psychology perspective. She makes it clear from the start that her 'theoretical position does not assume an equivalence between people's accounts and their internal experience and cognitive processes', and that in her analysis she will 'treat the narration of subjective experience and the construction of identity as situated productions that work to accomplish interactive business' (Horton-Salway, 2001: 249). Here, the participants' account of life with ME is, therefore, not taken at face value, as providing us with information about life with ME; instead, it is read through the theoretical lens of discursive psychology to tell us something about the way in which discursive resources are used by the participants and with what effects. In other words, the data is interpreted. Horton-Salway's (2001) analysis – her discursive interpretation – identifies various discursive strategies with which the participants manage their stake in the conversation with the interviewer and with which they account for themselves and their actions. Within a wider social context in which the social status of ME as an illness is contested as some attribute its symptoms to a psychological rather than a physical cause, those diagnosed with ME are required to account for their condition, and Horton-Salway's participants do this by disclaiming undesirable attributions (of psychological vulnerability and malingering, for example) and by constructing ME as a recognizable instance of organic disease (comparable to polio). Horton-Salway's analysis of the participants' account is not primarily concerned with the content of what they are saying about life with ME but rather with what the participants are *doing* with their talk; that is to say, with its action orientation. We do not know what the participants themselves would make of Horton-Salway's analysis of their account; however, it is likely that they would struggle to recognize themselves in the analysis and it is by no means certain that they would be comfortable with what they may perceive as an attribution of a preoccupation on their part with presenting themselves in a positive light to the interviewer. Furthermore, it could be argued that by not paying any attention to the participants' illness narrative as a form of self-expression, a discursive interpretation of the data serves to silence participants and interferes with their right to author their account, especially if participants consented to take part in a study because they believed that the researcher was interested in their story rather than in the way they were telling their story (see also Willig, 2004, for a fuller account of some of the ethical issues associated with discursive psychology research).

Other approaches to qualitative analysis

The psychoanalytic case study, phenomenological research, and discourse analysis are, of course, only some of the many available research methods in qualitative psychology. They are perhaps better known and more widely used than some of the other methods; however, there are many other well-established approaches such as grounded theory, narrative analysis, action research, and ethnography (see Willig and Stainton-Rogers, 2008a, for an overview) and it is important to also consider their relationship with interpretation. As has been explained in relation to discourse analysis, every study makes assumptions about the type of knowledge it seeks to produce and it is given direction by the types of questions that it asks of the data. Every study needs to be clear about what 'status' it attributes to the data; that is to say, what it wants the data to tell the researcher about. In this sense, every qualitative study, irrespective of which specific method of data analysis is used, interprets its data because the data never speaks for itself. The data must always be processed and interrogated to obtain answers to particular questions, to shed light on a particular dimension of human experience, and/or to clarify a particular aspect of an experience or a situation. Indeed, Emerson and Frosh (2004) remind us that even apparently practical decisions about which transcription method to use contain theoretical assumptions about which features of discourse are significant and meaningful and will shape the type of reading that can be produced. This is, of course, what hermeneutic phenomenologists mean when they talk about the impossibility of engaging with the world without at the same time interpreting it, or, as Heidegger (1962: 37) put it, 'The meaning of phenomenological description as a method lies in interpretation' (in Finlay, 2009: 11). It is also part of a conceptualization of understanding as being the product of intersubjectivity, of a 'fusion of horizons', as Gadamer (1991) puts it, whereby both the researcher (with his or her questions and assumptions) and the participant's account (with its meanings and propositions) blend together to produce the insights generated by the study. A study's theoretical orientation, its focus and its procedures in themselves are interpretative. This is why it is so important for researchers to be explicit about their frame of reference and their (personal, theoretical, emotional, conceptual) investments in the research; after all, in one way or another, these will be used to interpret the data.

However, as has become apparent in the discussion of the role of interpretation in the psychoanalytic case study, in phenomenological research and in discourse analysis, there are still differences in the extent to which qualitative researchers make use of interpretation during the process of data analysis. As Frosh and Emerson (2005: 310; italics in original) put it:

> there is still a variation among qualitative procedures between those that are *relatively* 'top down', dominated by theoretically-derived categories imposing an interpretive 'grid' on data in order to interrogate it according to the assumptions or perceptions derived from those categories, and those that are *relatively* 'bottom-up', eschewing theory as far as possible at least until the data has been examined performatively in terms of its own emergent properties.

For example, while psychoanalytic case study research seeks to unearth underlying psychic structures and mechanisms that generate the overt, manifest content that is represented by the data, more descriptive forms of phenomenological research take great care to (try to) stay with the data and to refrain from importing any theoretically informed meanings into the material. So while all qualitative research is interpretative, not all of it embraces interpretation as its primary method of data analysis. Grounded theory, for example, is interpretative in that it approaches its data as a form of evidence of what goes on, both in participants' minds and in their social encounters and practices. It is also interpretative in that the researcher, to be able to make sense of what participants are telling her, needs to use her own knowledge of the language spoken by the participants and of the meaning of common expressions and forms of communication, knowledge without which no understanding would be possible. However, grounded theory methodology does not then require the researcher to use a particular theoretical lens through which to read this evidence. In a sense, the data are taken at face value in so far as participants' accounts are not subjected to a 'suspicious' reading. It is assumed that participants mean what they say and say what they mean. In other words, they are treated as witnesses rather than suspects or patients. A similar approach is taken in ethnography and in action research, although the latter, particularly where the researcher's empowerment agenda is informed by a particular social theory such as feminism or Marxism, can be more thoroughly interpretative. Narrative analysis does not tend to produce 'suspicious' interpretations of participants' accounts, although it, too, approaches its data with the help of an orientating conceptual framework that assumes that people organize their experiences through telling stories about them and that this process is both helpful and natural. As Murray (2003: 116) puts it, constructing narratives about ourselves provides us with an opportunity 'to define ourselves, to clarify the continuity in our lives and to convey this to others' and, we may add, also to ourselves.

The 'psychosocial' approach

Over the last ten years or so, qualitative psychologists have engaged more explicitly than ever before with the question of interpretation. This 'turn to interpretation' (see also Willig and Stainton-Rogers, 2008b) can be understood as the product of qualitative psychologists' frustration with using methods which allowed them to identify, systematically represent, and map what research participants were saying and doing but which did not lend themselves to generating insights about why participants were having these experiences. In other words, (some) qualitative psychologists were becoming increasingly less content to see careful description of participants' thoughts and actions as the endpoint of their research and they wanted to find out more about the social and/or psychological structures and processes that generate and underpin such thoughts and actions. To do this they turned to the use of existing psychological theories, and psychoanalytic theory in particular, so as to generate richer interpretations and to produce explanatory accounts of their data. Perhaps the most well-known and most widely discussed manifestation of the 'turn to interpretation' is what has come to be known as the 'psychosocial' approach to qualitative psychology. This label is somewhat unfortunate as it is rather vague and all-inclusive and does not point to what really distinguishes the approach, namely its commitment to interpretation. In any case, psychosocial qualitative psychology is characterized by what Frosh and Young (2008: 109, 124) have described as 'binocularity', whereby both 'ground-up' (i.e. a descriptive focus on 'what is there') and 'top-down' (i.e. a theory-driven interpretation) perspectives are deployed in combination to make sense of the data. Here, a detailed description of the data is followed by a theoretically informed reading that seeks to explain the phenomenon under investigation. For example, an initial discursive analysis of some interview data may generate an account of which types of discursive resources participants are using in their talk and which subject positions they tend to occupy at particular points in the interview. This could then be followed by a psychoanalytic interrogation of the data that may generate a better understanding of what underlying psychic structures and processes may have led participants to invest in, and commit themselves to, the particular discourses and subject positions identified in the discursive analysis. Indeed, most of the published research taking a psychosocial approach combines discourse analytic and psychoanalytic perspectives in an attempt to 'thicken' the analysis of data (e.g. Frosh and Young, 2008; Frosh et al., 2003; Gough, 2004). The aim of such research is to recover an understanding of the dynamics of subjectivity without losing sight of the importance of the social and discursive contexts within which participants' narratives are produced. As Frosh and Young (2008: 111) put it:

> Developing a psychosocial account of relationships and subjectivity that can draw on psychoanalysis without dumping the significant advances produced by discursive social psychology thus requires openness to interpretation grounded in an understanding of the social as something that permeates apparently 'individual' phenomena.

Frosh and Young (2008) provide a helpful example of what is involved in a psychosocial analysis. In their study of narratives of brotherhood, the data consisted of transcripts of semi-structured interviews with eight men together with detailed notes taken by the interviewer straight after the interviews, recording her impressions of the participants' interactions with her and her own emotional responses to these interactions and to the men's presentation in the interview. The material was subjected to an initial discursive analysis which identified a number of core narratives which engaged with culturally available constructions of masculinity (for example, as tough, aggressive, and unemotional) in different ways and which participants were mobilizing as they talked about their relationships with their brothers. The researchers then examined these narratives in the light of the participants' personal biographies and the interviewer's notes about participants' style of interaction in the interview. With the help of psychoanalytic concepts and theory, the researchers were then able to develop an account of what in their psychic structure may have motivated individual participants to invest in particular constructions of masculinity and brotherhood. For example, one of the participants (Tom) was highly motivated to invest in a discursive construction of himself as a 'new man' and this could be traced back to his desire to differentiate himself from his half-brother who Tom had always experienced as something of a macho character and with whom Tom felt he had always needed to compete for their mother's attention. The researchers draw on Mitchell's (2000) theory of sibling rivalry to explain Tom's sustained attempts to differentiate himself from his brother throughout the interview. A psychosocial analysis of their data therefore enabled these researchers to understand participants' experience of brotherhood by 'conceptualising men as taking up socially available discourses in ways that resonate with the deeply personal', thus demonstrating 'the interweaving of the social and psychological in "doing brother"' (Frosh and Young, 2008: 124).

The increasing popularity of the 'psychosocial' approach in recent years has given rise to much discussion and debate regarding its methodological, epistemological, ethical, and political implications (e.g. Frosh and Emerson, 2005; Wetherell, 2003; see also Parker, 2005a). These debates resonate with some of the arguments developed in an earlier section in this chapter, which was concerned with 'interpreting beyond the data' (see pages 26–29), and are primarily concerned with the limits of interpretation, or, as Frosh and Emerson (2005: 308) put it, with 'what are the constraints operating on interpretation, what is allowable and what is not?' These questions will be revisited throughout the remaining chapters of this book.

3 The ethics of interpretation

Some of the ethical challenges associated with the process of interpreting other people's words and actions have been identified in Chapters 1 and 2. Chapter 1 established that the act of interpretation always involves a degree of appropriation because the process of making something meaningful necessarily involves a process of transformation as the interpreter digests and metabolizes the material that they are trying to make sense of. Whether we like it or not, we cannot attempt to understand something without transforming it at the same time. This means that power enters into the process of interpretation, as the interpreter has the power to shape what comes to be known about another person's experience. Chapter 1 provided some disturbing examples of the abuse of the power to interpret on the part of powerful social groups. Chapter 2 reflected on the ethics of interpretation in qualitative research by reviewing some of the debates about the politics of interpretation that have taken place between qualitative psychologists in recent years. Positions ranging from the desire to 'give voice' to participants to the adoption of the role of the expert interpreter were identified and their ethical dimensions were considered. The debates reviewed in Chapter 2 demonstrate that qualitative psychologists are very much aware of the ethical challenges associated with interpretative research. There are, however, differences in the ways in which qualitative psychologists meet these challenges, with some being prepared to risk the imposition of theory-driven meanings on participants' experiences in the interest of generating a deeper understanding of the underlying forces and structures that motivate and shape people's thoughts and actions (this has been described as a 'suspicious' approach to interpretation), while others prioritize the participants' right to generate their own meanings and refuse to adopt the role of the expert in making sense of psychological material (this has been described as an 'empathic' approach to interpretation). Chapter 2 concluded that while all qualitative research is by its nature interpretative, not all qualitative researchers embrace interpretation as their primary method of data analysis. Different approaches taken to interpretation entail different ethical challenges.

In this chapter, we return to the topic of ethics in interpretation by reflecting on the consequences of interpretation for those whose experiences and actions are being interpreted. The chapter introduces the notion of 'interpretative violence' and what happens when meanings are imposed on people. It is concerned with interpretative power and its potential and actual abuses. Questions are raised about who 'owns' interpretations and who has the right to produce them and use them. And three strategies are identified that qualitative researchers can use to help guard against some of the ethical risks associated with interpretative research.

Interpretation in everyday life

Interpretation as the act of assigning meaning to phenomena is something we do all the time. It is part of our lived experience of the world. It is also something we do to each other. To make sense of other people's actions, we give them meaning, often on the basis of little evidence and more often than not by drawing on psychological discourse. Consider casual comments such as the following, all of which are taken from 'real life' conversations:

> 'Ooh, you want to be in charge!' says a student commenting on another student who has volunteered to write on the blackboard.
>
> 'It looks like she is trying to hide something' says a woman about a girl she has seen who is wearing heavy make-up.
>
> 'He's like a child with his dummy' says a man who sees another man sitting on a park bench clutching a bottle of scotch.

Here, people are spontaneously producing interpretations of phenomena to make them meaningful. Since what presents itself (the fellow student getting up to write on the board; the heavily made-up girl; the man with a bottle) does not speak for itself, it is given meaning and significance by those who perceive it. The interpreter selects one of the many possible interpretations of the phenomenon and foregrounds this by putting it into words.

   Once an interpretation has been selected and foregrounded, it structures the phenomenon in a particular way, emphasizing some features and minimizing others. The interpretation makes its version of reality appear and leads us to respond to this, rather than to an alternative reading of the situation. So, for example, the student who has interpreted his colleague's readiness to write on the board as a desire to dominate may be uncooperative in an attempt to resist being dominated. The woman who has interpreted heavy make-up as a form of disguise may start to ask searching questions in an attempt to find out what is being hidden beneath the mask of make-up. The man who has likened the bottle of scotch to a dummy may adopt a parental role when approaching the man on the park bench. This demonstrates that interpretations have consequences for those whose conduct has been interpreted.

   In his discussion of 'being-for-others', the social dimension of his phenomenological ontology, Jean-Paul Sartre (2003) reflects on what it means to exist for others. He identifies the moment when we experience being seen by another person as the moment when we become aware of ourselves as an object within the other's world. He describes this moment as highly disturbing and he invokes 'the shock which seizes me when I apprehend the Other's look' (Sartre, 2003: 288). This is because the other person's look reminds us of the fact that it is the other person, not ourselves, who gives meaning to the object that we constitute in their world. It is the other's interpretation of me that makes me 'real' for him or her. Through the other's look we are trapped in the other's world and have to live with the consequences. As Sartre (2003: 291) puts it, 'being seen constitutes me as a defenceless being for a freedom which is not my freedom'. In other words, I am at the mercy of the other's interpretation of my being, and all I can do is 'wish that others should confer upon me a being which I can recognise' (Sartre, 2003: 286) as, ultimately, in the social world, I need to accept responsibility for 'this stranger who is presented to me' (p. 298).

The consequences of interpretation

Although it could be argued that Sartre's account tends to over-emphasize the disempowering and restrictive dimensions of the experience of being interpreted, he draws attention to some very important features of the process of interpretation, namely its social consequences and their ethical implications. There are numerous striking and often disturbing historical examples of the power of interpretation, many, though not all, of which involve the abuse of interpretation in the interests of ruling elites (see Chapter 1). Social historians such as Shorter (1992), Porter (1997), and Cushman (1995) have provided fascinating accounts of the diverse ways in which various expressions of physical and/or psychological distress have been interpreted and treated over the course of history. For example, the appearance of palpitations, breathing difficulties, dizzy spells, fainting fits, and temporary paralysis in a person could be perceived and, therefore, dealt with as a manifestation of divine inspiration, as evidence of possession by evil spirits and involvement with witchcraft, as symptoms of a hysterical disorder or as the somatic expression of socio-political oppression on the part of a person who does not have access to other forms of resistance, all depending on the historical and cultural context within which the interpretation is made, thus demonstrating how a phenomenon can accommodate a very wide range of interpretations that have very different consequences for those at the receiving end of them. Santomauro and French (2009; see also French and Santomauro, 2007) present an interesting case study of the experience of sleep paralysis and its interpretations over the course of history and across cultures. Sleep paralysis involves the experience of being fully conscious but unable to move. It usually occurs when the person is lying on a bed on their back, facing upwards, and can last up to ten minutes. Sleep paralysis can be accompanied by hallucinations as well as by acute anxiety and/or other intense feelings. Santomauro and French (2009) observe that the experience of sleep paralysis appears to be near universal (its experiential elements have been reported from many countries and cultures) while its nature and significance have been interpreted in many different ways. Examples include the Inuit of Canada who interpret sleep paralysis as an attack from evil spirits, Japan where it used to be said that monks could use magic to paralyse people in their sleep, and St. Lucia where sleep paralysis was alleged to be caused by the spirits of unbaptized babies. In sixteenth to eighteenth century Europe, sleep paralysis was interpreted as being the work of vengeful witches who punished their enemies by disturbing their sleep. It could also be associated with an attack by demons intent on sexually molesting the sleeping victim. More recently, in the USA and elsewhere the experience of sleep paralysis has been explained in terms of alien abduction. Modern scientific explanations understand sleep paralysis as the result of an intrusion of rapid eye movement (REM) sleep characteristics (in the form of deep muscle relaxation and hallucinations) into wakefulness. Clearly, each of these diverse interpretations indicates a different response to the phenomenon of sleep paralysis and to those who experience it.

In the next section, we take a closer look at the relationship between interpretation and social practices. I have chosen the topic of ill health in general, and cancer in particular, as the terrain upon which some of the ethical challenges and dilemmas associated with interpretative activity can be explored as we trace some of the ways in which dominant interpretations of ill health can shape the illness experience (see also Willig, 2009b, 2011).

Interpretations of ill health

Experiences which are potentially disturbing and/or unsettling and which, therefore, have a strong emotional impact tend to provoke interpretative activity as we try to make sense of them and to find ways of responding to and dealing with them. As Santomauro and French (2009) indicate, an experience such as sleep paralysis is a potential threat to one's sense of self and needs to be explained in a way that protects the self. Accounts that invoke external forces such as evil spirits or aliens are preferable to those according to which sleep paralysis is a private experience generated by the self and, therefore, potentially an indication of pathology or madness. Similarly, death and illness are phenomena that attract interpretation. It seems that, faced with the anxiety generated by a confrontation with the vulnerability of our physical being and the reality of human mortality, we feel compelled to create protective meaning. Often this means interpreting other people's experiences of death and illness as the product of predispositions or behavioural practices that we ourselves do not share or take part in. In this way, they are turned into things that happen to other people, not ourselves. Such causal attributions, made in the absence of any medical information about the particular case and made purely on the basis of cultural representations, can be distressing for those on the receiving end. Consider Patrick Weir's (2010) account of what it is like to live with gout. Having described the physical symptoms and discomfort associated with gout, he goes on to say that:

> [O]ne of the difficult aspects of the illness for me is the assumption that it is brought on by rich living. Mention gout and people automatically assume that you gorge on rich food and down the booze in equal measure. Having limped in agony to the local shop, I mention the g-word and am greeted by a smile and words along the lines of 'Too much of the good life, eh? You like your food and drink, eh?' And I have to put up with this whenever I explain my laboured gait.
>
> (Weir, 2010: 14–15)

It seems that, once diagnosed with a medical condition, we become the targets of other people's interpretative efforts. As Fleischman (1999: 21) puts it, '[W]hen you contract a disease, you contract with it the world of that disease, including all its affective and culture-specific meanings, which are frequently symbolic or metaphorical'.

The power of words

Being diagnosed with a serious illness is an interpretative event twice over. First, diagnosis marks the moment when a number of phenomena (such as an array of signs and/or symptoms, a series of test results, episodes of feeling unwell) are transformed into disease categories. Such categories constitute medical interpretations of experiential and social phenomena, and they usually offer both aetiological as well as prognostic meanings that organize the illness experience. This includes treatment options and procedures. Second, diagnosis inserts the patient into the wider discursive field associated with the diagnosis they have received. Disease categories, once applied to a person, position them as a 'patient' and as a 'sufferer' of the pathological condition that has been diagnosed, and with this as a target for culturally available interpretations of the condition. This means that, once a person's diagnosis is known to others, the diagnosed person is subject to lay interpretations of their condition.

Medical sociologists and linguists have drawn attention to the 'transformative power' (Fleischman, 1999: 10) of language in the process of diagnosis. For example, Fleischman (1999) reflects on the significance of the choice of words for describing the rare blood disorder with which she herself has been diagnosed. Available diagnostic labels include 'refractory anaemia', 'preleukaemic disorder', and 'myelodyplastic syndromes'. Fleischman notes that each of these labels constructs the haematological pathology in a different way, foregrounding different dimensions of the condition, with the reference to 'preleukaemia' constructing a particularly threatening and, therefore, emotive version of it. Diagnosis initiates a struggle for meaning as the patient and his or her social contacts try to understand what it means to be diagnosed with this condition, and at the same time it provides some of the discursive resources with which meaning can be made. Fleischman (1999: 13; italics in original) writes:

> For the afflicted individual, illness becomes a trope for new attitudes toward the self; it also influences perceptions of that self by others ... if the diagnosis is *refractory anaemia* the impact on all concerned is dramatically different from a diagnosis of *preleukemia*.

Several authors have drawn attention to the fact that we are particularly sensitive to the meanings and resonances associated with terms and expressions when we find ourselves in a position of having to find new meaning and make sense of a challenging situation. Fleischman (1999: 7) observes that:

> [W]hen the body is seriously out of kilter, particularly if the condition is likely to endure, your sensitivity to the nuances of words used to describe it is inevitably heightened. You become critically aware of the subtle ways in which lexical choices define you as a person.

Fleischman (1999) points out that languages differ in the way in which they construct the relationship between a person and their illness whereby some languages allow for the possibility of an existential identification with one's health problem (e.g. by saying 'I am a diabetic') whereas others do not, instead preferring a subject–object split between person and disease (e.g. by using the construction 'I have diabetes'). In addition, in most languages and cultures, the body and its various constitutive parts take on symbolic meanings, acting as metaphors for mental and physical states and conditions (e.g. in English, 'blood' signifies transmission of qualities or characteristics via the notion of lineage as well as of contagion) that are activated when a body part or organ is diagnosed with a pathology. All of these have implications for the ways in which the person thus described experiences their condition including their relations with others in the social world.

Being diagnosed with a serious illness requires major adjustments, including modifications to one's sense of self. It means that assumptions about one's life course and expectations regarding the future may need to be reviewed and adjusted. A new narrative that makes sense of the new experience needs to be constructed and at such times we are particularly vulnerable to what Frank (1995: 6) has described as 'narrative surrender'. This involves a submission to a dominant narrative that frames one's experience in a way that does not accommodate one's own personal meanings. In other words, it means interpretative capture.

In recent years, an increasing number of authors have written about the experience of being the target of unwanted interpretations of what it means to be ill. For example, Sontag (1991), Stacey (1997), and Ehrenreich (2009) evoke the sense of vulnerability and mortification that accompanied their experience of being constructed by and positioned within dominant cancer narratives. These authors describe a sense of loss of control over the story that they can tell about themselves once diagnosed and the struggle over the meaning that is given to their experience.

A large body of evidence demonstrates that cancer patients in particular encounter considerable difficulties in their relations with other people as a result of their diagnosis (Wortman and Dunkel-Schetter, 1979). It seems that in addition to the physical and psychological challenges associated with the diagnosis, the encounter with culturally available and widely used interpretations of what it means to have cancer adds significantly to many cancer patients' distress. They can, as Ehrenreich (2009: 43) puts it, 'weigh on a cancer patient like a second disease'.

In an interview study of nineteen female breast cancer patients' experiences of the impact of an altered appearance during chemotherapy treatment, Harcourt and Frith (2008) identified two key themes within the data: (1) anxiety that chemotherapy would render them identifiable as a 'person-with-cancer', and (2) problematic interactions with others. In particular, the loss of hair (including any attempts to disguise this, for example by wearing a headscarf or a wig) was feared, as it was seen to impart information about their disease status to others and, therefore, to lead to them being identifiable as a 'person-with-cancer'. Such identification, in turn, led to a loss of control over how to define oneself and over how one was treated by others (e.g. with unwanted attention, with sympathy or pity when they just wanted to 'blend in', with unwanted advice or unsolicited opinions about the causes of their cancer). In other words, the women experienced a loss of control over who they were and who they could be within a social context. For some participants, their attempts to regain control over their sense of self led them to avoid social interactions altogether.

In what follows, we take a closer look at some of the dominant interpretations of what it means to be diagnosed with cancer in contemporary Anglo-American cultures and reflect on their implications for the experience of those who encounter them (see also Willig, 2011).

Dominant constructions of cancer and their phenomenological implications

A review of recently published analyses of cancer discourse (e.g. Clarke, 1992; Ehrenreich, 2009; Seale, 2001; Stacey, 1997; Stibbe, 1997; Van Rijn-van Tongeren, 1997; Williams Camus, 2009; Willig, 2009b) reveals that there are several widely used constructions of what it means to have cancer and these dominate the cultural terrain. They include: (1) the imperative to 'think positively', (2) the construction of cancer as 'war', and (3) the construction of cancer as a moral concern.

The imperative to 'think positively' requires the person with cancer to demonstrate faith in the belief that things will turn out well and to display an optimistic outlook. It requires the person to emphasize and foreground positive aspects of their situation (e.g. the considerable medical advances that have been made in cancer treatment, the support that is available, their desire and determination to be cured, and so on) while minimizing negative aspects (e.g. the fact that not all cancers can be cured, the amount of suffering that cancer can involve, the unpleasant nature of the treatments, and so on). The imperative of 'positive thinking' also means that death as a possible outcome of the diagnosis is not acknowledged or talked about. In her aptly entitled book *Smile or Die*, Ehrenreich (2009: 45) argues that '[E]xhortations to think positively – to see the glass half full, even when it lies shattered on the floor' pervade North American culture including breast cancer culture where '[P]ositive thinking seems to be mandatory ... to the point where unhappiness requires a kind of apology' (Ehrenreich, 2009: 26). The imperative to 'think positively' constructs cancer as a 'wake-up call', an opportunity to rethink one's life and to make a fresh start leading to a better, healthier lifestyle.

Recent research into the social and emotional consequences of word choice (Mosher and Danoff-Burg, 2009) demonstrates how the cultural imperative to think positively about cancer is reflected in interpretations of linguistic classifications of individuals with cancer. Mosher and Danoff-Burg (2009) found that across two studies that compared reactions to the use of the terms 'cancer survivor' and 'cancer patient', a large sample of undergraduate students attributed consistently more positive qualities to someone described as a 'cancer survivor' (as opposed to 'cancer patient') and they expressed more positive attitudes towards them. In the second study, participants also expressed a significantly greater willingness to interact with 'cancer survivors' than with 'cancer patients'. This suggests that a 'positive' stance towards having cancer, one that focuses upon survival and active living ('survivor') as opposed to one that foregrounds passivity and suffering ('patient'), is socially desirable and rewarded. Interestingly, Mosher and Danoff-Burg (2009) cite three recent studies that found that people who are receiving health care themselves actually prefer the label 'patient' to alternatives such as 'survivor' or 'consumer' (see Deber et al., 2005; Lloyd et al., 2001; Nair, 1998).

The construction of cancer as 'war' and the use of military metaphors that instruct patients to 'fight their illness' (see Lupton, 1994; Ross, 1989) are extremely widespread. Obituaries and other references to cancer-related deaths in the media almost inevitably construct the death as a casualty of a 'battle with cancer'. It seems as though it is not acceptable to simply die of cancer – one must first 'do battle' with it. Williams Camus (2009) presents a comprehensive analysis of the use of metaphor in popularizations of scientific articles on cancer in the English press. 'Cancer is War' was found to be the most frequently used metaphor, a finding that is supported by earlier research (e.g. Clarke, 1992; Seale, 2001; Van Rijn-van Togeren, 1997). This construction is also something that Sontag's (1991) early polemic against the use of metaphor in cancer discourse identified and challenged. 'Cancer is War' constructs cancer as an enemy who must be fought at all costs and by any means necessary. It instructs patients to not give up the fight, positioning the body as a battlefield upon which the struggle between life and death is fought. Collateral damage (to the body, to the patient) is to be expected and must be accepted as an inevitable part of this process. Soldierly bravery and stoic acceptance together with an optimistic attitude and a belief in one's ability to 'win the battle' are required and expected. It is suggested that if the patient shows enough determination to win and fights hard enough they can win the war. 'Not giving up' is valued more highly than any other stance within this context.

The construction of cancer as a moral concern involves attributing responsibility for their cancer to the cancer patient. Stacey (1997: 175) identifies a contemporary 'model of cancer as a disease "occasioned" by the self', according to which the cancer is understood as the patient's own creation (be it through their lifestyle, their body's inability to recognize and destroy the cancer cells, or their psychological predisposition to suppress negative emotions) and, therefore, their own responsibility. Cancer as a moral concern legitimizes the question 'What is it about this person that invited cancer into their lives?' and, by implication, 'What did they do wrong?' In this way, cancer is constructed as a sign of some (moral) failing on the part of the patient.

The three dominant constructions of what it means to have cancer identified above (i.e. the imperative to 'think positively'; the construction of cancer as 'war'; the construction of cancer as a moral concern) each foreground particular dimensions of meaning around which the experience of cancer is organized while obscuring or excluding others. As such, they constitute interpretative frameworks which prescribe legitimate ways of being a cancer patient and which structure the experience of those who are positioned within them.

For example, the cultural imperative to 'think positively' foregrounds the patient's responsibility to do all they can to regain health. It privileges a 'restitution narrative' (Frank, 1995) that constructs illness as a temporary interruption of the 'normal' state of being, which is health. This means that acceptance (of illness, of suffering, of mortality) is not a legitimate way of finding meaning in a cancer diagnosis. The cultural imperative to 'think positively' constructs acceptance as 'giving up' and it taints the patient who chooses to accept their fate with the undesirable qualities of the deserting soldier, the one who surrenders, who lacks the moral courage to continue to fight the enemy. Staying with the experience of suffering and finding meaning within it without 'making it better' is not a socially acceptable option. The cultural imperative to 'think positively' instructs those diagnosed with cancer to fight back and not give up. It positions the patient as active agent in the cancer drama and it attributes ultimate responsibility to the patient for the outcome of their battle where, morally speaking, not giving up is as highly valued as winning (as demonstrated by the obligatory reference to the 'battle with cancer' in obituaries and media reports of cancer-related deaths). Similarly, the construction of 'cancer as a moral concern' also positions the patient at the centre of events. This time, responsibility is attributed retrospectively, by scrutinizing the patient's psychological make-up and lifestyle in the search for aetiological factors. As Stacey (1997: 175) points out, the construction of cancer as 'a disease "occasioned" by the self' implicates the very core of the cancer patient's identity, their character and personality, in the aetiology of the disease. This means that it can be difficult for the patient to separate 'self' and 'disease' leading to a sense of overall corruption and inadequacy. The malaise then transcends the medical frame of reference and begins to require moral adjustments, the first of which is the acceptance of responsibility for the disease, followed by the promise to heed the 'wake-up call' and to change one's ways. Experientially, this means that, for the cancer patient to gain social approval, they need to reject their former self and to engage in a process of moral renewal. Refusal to do this may mean losing social support and missing out on empathy.

We have seen that military cancer metaphors construct cancer as a formidable enemy which has invaded and colonized the body and which must be fought by any means necessary. They present the patient's body as the battleground upon which the war against cancer must be fought and where collateral damage is inevitable. Within this perspective, the cancer patient as a person is separated from their body, which itself becomes the enemy since the cancer resides within the body's own cells. Experientially, this means that the patient's relationship with their own body is likely to be ambivalent, as it is not obvious to what extent the body is an ally and to what extent it is the enemy (see also Williams Camus, 2009, for a discussion of the social psychological consequences of martial cancer metaphors). In addition, the patient's physical needs as a person (e.g. for physical closeness to others, for physical intimacy) can easily disappear from view when the body becomes a battlefield and the patient may feel that a desire for physical comfort and human contact is inappropriate and needs to be suppressed, particularly during treatment.

Overall, dominant interpretations of what it means to have cancer are characterized by an individualistic orientation. From the suggestion that the individual's commitment to their 'battle against cancer' can make the difference between life and death, to the notion that cancer is a disease occasioned by the self, interpretations foreground the individual patient's role in their illness. A preoccupation with control and the assumption that gaining control over events is always possible and desirable are also evident. Dominant interpretations of what it means to have cancer position the person with cancer as the protagonist in a moral tale about overcoming obstacles and rising to the challenge of constructing a better life. As such, these culturally preferred interpretations resonate with the individualism which characterizes the thinking of Western industrialized societies and which underpins their socio-economic structures.

'Interpretative violence'

Our discussion of the ways in which dominant interpretations of what it means to be diagnosed with cancer has drawn attention to the power of interpretation. It has demonstrated how vulnerable people's experiences can be shaped by culturally available interpretations that privilege certain aspects of the experience (e.g. individual responsibility, the need to fight) while marginalizing others (e.g. the possibility of acceptance, the experience of suffering). It has become clear that encountering dominant interpretations can severely constrain the individual's freedom to give meaning to their own experience and can be restrictive or even oppressive.

The act of interpretation has ethical implications because, as we have seen, interpretations are actions with consequences that can be evaluated (see Teo, 2010: 299, citing Austin, 1975). When interpretations have consequences that hurt, damage or disadvantage those at the receiving end of them, such interpretations can be described as unethical. Teo (2010; see also Teo, 2008) has developed the argument that interpretations of social-scientific data (for example, on differences in IQ or personality measures) that construct entire social groups (such as ethnic minorities or women) as inferior even though the data allow for equally viable alternative interpretations that do not involve the depreciation of these groups, then these interpretations constitute an instance of 'epistemological violence'. This is because the observed differences in the measures of interest to the researcher (be they IQ, personality, or some other measure of performance) do not, in themselves, mean anything. They are made meaningful by the researcher's use of theory to account for the differences. However, the role of interpretation is not openly acknowledged when one theory is selected to explain the findings (e.g. the proposition that genetic factors are responsible for the observed differences) while other possible explanations are overlooked (e.g. the possibility that the differences are the product of inequalities). The result is the presentation of one interpretation as 'knowledge'. Teo (2010: 296) proposes that 'if concrete interpretations have negative consequences for groups – even though alternative, equally plausible interpretations of the data are available – then a form of violence is committed'. Teo's use of the expression 'epistemological violence' builds on the notion of 'epistemic violence' developed by post-colonial researchers such as Spivak (1988), which refers to the construction of those who are defined as 'Other' (and, therefore, problematized) in society. Teo draws attention to the role of social scientists in general, and psychologists in particular, in perpetrating interpretative violence within the process of knowledge production. He defines 'epistemological violence' as follows:

> Epistemological violence is a practice that is executed in empirical articles and books in psychology, when theoretical interpretations regarding empirical results implicitly or explicitly construct the *Other* as inferior or problematic, despite the fact that alternative interpretations, equally viable based on the data, are available.
>
> (Teo, 2010: 298)

The negative impact of such interpretations can take the form of misrepresentations and distortions, the silencing of the voices of those who are being thus interpreted, propositions of inferiority, and, most seriously, the infringements of their rights through adverse practices and/or policies. Some examples of such practices have been provided in Chapter 1 (see p. 19). Teo (2010) argues that those who produce interpretations of social-scientific data need to understand that they have an 'epistemological responsibility' to be mindful of the potential and actual consequences of their interpretations, particularly when the research is concerned with differences between social groups – between 'us' and 'the Other' (see Teo, 2010: 301). Teo's argument here echoes the concerns voiced by Barker et al. (2007) and Flowers and Langdridge (2007) regarding 'suspicious' interpretations of the actions of marginalized communities, discussed in Chapter 2 (see pp. 29–32).

Ethics of interpretation in qualitative research

So what are the implications of all this for qualitative research? And how can qualitative researchers navigate the ethical challenges involved in the process of interpretation?

I would agree with Teo (2010: 300–1) in emphasizing the need for researchers to be self-reflective and to ensure that they have the awareness and necessary training to fully understand the relationship between data and interpretation. In fact, the desire to raise awareness regarding the theoretical, ethical, and practical implications of interpretation is one of the reasons for writing this book. Responsible interpretation also requires a good understanding of the social and political context of one's research and an awareness of the possible limitations of one's interpretations. Interpreting the experience, conduct, and/or performance of those who come from different traditions, cultures or social groups requires particular care and sensitivity on the part of the researcher.

In the remainder of this chapter, we shall identify some strategies qualitative researchers can use to foreground and, hopefully, address ethical concerns in their interpretations. These include: (1) keeping the research question in mind and being modest about what the research can reveal, (2) ensuring that the participant's voice is not lost, and (3) remaining open to alternative interpretations.

As Brinkmann and Kvale (2008) point out, however, being an ethical researcher involves far more than following ethical rules and guidelines; it requires the ability to remain open to the ethical conflicts, dilemmas, and ambivalences that will arise throughout the course of the research, and to respond to them on the basis of one's own ethical capabilities rather than simply by applying pre-defined rules. As such, qualitative researchers need to engage continuously with what Brinkmann and Kvale (2008: 265) call 'fields of uncertainty' while trying to practise 'morally responsible research behaviour' (Brinkmann and Kvale, 2008: 268).

Strategy 1: Keeping the research question in mind and being modest about what the research can reveal

It is impossible to analyse data without a research question in mind. As we have seen, the data never speaks for itself and to render the data meaningful the researcher needs to interpret the data. This, in turn, is only possible if the researcher interrogates the data; that is to say, if she asks questions of the data. The researcher approaches the data with a question in mind, something she wants to find out. It is essential that the researcher is fully aware of her motives in approaching the data, as these will inevitably shape the research findings. For example, a semi-structured interview with a young woman about her experience of 'coming out' to family and friends as a lesbian could potentially answer a whole range of research questions. The researcher needs to know what it is she wants from the data. Does she want to know what it was like for the woman to tell her friends and family about her sexuality? What it felt like? Does she want to know how others reacted to the woman's news? What it was like for them? Does she want to know how the woman talked about her experience? What kind of language she used? Or what kind of impact her account had on the interviewer? It is impossible to simply 'analyse the data', because to do this would mean to claim to be able to find out what the young woman's account meant as such, rather than to see it as a potential source of information about specific dimensions of the phenomenon of 'coming out'.

Responsible research means being modest about what we can come to know. It is important to remember that any research project is motivated and driven by a research question, which specifies what aspect or dimension of social/psychological reality the study aims to shed light on. No study ever seeks to simply study 'life' as such or to understand 'the world' in general. Even realist research only ever seeks to establish the truth about something in particular rather than simply 'the truth'. In addition, every study will have to work within a set of practical constraints (such as available time and finances), which set limits to what it can aspire to find out.

This means that even the most carefully designed study can never do more than to shed light on one small part of a much bigger whole. Different research methods such as grounded theory, discourse analysis, or phenomenological methods can shed light on different aspects of human experience; none of them can capture all of it. From this point of view, qualitative research is about attempting to discover new aspects of a totality that can never be accessed directly or captured in its entirety. Kvale (2003) suggests that a mixed methods design whereby the researcher uses multiple research strategies to shed light on a phenomenon from different angles can help to ensure that data are not over-interpreted and/or over-generalized. This may indeed help to remind the researcher (and her audience) that no one reading can provide an answer to all the questions we may have about a phenomenon. The knowledge claims a researcher can make on the basis of her research, however, are always limited and it is imperative that she is clear about this.

Strategy 2: Ensuring that the participant's voice is not lost

The relationship between the data (that is, the original texts that research participants produce) and the analysis (that is, the stories that the researcher tells about such texts) is a complex one. In see Chapters 1 and 2, we acknowledged that the researcher's own prior understandings, their expectations, interests and preferred theoretical frameworks, and, indeed, their research question(s), provide a necessary starting point, a way-in to the data, which allows the process of interpretation to take place. This means that the analysis of the data and the insights generated on the basis of it are always a synthesis of the participant's original account and the researcher's own perspective. Any sense that is made of the phenomenon and any meaning that is attributed to it come from both the participant and the researcher. On the basis of our discussion of 'suspicious' and 'empathic' interpretations (see Chapter 1), we have established that some interpretations are more openly informed by the researcher's agenda than others. We have drawn attention to the power issues involved in such interpretations and we have raised questions about the potentially harmful effects upon research participants of 'suspicious' interpretations of their words and actions (see Chapter 2).

Interestingly, the effects of the interpretations of the data on those who generated the data in the first place are rarely discussed in the literature on research ethics (see Parker, 2005a, for an exception to this). In line with this, ethical clearance procedures tend to be concerned with the effects on participants of taking part in the research rather than with the effects on them of the 'knowledge' produced by the research. For example, researchers are expected to have considered the psychological effects of talking about sensitive issues within research interviews and they are expected to provide appropriate referral options for those participants who become distressed as a result. By contrast, the ethical dimensions of the process of analysis are often neglected. And yet, in qualitative analysis, much more so than in counselling and psychotherapy, it is often the researcher alone who gives meaning to the data. The research participant, having provided an account of their experience, tends to disappear from the scene. Occasionally, they may be consulted again, once or twice, in a process referred to as member checking or participant validation. While there are exceptions to this pattern, most notably within the context of participatory action research projects, in most qualitative studies in psychology the participants are not involved in the interpretation of their data and they have no say over how the results from the study are to be used. However, it could be argued that potentially the effects of the interpretations (and their uses) are longer lasting and perhaps more profound than the effects of the experience of generating the data. For example, while it may be relatively undemanding and perhaps even fun for a teenager to join a focus group to talk about cigarette smoking, if the focus group research was funded by a tobacco company, the findings could be used to market cigarettes more effectively to teenagers, thus impacting upon the participants (and their peer group) in a way they may not have anticipated or be desired by them and which may do them harm (see Brinkmann and Kvale, 2008: 274).

So how can we make sure that the participant's voice is not lost from the research? And how can we find ways of ensuring that informed consent is obtained throughout and for all aspects of the study (including the analysis and interpretation of the data), not just for the data collection phase?

Kvale (2003; see also Brinkmann and Kvale, 2008) invokes Latour's (2000) argument about the importance of allowing the objects of research to object to what is said about them. Latour (2000) reminds us that scientists learn about the objects of research in the physical sciences (i.e. physical or chemical processes and entities) precisely through these objects' (often very powerful, even violent) reactions to experimental conditions and manipulations. He argues that if humans were given the opportunity to object to the researcher's constructions of them in the same way, '[T]hen, humans would start to behave in the hands of the social scientists as interestingly as natural objects in the hands of natural scientists' (Latour, 2000: 116, cited in Kvale, 2003: 35). The resulting knowledge would then, according to Latour, be more objective and more valid, and as Kvale (2003) emphasizes, also more ethical, as participants' objections to the researcher's interpretations would be incorporated into the analysis. Brinkmann and Kvale (2008: 275) propose that:

> an important ethical and scientific attitude that should be cultivated in qualitative researchers is a willingness to let the object object and frustrate the investigations, since this is often at once a sign of important knowledge and of ethical issues.

This does not, of course, mean that researchers should confront participants with challenging interpretations to provoke strong responses and/or objections. The effects of an interpretation on the self-understanding of the participant needs to be carefully considered even when there is an opportunity for the participant to object to it.

Ideally, therefore, research participants ought to be maximally involved in the production of knowledge about them and research procedures ought to ensure that they are 'interested, active, disobedient, fully involved in what is said about them by others' (Latour, 2000: 116, cited in Brinkmann and Kvale, 2008: 276). However, in the absence of ongoing collaboration with research participants, ethical inter- pretation must acknowledge the considerable distance between the account and any claims about its meaning. This means that in such instances the interpretation belongs to the researcher and it must be understood that it may tell us just as much (or more!) about the researcher as it does about the participant. It also means that the aim of an ethical analysis ought to be the amplification of meaning; that is to say, the exploration of layers of meaning associated with the account without claiming that the account can be reduced to any one of them. Most importantly, it means respecting the integrity of the original account, acknowledging its value in its own right. This is to say, it means not claiming that the researcher knows what the participant's account 'really' means.

Strategy 3: Remaining open to alternative interpretations

It is important to reduce the risk of producing interpretations that close down (rather than open up) meaning. Interpretations which impose pre-conceived nar- ratives upon the data and which squeeze the data into an existing theoretical framework to confirm the researcher's expectations are both unethical and also unlikely to increase our understanding of the phenomenon under investigation. Even 'suspicious' approaches to interpretation can be cautious and allow the data to object. For example, Frosh and Young's (2008) account of the application of a psychosocial reading to interview data from a study on the experience of broth- erhood constitutes an excellent example of a tentative and cautious formulation of a 'suspicious' reading. Kvale (2003) also provides a sensitive and ethically at- tuned discussion of the value of psychoanalytically inspired qualitative research. Remaining open to alternative interpretations, even when using a specified theor- etical perspective, means avoiding ' "top down" assertions of expert knowledge' and instead engaging in 'careful examination of textual material' (Frosh and Emerson, 2005: 322). Brinkmann and Kvale (2008: 277) recommend that qual- itative researchers 'contextualize' and 'narrativize' to help them achieve a fuller understanding of the data. Contextualizing involves paying attention to the con- text within which something is said or done, while narrativizing means situating an account temporally and understanding the events that are being described in it as forming part of a bigger whole (such as a story or a project). Brinkmann and Kvale (2008: 277) advise against '[L]ooking at a situation as a "snap-shot", outside its temporal and social narrative context', as this removes its moral meaning and can lead to misunderstandings and misrepresentations. Teo (2010) also draws at- tention to the importance of the context of reflection and discovery within which the researcher is working. Ethical interpretation requires that we think about why it is that a researcher may be interested in asking a particular research question. For example, why is it that particular social groups' actions and conduct are the focus of much research (e.g. young people or minority groups) while other groups (e.g. middle-aged, middle-class men or very wealthy people) escape such scrutiny? And who wants to know about their behaviour and why? Teo (2010) encourages researchers to think about the social origins of our research questions, hypotheses and theories, and to consider their relationship with the various social, political, economic, and cultural interests that exist in the society within which the research is taking place.

Conclusion

In this chapter, we have been concerned with the ethical dimensions of the act of interpretation. We have established that interpretations are much more than the products of our analysis, more than interesting stories about our research participants' experiences. Interpretations are actions that can have powerful consequences, as they impact upon people in all kinds of ways. These consequences can be immediate and personal (as in the example of the women undergoing chemotherapy who avoided social interactions to protect themselves against encountering certain interpretations of their cancer) or they can be delayed and socially dispersed (for example, where an interpretation is picked up by policy-makers and begins to inform the work of providers of social services).

This chapter has emphasized the constraining and potentially oppressive aspects of interpretation because we need to be keenly aware of these to ensure that our interpretations are as ethical as possible and that we do not (knowingly) damage those whose accounts our interpretations are based on (and others like them). However, before bringing this chapter to a close, I want to acknowledge that interpretations can also be extremely helpful and, indeed, liberating to those who receive them.

Narrative psychology has demonstrated that especially at times of major change in a person's life circumstances, at times when a person's sense of identity and of their place in the world is disrupted, people seek to create new stories about themselves and their lives. They try to make sense of what is happening to them by making the disruptive events meaningful and they do this by making them part of a new narrative that turns chaos into something that can be understood, thought about, and shared with others. For example, research has established that there are positive (social and psychological) consequences of receiving a medical diagnosis, especially if this follows a lengthy period of uncertainty about the meaning of one's symptoms. Diagnosis, which is after all a medical interpretation of a variety of unexplained phenomena, can provide a sense of validation of one's medical condition, access to a collective identity, and a reduction in social isolation, for example through access to support groups. Receiving a diagnosis entails an entitlement to take up the sick role with all its attendant social benefits and this, in turn, can lead to a reduction in distress for the patient (e.g. Reid et al., 1991;

Stewart and Sullivan, 1982; see also Radley, 1994). Being diagnosed, especially if this occurs after a long period of pre-diagnostic health problems and health-related uncertainty, can come as a great relief.

Thus, interpretations (even those, such as a medical diagnosis, which are imposed by an expert) can both limit and constrain as well as open up and facilitate what those labelled with them can experience. On the one hand, embracing a diagnostic label can empower a person to join with others to request treatment and support, while, on the other, it can severely limit a person's options within their social world, as has been discussed earlier in this chapter. Whether a particular interpretation is desirable or undesirable depends on how it is used, by whom, and for what purpose.

Finally, it is important to acknowledge that avoiding interpretation, for example by taking a person's comments or behaviour at face-value and by refusing to 'read between the lines', can also carry ethical risks. Think of the therapist who does not simply accept a client's assertion that she 'is fine' when there is non-verbal evidence to the contrary such as eyes bathed in tears and shaking hands. Or the parent who does not believe her son when he tells her 'I hate you' and instead interprets his statement as an expression of frustration and the desire to have more control over his life. In both of these examples, the interpretation of the words ('I am fine'; 'I hate you') takes into account the context within which they are spoken and, by doing that, it allows for a deeper understanding of their meaning. It could be argued that in both cases the interpretation is in the interest of the speaker as a literal reading would close down further communication and with that the possibility of really being heard. However, ultimately, the helpfulness or otherwise of an interpretation can only be evaluated by its consequences for those to whom it was applied and their own experience of them. This means accepting that there are times when people do not wish to 'be understood'.

We need to accept that the solution to the ethical challenges associated with the act of interpretation is not to avoid interpretation altogether. For one thing, as we have seen in Chapter 1, it is impossible to understand something without interpreting it at the same time. In addition, a refusal to interpret other people's actions can actually impoverish their experience and limit their options. However, I hope it has become clear that the act of interpretation carries an enormous responsibility and that striving to produce ethical interpretations ought to be a priority for every qualitative researcher.

Box 2 'I Remember My Mother Dying' by Craig Raine

Even in the world of artistic expression, which in many ways is all about the freedom to create new meaning, the ethics of interpretation cannot be sidestepped. A good example of how the ethics of interpretation can become an issue within this context is a poem published by Craig Raine following the death of his mother. In the poem, Raine tells the reader how, two days before her death, his mother asked him to pluck the hairs out of her chin. He goes on to describe his mother's response to having her hairs plucked with a tweezer. He does this by comparing her expressions of satisfaction (her sighs, her saying 'yes, yes') to the expression of sexual pleasure, likening his mother's response to 'someone being slowly fucked'. Raine interprets his mother's experience through a sexual lens. In an article for the *Guardian* newspaper, he himself acknowledges that she would not have liked the poem because it violates her privacy. He still went ahead and published the poem, against the advice of his wife and friends, because he believed that 'the morality of art is its accuracy'. Note how the poet justifies his decision to publish by suggesting that his interpretation is 'accurate', thus implying that he is merely telling the truth about his mother's experience. However, another take on this poem is that it constitutes an act of interpretative violence, perhaps all the more ethically problematic because its target, the poet's mother, has died and cannot challenge it.

Based on Raine, C. (2005) I remember my mother dying, *The Times Literary Supplement*, 25 November, p. 5.

4 Language and interpretation

Our concern in this chapter is the role of language in interpretation, the way in which the medium we use to construct and communicate meaning (i.e. language) is implicated in the character and make-up of this very meaning. Within this context, in this chapter we invoke what Forrester (1996: 32) describes as the 'language-dominant view of language'. According to this view, language and thought are inextricably bound up with one another, with language producing 'versions and visions of reality as codes and conventions embedded within particular cultural contexts' (Forrester, 1996: 33). An early version of this view can be found in what has become known as the Sapir/Whorf hypothesis (Whorf, 1956), which proposed that the language one uses shapes one's worldview.

Lowe (1985: 4) captures these propositions very clearly in the following account of the relationship between experiential 'reality' and language:

> Reality, the world of experience, consists of a *continuous*, uninterrupted flow of impressions of all sorts which man [*sic*] can perceive with his physical senses. Human language, by categorizing these impressions through the various representational systems it has developed, has introduced some sort of *discontinuity* into the flow of impressions – hence the expression 'to split' the world of experience – by providing man [*sic*] with a mental vision or representation of experience. In fact, by providing man [*sic*] with a certain conceptualization of reality, every language proposes an original, discontinuous vision of the universe of experience. And in a sense, every meaningful unit of a given language participates in some way in the creation of the global mental vision of the world this particular language proposes to its speaker.
>
> (cited in Galántai, 2002: 191; italics in original)

In his 'Letter on Humanism' (1993), Martin Heidegger describes language as 'the house of Being'. While Heidegger's reflections on the nature of language and its relationship with human existence are too complex and multifaceted to be discussed here, his image of language as 'the house of Being' does capture something that is very relevant to our discussion. Language is the medium through which we humans construct meaning, and language seems to be required for us to know ourselves in particular ways. In his discussion of culture and private discourse, Moghaddam (1999) points out that personality descriptions (such as 'shy', 'helpful' or 'honest') are extremely rare in some societies and that some languages do not have words with a meaning of 'self' equivalent to that in the West. As a result, different kinds of subjectivities emerge and not all of them are characterized by individualized self-reflection. In a similar vein, Cushman (1995: 39) argues that historical and cultural contexts 'promote particular configurations of the self', which make available radically different ways of being for those who are positioned within them. Cushman (1995: 28) writes:

> Our contemporary idea of what it means to be human, of what is the proper and natural way of being, was probably not shared by our ancestors, and it certainly is not shared by peoples of other cultures. This might help us better understand why the current configuration of the self, the masterful, bounded self of the twentieth century, is considered an aberration by many other cultures and would have been unthinkable (literally) by Westerners in earlier times, say six hundred, a thousand, or two thousand years ago.

Although socio-economic structures and socio-cultural practices condition these configurations of the self, it is language that captures them and allows us to internalize them, thus structuring our subjectivities in particular ways. It seems that language is indeed more than a tool for communication – it constitutes 'the home' within which we 'dwell' (Heidegger, 1993: 217) and which makes us who we are.

Within the language-dominant view, then, language plays a foundational role in human psychology, bringing into being the very notions of the 'self' and 'other'. As Berger and Luckman (1967: 35) put it, '[L]anguage forces me into its patterns', with the result that, and here Forrester (1996: 48) cites Wittgenstein, 'the limits of my world are the limits of my language'.

Our discussion of the process of interpretation and the ethical challenges associated with it (see Chapters 1–3) has already indicated the close connection between language and interpretation. For example, our examination of the transformative power of language during the process of diagnosis (see Chapter 3) demonstrated how the choice of a label for a disease informs the way in which a patient constructs meaning around their diagnosis and how this in turn shapes their experience of the condition. We showed how our choice of label and the grammatical constructions associated with it construct the very relationship between a person and their illness (e.g. illness as being our possession as in 'I have diabetes', or as being identical with the self as in 'I am diabetic').

This chapter explores in more detail the intimate relationship between language and interpretation. It foregrounds the connection between the process of meaning-making and the use of language, and it reflects on the ways in which different qualitative methods engage with this. The chapter identifies some of the challenges associated with the (inevitable) use of language in qualitative research. It addresses issues around the transformation (e.g. from spoken to written language through transcription; through descriptions of non-linguistic data in words; through translation from one language into another) of qualitative data and their implications for the act of interpretation. The aim of the chapter is to sensitize the reader to the role of language in qualitative research and to emphasize that the use of language always involves a degree of interpretation.

Language and meaning

The intimate connection between the process of meaning-making and the use of language constitutes a challenge to qualitative researchers. Since all qualitative data is either language-based in its original form (e.g. semi-structured interviews, transcripts of focus group discussions, diary entries) or transformed into language by the researcher (e.g. descriptions of participants' non-verbal behaviours and actions, accounts of social processes, discussions of the meanings found in non-linguistic data such as drawings or photographs), it is impossible to access its meaning outside of language. In other words, the interpretation of the data always requires a simultaneous interpretation of the language used to capture it. This, in turn, means that the researcher needs to adopt a perspective on language. In other words, the researcher needs to decide how to conceptualize the contribution made by the particular use of language (the choice of words, terminology, figures of speech, style of expression, etc.) to the meaning that is being created and communicated in and through the research.

Polkinghorne (2005) points out that the relationship between experience and its description in language remains a contested issue. He identifies an array of positions on this question, which range from viewing language as predominantly expressive to viewing it as largely performative. A view of language as expressive approaches language as a means to an end whereby it is used to express pre-existing thoughts and feelings. Here, experience is seen to precede language (as in Husserlian versions of phenomenology). From this point of view, language is a medium for encapsulating and transmitting meaning that pre-exists its capture in language. For example, this perspective would suggest that, when someone says 'I love you', they are putting into words an inner feeling that was there before the person decided to express it. Although they could have used a different phrase to describe the feeling (for example, they could have said 'Je t'aime' or 'I have the deepest feelings of love and affection for you' or 'I am in love with you'), the words used are secondary to the feeling that they attempt to capture. From this point of view, although language is important as a major way in which thoughts, feelings, and experiences can be expressed and communicated and, therefore, be made accessible to others, it remains a means to an end rather than being an end in itself.

An opposing view of language would be that experience is constructed by, and therefore the product of, the language that is used to talk about it (as in Derrida's postmodern position). Here, language is seen as performative. This perspective presents language as more than a medium because language is seen to construct meaning rather than simply reflect it. Such a constructionist view of language argues that our thoughts, feelings, and experiences are produced as we take up positions within discourses. For example, from this point of view, saying 'I love you' to one's partner on Valentine's Day is part of a culturally specific repertoire, the discourse of romantic love, which sets up subject positions (of the lover, of the beloved, of the broken-hearted, of the betrayed, and so on) that require particular routines and rituals. Here, talk about 'love' does not refer to an inner feeling that can be diagnosed by looking out for the signs and symptoms of 'being in love'; rather, saying 'I love you' is part and parcel of a socio-cultural practice which many of us engage in and which helps us to structure our relationships in ways that fit in with the discourses and institutions of our particular culture.

It is important to point out, however, that the above presentation of these two perspectives has emphasized their differences so as to bring out the contrast between the view of language as *expressive* and that of language as *constructive* or *performative*. Most people who subscribe to either of these views would probably adopt a more moderate version of them than the ones presented here. For example, seeing language primarily as a medium does not mean that one would claim that expressing thoughts and feelings is unproblematic. Even where language is conceptualized as a means to an end (e.g. for the expression of inner feelings), the words chosen to do this (e.g. whether I say 'I love you', 'I am in love with you', 'I care for you') introduce subtle differences into the meaning that is being expressed. No-one would claim that an unambiguous matching of feelings with the 'right' words that correspond to them can ever be achieved.

Similarly, a social constructionist view of language does not require that we deny that people have feelings. However, the argument is that feelings, even those that we experience as arising from within ourselves, are only made possible because we have been socialized into a discursive universe that makes these particular feelings and their peculiar meanings available to us. They are part of a culturally specific repertoire within which we experience ourselves.

Indeed, Polkinghorne (2005) describes a middle position, as exemplified by the work of Ricoeur, whereby experience is seen as more complex and nuanced than literal language is capable of capturing; however, at the same time, the use of figurative expressions such as metaphors that come closer to the richness of experience does more than to (imperfectly) reflect it; instead, it adds to the original experience, congealing, differentiating, and perhaps amplifying it. Hammersley (2010: 559) adopts a similar (hermeneutic) position in relation to language.

To obtain a clearer understanding of the different ways in which qualitative research can engage with the problem of language, it may help to consider to what extent the research is concerned with the *content* (e.g. what participants are saying about their experiences) and to what extent it is concerned with the *form* (e.g. how participants are talking about their experiences) of the data. If the primary purpose of the research is to get closer to participants' experiences and to find out what is going on for them, then the *content* of the data is the most important feature and language is approached as a medium (i.e. as *expressive*). If, however, the aim of the research is to obtain a better understanding of how meaning is constructed around a particular phenomenon, then the use of language and its strategic deployment (i.e. the *form* the data takes) will be of interest. In this case, language is seen as *constructive* and *performative*. However, again, in reality things are not quite so clear-cut and there is, of course, some interdependence between form and content. As Smith et al. (2009: 194) point out, human experience is 'inevitably "always already" enmeshed with language and culture' and this means that it is impossible to study the meaning of an experience without at the same time paying attention to the resources (such as narratives, discourses, and metaphors) with which such meanings are made.

Let us take a closer look at the ways in which different qualitative approaches engage with the problem of language and how their different perspectives on language shape the interpretations that emerge from such research. For the purpose of this discussion, approaches to qualitative research are categorized into three broad orientations to knowledge production: *realist, phenomenological,* and *social constructionist*. This classification (and the characterizations of each of the three orientations) is taken from Willig (2012).

Realist research

Realist research in qualitative psychology can be characterized as research that uses qualitative methods of data collection and analysis to obtain a rich, accurate, detailed, and comprehensive picture of (some aspects of) the social world or of human psychology. The type of knowledge sought in this case is the type that aspires to capture and reflect as truthfully as possible something that is happening in the real world and that exists independently of the researcher's, and indeed the research participants', views and/or knowledge about it. The sorts of things a researcher who aspires to generate this type of knowledge might study include social processes (for example, what happens when a new member joins an established reading group or what happens when an organization implements a new equal opportunities policy) and psychological mechanisms or processes (for example, how a person who suffers from panic attacks plans a journey on public transport or how people who lost a parent at an early age approach intimate relationships). The assumption that underpins this type of research is that there are certain processes or patterns of a social and/or psychological nature that characterize and/or shape the behaviour and/or the thinking of research participants, and that these can be identified and conveyed by the researcher. This means that the researcher assumes that the (material, social, psychological) world they investigate can potentially be understood provided that the researcher is skilled enough to uncover the patterns, regularities, structures, and/or laws of behaviour which characterize it and which generate the social and/or psychological phenomena which we witness (and which constitute our data). The researcher can succeed or fail in this, which means that the researcher aspires to generate valid and reliable knowledge about a social and/or psychological phenomenon that exists independently of the researcher's awareness of it. As such, this type of research is characterized by a *discovery orientation* (see Madill et al., 2000). The role of the researcher in this situation is akin to that of a *detective* who uses their skills, knowledge, and experience to uncover hitherto hidden facts and who, through their labour, makes what appeared puzzling or mysterious intelligible. The kinds of methods used by qualitative researchers who aim to produce this type of knowledge include (realist versions of) ethnography and grounded theory methodology as well as some varieties of interpretative analysis, such as psychoanalytic approaches (but note that these methods can also be used from within a less realist epistemological framework).

Most realist research is primarily interested in the *content* of the data and the extent to which this can shed light on the phenomenon of interest to the researcher. Research participants act as *witnesses* who can provide the researcher with information about the phenomenon under investigation. Within this context, language is a medium for transmitting information from the participants to the researcher. Its function is, therefore, *expressive*.

To illustrate how realist research may approach language, let us imagine that we have conducted a semi-structured interview with a man who has witnessed a street robbery. Here is what our participant might have said:

> Well, I was on my way to the shops, just walking down the high street, when I heard this noise. It was right behind me. I looked round and I saw a commotion, people being shoved and pushed, and there is this young girl in the middle of this melee and she's struggling, her eyes looked really wild and I immediately thought, they're trying to hurt her. I was going to turn around and go back to help her of course, but then I saw what I thought was the blade of a knife and I got scared. I've got a bad back so I can't move very fast so I didn't think it was a good idea for me to get involved. I'm in my sixties now so I don't feel as strong as I used to. I know it's bad but I just didn't feel like I was going to be of any use to the girl. Luckily a couple of young lads stepped in and scared them off so it had a good ending.

From a realist perspective, this extract provides us with a description of the events that our participant witnessed. Here, language is seen to be used by the participant to express and communicate external (e.g. the setting; other people's actions) as well as internal (e.g. his thoughts at the time) events so that the interviewer can obtain an understanding of what transpired during the course of the robbery. The interviewer may ask further questions to obtain more detailed descriptions. For example, she may ask how many people were involved in what the participant described as a 'melee', or ask for more information about the girl (e.g. her age, her height, whether she was wearing expensive clothing or carrying valuable items such a mobile phone). The researcher may be interested in social aspects of street robberies and wants to find out which types of situations encourage bystander apathy. Alternatively, she may be interested in the psychological processes that occur within those who witness robberies, which may help her to understand how witnesses make decisions about whether or not to intervene. In any case, language is very much a means to an end: it is the medium through which research participants provide the researcher with the information she needs to understand what was going on and why.

There are realist approaches to research that go a step further in that they do not assume a straightforward relationship between the participant's account of their experience and what 'really happened'. For example, psychoanalytic approaches invoke the notion of the unconscious to explain why a participant says something in just the way that he does. So here the researcher needs to do additional work to establish what the participant's reference to, say, the blade of the knife that he thinks he saw 'really' means; for example, it could point to an underlying castration anxiety on the part of the witness. However, even then there is still an assumption that language does point to something that exists independently of the participant's (or the researcher's) awareness of it, and there is a belief that language is the route that gives the researcher access to this reality.

Phenomenological research

Qualitative research that aims to produce knowledge about the nature and quality of the subjective experience of research participants can be described as *phenomeno-logical*. In this case, the researcher still aspires to capture something that exists in the world (namely the participant's feelings, thoughts, and perceptions – their *experience*); however, no claim is being made regarding its relationship with other facets of the world or indeed regarding the accuracy of the participants' accounts of their experience (e.g. whether a phenomenological account of an embodied experience such as anger or anxiety matches up with objective physiological measures such as blood pressure or galvanic skin response). Such research aims to *understand* experience (rather than to discover what is 'really' going on). In other words, it does not matter whether what a research participant describes is an accurate reflection of what happened to them or a fantasy; instead, the type of knowledge the researcher is trying to obtain is *phenomenological* in nature – that is, knowledge of the quality and texture of the participant's experience. For example, a researcher might want to find out what it is like to be living with a diagnosis of psychosis or how a participant experiences the process of going through a divorce. Finding that a participant experiences herself as 'rejected by the whole world', for example, constitutes phenomenological knowledge irrespective of whether the participant really is being rejected by everyone she encounters. The task of the researcher in this type of research is to get as close as possible to the research participant's experience, to step into their shoes and to look at the world through their eyes, that is to say, *to enter their world*. Here, the role of the researcher is similar to that of the *person-centred counsellor* who listens to the client's account of their experience empathically, without judging and without questioning the external validity of what the client is saying. This means that the researcher assumes that there is more than one 'world' that can be studied. This is because researchers who seek this type of knowledge are interested in the *experiential world* of the participant (rather than the material, social, or psychological structures that may give rise to particular experiences; for example, the biochemical changes associated with psychosis or the social processes that can give rise to stereotyping); what appear to be the 'same' (material, social, psychological) conditions (e.g. a divorce, a diagnosis, an accident) can be experienced in many different ways, and this means that there are potentially as many (experiential) worlds as there are individuals. A researcher who attempts to generate this type of knowledge asks 'What is the world like *for this participant*?' The kinds of methods used by qualitative researchers who aim to produce this type of knowledge, unsurprisingly, tend to be phenomenological methods (such as interpretative phenomenological analysis or descriptive phenomenology).

Phenomenological research is still primarily interested in the *content* of the data and the extent to which this can shed light on the phenomenon of interest to the researcher. However, since the phenomenon of interest here is not, as it is in realist research, something that can be conceptually separated and isolated from the research participant who provided evidence of or about it (such as an underlying psychological structure, a social process, a psychological trait), in phenomenological research the participant is not so much in the role of a witness as that of a *story-teller* or the *author of an autobiography*. What is of interest here is the participant's experience as a whole, not an isolated part of it. Within this context, language is still a medium for transmitting information from the participant to the researcher and its function is still primarily *expressive*. However, as the quality and texture of the participant's experience is of interest (rather than factual information about it), the language used by the participant is of great interest to the researcher who will pay attention to the resonances and particular meanings invoked by the participant's choice of words and phrases.

Let us return to the interview extract describing our hypothetical participant's experience of witnessing a robbery. How might a phenomenological approach to research make sense of the account? The primary focus of phenomenological research is subjective experience. This means that the participant's account is taken to provide us with information about his experience rather than about the robbery itself. A phenomenological approach to language requires us to pay attention to the experiential meanings that are invoked by the words and expressions used by the participant. For example, we would be interested in the way in which his references to himself as having 'a bad back', as being 'in his sixties', and as not feeling as 'strong' as he used to be suggest that our participant is experiencing himself as fragile, as physically compromised, and somewhat delicate. He does not experience himself as the sort of person who is robust enough to challenge the robbers. This is confirmed by his reference to the 'young lads' who eventually did what he himself did not feel capable of doing. Another feature of our participant's account that would be of interest to phenomenological research is his repeated references to his senses. He describes himself as 'hearing a noise' and locating this as being 'right behind him'. He 'looks around' and 'sees a commotion'. He 'sees' what he believes to be the blade of a knife. These references indicate that our participant was alert and that he experienced himself as being tuned in to his physical environment. He is aware of what is going on and, in addition to this, he experiences himself as being called upon, by the events that he is witnessing, to act. It is only his rational considerations (of his fragility, his limited strength, his inability to move fast) that stop him from acting upon this impulse. A phenomenological analysis of our participant's account suggests that witnessing the robbery drew our participant's attention to his physical fragility and that this generated within him a struggle between his desire to help the victim of the robbery and his fear of being hurt in the process as a result of his lack of physical strength and agility.

Social constructionist research

Finally, a qualitative researcher can adopt a much more sceptical position in relation to 'knowledge' and argue that what is of interest is not so much what is really going on (*realist* approach to knowledge) or how something is actually experienced by participants (*phenomenological* approach) but rather how people talk about the world and, therefore, how they construct versions of reality through the use of language. Here, the type of knowledge aspired to is not knowledge about the world or knowledge about how things are experienced, but rather knowledge about the process by which such 'knowledge' is constructed in the first place. This means that questions about the nature of social/psychological events and experiences are suspended and instead the researcher is concerned with the social construction of 'knowledge'. Since language plays such an important part in the construction of 'knowledge', qualitative researchers who adopt a *social constructionist* orientation to knowledge generation tend to study discourses and the ways in which they are deployed within particular contexts. For example, a researcher might analyse the language used in policy documents about antisocial behaviour to understand how the phenomenon of concern – 'antisocial behaviour' – is constructed within these documents and how the discourses used in the documents position those who are constructed as the targets of proposed interventions. Such an approach to research is based upon the assumption that all human experience is mediated by language, which means that all social and psychological phenomena are constructed in one way or another. It also means that all knowledge about the world and experience of the world is very much socially mediated and that individual experiences are always the product of internalized social constructions. In other words, when participants are telling the researcher about their experiences, they are not seen to be giving voice to an inner reality (as in *phenomenological* research) or to be providing information about social/psychological processes (as in *realist* research); instead, the researcher is interested in how socially available ways of talking about the phenomenon of interest (i.e. discourses) are deployed by the participant on a particular occasion and perhaps also how these may shape the participant's experiences. Here, the role of the researcher is to draw attention to the constructed nature of social reality and to trace the specific ways in which particular phenomena are constructed through discourse and to reflect upon the consequences of this for those who are affected (that is to say, who are 'positioned') by these social constructions. As such, the role of the researcher is akin to that of an *architect* who looks at the phenomenon of interest with a view to how it has been constructed and from what resources and materials. The most commonly used method to produce this type of (*social constructionist*) knowledge is discourse analysis (of which there are several versions, including discursive psychology, Foucauldian discourse analysis, and critical discourse analysis); however, other methods such as narrative analysis and memory work can also be used.

Social constructionist research is, therefore, primarily interested in the *form* of the data and the extent to which this can shed light on the way in which 'reality' has been socially constructed on a particular occasion. Research participants whose talk is being sampled provide the discursive fabric that is unravelled by the researcher as she deconstructs the discourses that constitute their world. Here, language is seen as *constructive* and its function is *performative.*

Returning to our account of the robbery, how may a social constructionist perspective approach this text? Key questions to guide a social constructionist analysis include 'What is the participant doing when he is describing the robbery in this way?' and 'How exactly is he doing this?' Here, the language used by the participant to describe his experience is seen to construct a particular version of the event. The participant has a stake in this version as it constructs him and positions him in particular ways, too. A social constructionist approach to the account is based on the assumption that the event (in this case, the robbery) could have been described in a number of different ways. Such an approach is interested in how the event is constructed in this particular case and what the consequences and implications of such a construction might be. For example, our participant's references to his bad back, his age, and his lack of strength and agility within the context of the robbery position him as someone of whom heroic interventions could not be expected. As such, the participant's decision to foreground these qualities (as opposed to other qualities that he may have and that may have made him seem more eligible for intervention, such as a history of involvement in the Territorial Army or the presence of a strong walking stick) serves to ward off potential accusations of bystander apathy, selfishness, or cowardice. In addition, our participant's account is characterized by a lack of detail and some vagueness, especially in relation to the 'melee' which he witnessed ('I saw a commotion'). Note how he fails to specify how many people were involved, who shoved whom ('people being shoved and pushed'), and what was actually done to the girl (she is merely 'in the middle'). This way of constructing the event introduces a sense of confusion and lack of clarity that positions our participant as someone who is caught up in events he does not fully understand. Again, this implies that he could not be expected to intervene in the events in any meaningful way. From this perspective, language is not primarily expressive but rather performative in that it has an action orientation. The participant's account of his past experience (i.e. witnessing the robbery) cannot be separated from what he is doing in the present (in this case, trying to disclaim potential negative attributions and blame for not helping the girl).

We have seen that each of the three different epistemological orientations engages somewhat differently with language. Each one adopts a different view of what language represents, and this means that each approach to interpreting the data generates different insights. In the case of realist research, these take the form of claims about how the world works (including human psychology). Here, language provides a means of accessing information about the world. By contrast, phenomenological research attempts to capture experience and explicate its meaning. Here, the language people use to describe their experience sheds light on its texture and quality. However, from a phenomenological point of view, the use of language is also a part of the experience itself, giving it its shape and structure.

Finally, a social constructionist take on language engages with the constructive and performative dimensions of discourse, which means that the insights generated by social constructionist research are insights about how people construct versions of reality through language.

Transforming qualitative data: the case of translation

Whichever approach to language the researcher takes, additional challenges are presented when the research involves translation from one language into another. It is increasingly common for qualitative researchers to interview participants in their first language and to then translate the data before conducting the analysis. For example, research into social psychological aspects of migration, of cross-cultural phenomena, or of the experiences of refugees may require that data are translated. Translating qualitative data is particularly challenging because the aim of the work of translation is to get as close as possible to the meaning intended by the participant. It is not enough to capture the gist of what is being said and there is little room for poetic licence. Since qualitative analysis tends to involve a close reading of the data, paying particular attention to the participant's choice of words, phrases, and expressions, the transformation of the data which translation constitutes can be a problem. Scholars in translation studies have drawn attention to the extent to which translation involves much more than replacing words from one language with those of another. Galántai (2002) discusses the difficulties in trying to achieve a literal translation of a text from one language into another, citing Ortega y Gasset's (2000: 51) observation regarding the incommensurability of the meanings contained in words from different languages:

> It is utopian to believe that two words belonging to different languages, and which the dictionary gives us as translations of each other, refer to exactly the same objects. Since languages are formed in different landscapes, through different experiences, their incongruity is natural.
>
> (cited in Galántai, 2002: 170)

For example, it has been noted that emotional experiences are modulated differently in different languages. Besemeres (2006) observes that the term 'anxious', for instance, has acquired a meaning that invokes psychology (and psychopathology) in modern English, whereas the Polish term ('boję się') signifies something more natural and part of everyday life.

Ortega y Gasset (2000) argues that different languages structure experiential reality in different ways and that the work of translation involves a restructuring of reality in line with the language being used. Thus, to produce a translation, we need to 'reconstruct our conception of the world' (Galántai, 2002: 182). This means that translating an account of an experience from one language into another transforms it in such a way as to make the meanings invoked in one language accessible to speakers of another language. In the process of doing this, some meanings are lost and some are added. The result is something inspired by the original account yet different from it. In other words, by translating the account the researcher has interpreted it.

As we have seen in Chapter 3, the act of interpretation carries with it ethical responsibility. It is no different when interpretation takes the form of translation. As Temple and Koterba (2009) point out, when we translate other people's words we make choices about how we represent them and their lives. This means that translation is a political act and it is therefore important, argue Temple and Koterba (2009), that researchers engage with the implications of this and take responsibility for their choices. Power resides in the act of translation just as it is implicated in every act of interpretation.

For example, when translating their participants' accounts researchers have a choice about the extent to which the translated text should be tidied up and rendered into standard English, and the extent to which it should retain its foreign features. Temple and Koterba (2009) provide the example of Polish-speaking interviewees using the term 'Panem Bogiem', which literally translates as 'Mr God'. In the translation, the original construction could be retained and translated as 'Mr God', thus emphasizing the gendered aspect of it (i.e. 'Mr God' as opposed to 'Mrs God' or simply 'God'), or it could be translated into its English meaning equivalent – 'God'. There is a difference in meaning between the two options and there is also a differential construction of the interviewees, with the former option ('Mr God') emphasizing their foreignness and the latter ('God') minimizing any cultural differences. The option of minimizing differences has been described as 'domestication' of texts (Venuti, 1995, 1998) and as 'translatese' (Spivak, 1992) whereby all texts, regardless of their original language, sound as though they had been written in English in the first place. Temple and Koterba (2009) recommend that researchers produce what they call 'translation histories' in which they provide information about the various versions of the translation and a trail of decisions about word choice, and that this should form a part of the research itself.

Qualitative researchers who work with accounts that require translation can approach their task in a number of ways. Each of these has advantages and disadvantages and none of them is perfect. The important thing is to be aware of how each strategy shapes the product of the translation process and how this, in turn, has implications for what can emerge from the analysis of the translated data.

Perhaps the most common approach to working with qualitative interview data that requires translation is to transcribe the interview in its original language, to translate the transcript, and to then analyse the translation. An advantage of this way of working is that producing a full transcription in the original language first means that any translation that is produced is made on the basis of a full written record that can be re-visited, checked, and revised by the original or indeed other translators. This is quite different from translation that takes place as the interview proceeds in real time and is, therefore, made without much time for reflection, and where it is only the interpreter's original version of the translation that is available for inspection. Any errors made at the time of translation will remain and enter the analysis. Another advantage of this first approach is that the availability of a full translated transcript means that people other than those speaking the language in which the interview was originally conducted can work with the transcripts. This is important where research is supervised or the team of researchers have different language backgrounds. However, carrying out qualitative analysis of a translated interview transcript also has disadvantages. Given that, as we have seen above, there is no straightforward word-for-word equivalence between languages, the act of translation means that the transcript the researchers are analysing is, in fact, no longer the original document. The researchers are effectively analysing an interpretation (made by the translator) of the original interview data. This means that any decisions made by the translator (for example, about appropriate terms for emotional states and other categories of meaning) will unwittingly be carried over into any analytic categories constructed by the researchers and will, therefore, shape the findings of the study. In this situation it is desirable that either the translators are the researchers themselves or that the translator is consulted during the analytic process.

Another way of approaching the task of translating qualitative interviews attempts to avoid any problems associated with analysing a translated version of the data by analysing the original transcript in the original language and then translating the analysis. Here, the analysis can stay close to the original data as any analytic categories that emerge from the analysis are directly informed by the original text. Initially, analytic categories are also labelled in the original language and any notes, memos, and reflections by the researcher are in that same language, too. It is only when the researcher has gained an understanding of the meaning of the data and has developed insights into what is going on in the data that they begin to formulate these ideas in the second language. In this situation, the act of translation required by the research ceases to be an attempt to match participants' words in their original language with their closest equivalents in the second language (as was the case when translating the interview transcripts from one language into another), and instead becomes a quest to capture the researcher's own understanding gained in the original language in a second language. An obvious disadvantage of this approach is that those who do not speak the original language will have to trust the researcher's claims about the insights their data has thrown up without being able to establish these for themselves. And although this approach does circumvent the problems associated with analysing a translation, it cannot evade entirely the transformation of meaning associated with the act of translation; it simply moves it further down the line and encounters it when the analysis is translated into the second language.

It is clear that whichever way we approach the task of translating qualitative research we cannot get away from the fact that translation adds further layers of meaning while at the same time obscuring others. As Temple and Koterba (2009: 12) put it:

> As many philosophers have shown there is no final translation. Alternative words and concepts can always be chosen to re-write accounts. These will be situated within the context of their own production processes and the translation memories and histories of translators.

If language itself is 'a medium of obfuscation as well as revelation' (Sullivan, 2010: 14), then the act of translation further complicates the researcher's relationship with the narrative accounts they work with. At the same time, of course, an awareness of the role of language in the construction of meaning and the inclusion of reflections on one's own relationship with the language(s) used in one's qualitative materials can generate further insights and improve the richness and scope of the analysis itself. Temple and Edwards (2002) provide an excellent example of how qualitative researchers can practise critical language awareness and reflexivity in such a way as to generate deeper insights into their data when they describe how they incorporated their interpreters' perspectives on the data into the research process.

Other transformations of data

While the translation of verbal or written accounts from one language into another is perhaps the most obvious manifestation of the transformation of qualitative data, there are other, more subtle conversions that also have important interpretative implications. For example, the transcription of recordings of semi-structured interviews or the verbal description of non-linguistic data constitute radical transformations of data from one medium into another and, as such, deserve consideration. Indeed, transcription has been described as an interpretative act by a number of qualitative researchers (e.g. Kvale, 1996; Ross, 2010; Tilley and Powick, 2002).

Most qualitative research involves semi-structured interviewing of some kind. Such interviews are normally recorded and transcribed before analysis takes place. Several transcription notations are in use and a researcher's choice about how to transcribe their data has implications for the type of analysis that can be carried out. For example, if the researcher is interested in the subtleties of communicative interaction between interviewer and interviewee, she would need to capture more than the words spoken by them; transcription in this case would need to include information about non-linguistic features such as pauses, interruptions, hesitations, intonation, volume, pitch, emphasis, and so on. If the researcher is interested in the participant's emotional relationship with the material she is talking about, the transcription would also need to pay attention to features such as incomplete sentences, false starts, crying, laughter, clearing of the throat, the audible intake of breath, repetitions, and so on. Alternatively, if the researcher is concerned only with the content of the information provided by the participant, then transcription would aim to do nothing more than to capture the explicit content of what was said in words.

Approaches to transcription, just like approaches to translation, can aim to generate naturalized (overt) or de-naturalized (covert) versions of the original material. Naturalized transcription involves the attempt to capture as much detail as possible of the original utterance (by including repetitions, hesitations, interruptions, stutters, pauses, etc.) while de-naturalized transcription produces a tidied-up version (including corrections of grammatical errors, standardized accents, re-moval of pauses, etc.) that is primarily concerned with capturing the meaning of the content communicated in the utterance (see Bucholtz, 2000; Oliver et al., 2005; Ross, 2010). The former (overt) approach does not try to hide that it is not the original and, paradoxically, by staying as close as possible to the original, it openly identifies itself as a transformation of the original. By contrast, de-naturalized (covert) transcription produces text that looks as though it has been 'born textual' (Ross, 2010: 13), thus making for an easy and smooth read without reminders that the original was in fact speech.

Whatever approach to transcription is taken, however, it is important to ac-knowledge that the very act of transforming the spoken word into a written ver-sion means that a transcript can never simply be the mirror image of an interview; rather, a transcript always constitutes an interpretation in its own right. This is because it is the product of a number of choices made by the researcher. Ham-mersley (2010: 556) points out that none of these choices 'is open to a single rational solution, so that there cannot be one correct transcription of any stretch of audio- or video-recording'. Decisions about transcription are informed by the research question(s) the researcher is trying to answer and the research tradition within which she is working. As such, transcriptions are much more than a tech-nical matter – they 'document and affirm theoretical positions' (Mishler, 2003: 310, cited in Ross, 2010: 3). Hammersley (2010: 556–7) discusses nine key deci-sions involved in transcription, all of which involve some constructive activity on the part of the researcher. Selectivity (i.e. what to include and what to leave out) and the (inevitable) application of cultural knowledge to make sense of what the researcher is hearing (and in the case of video-recordings what she is seeing) are always implicated in transcription work.

Even though qualitative psychology is dominated by linguistic data, increasing numbers of qualitative studies are using visual approaches in which images such as photographs, videos or other artworks are used as data (see Reavey, 2011). The use of imagery to represent and/or express emotions, social identities or subjective meanings allows the researcher to gain access to those aspects of experience that may be hard to capture in words. This means that '[u]sing visual material can open up a range of new and exciting possibilities for qualitative researchers in psy-chology' (Reavey and Johnson, 2008: 299). At the same time, such research raises questions about how visual data may be transformed (for example, into words) so as to allow the researcher to analyse it. For example, visual data could be used as a trigger for further verbal reflection on and/or discussion of its possible meanings by those who generated the images, which could then be transcribed and ana-lysed. As part of this process, abstract images could be made meaningful through their authors' descriptions of them and a discussion of the thoughts and feelings associated with them, a process whereby participants themselves interpret their own images. Alternatively, the researcher could work directly with the images, at-tributing meaning to particular features of them that would have been identified and labelled beforehand by the researcher (e.g. the presence/absence of colour; representations of gender). The researcher could also attempt to identify relevant symbolisms contained within the images. Here, it is the researcher who interprets the images. In some cases, of course, the roles of researcher and participant are merged and researchers themselves produce and analyse their own visual data (e.g. Gillies et al., 2005). Whatever approach is chosen by the researcher, she needs to make a decision about what she takes the image to represent (e.g. is it a visual representation of its author's inner feelings?, a representation of cultural meanings associated with the topic?, an existential 'truth' about a particular experience?, or something else entirely?) and put this into words. The researcher needs to acknowledge that this decision will inform how the image is transformed and what can emerge from the analysis. As Radley and Taylor (2003) emphasize, images are not somehow more 'real' than words and they cannot stand alone and speak for themselves. At the same time, the transformation of visual data into something else (either through or prior to analysis) means that some 'scaling down of meaning from a polysemic image to a mono-modal account', as Reavey and Johnson (2008: 304) put it, will inevitably take place. As a result, some of the richness of the data will be lost in each transformation.

To conclude, any transformation of data prior to analysis constitutes an important (and often unacknowledged) stage in meaning-making in qualitative research. Interpretation enters the picture from the very beginning and it is not something we can put to one side until we settle down to formally 'analyse' our data. In this chapter, I have argued that as soon as language is involved, interpretation has been initiated. It is important for qualitative researchers to recognize and accept this, to work with rather than against this, and to be transparent about their relationship with language and interpretation throughout the processes of data collection, transformation, and analysis.

Box 3   Translation as an Act of Interpretation: The Case of the King James Bible

Soon after he became king, James I called a conference to discuss, review, and clarify the role of the Church in English politics, or as he put it 'for the hearing, and for the determining, things pretended to be amiss in the church' (see Vance, 2011: 1). The Hampton Court Conference took place in January 1604 and was attended by bishops, clergymen, and professors representing the various strands and factions of the Church of England at the time, including High Churchmen and Puritans. The conference decided that a new authoritative translation of the Bible would be desirable and it resolved 'That a translation be made of the whole Bible, as consonant as can be to the original Hebrew and Greek; and this to be set out and printed, without any marginal notes, and only to be used in all churches of England in time of divine service' (Vance, 2011: 1).

However, James knew that translating the Bible was no straightforward matter and that clear guidelines were required to ensure that the product of the translation met his objectives. After all, the purpose of producing a new translation was to create a version that would be acceptable to all members of the Church of England (including those with Puritan affinities) while at the same time affirming and reinforcing the existing structures of the established Church of England and its relationship with the Crown.

The process of translating the Bible was shaped throughout by these objectives, starting with the selection of those who would carry out the work of translation. James I recruited fifty-four biblical scholars and linguists, all of whom were members of the Church of England and all except one were members of the clergy. Forty-seven of these eventually took part in the translation. Fifteen rules were established that were to guide the translators in their labours. They included the following instructions designed to maintain tradition and to ensure that the new translation would not challenge the episcopal structure of the Church of England (see Vance, 2011: 2):

- Rule 3: The Old Ecclesiastical Words to be kept, viz. the Word Church not to be translated Congregation &c.
- Rule 4: When a Word hath divers Significations, that to be kept which hath been most commonly used by the most Ancient Fathers, being agreeable to the Propriety of the Place, and the Analogy of the Faith.

These rules meant that certain words would be translated in such a way as to correspond to their traditional usage in the established Church, thus reinforcing its structures and practices by implying that they were derived directly from the holy book. For example, references to 'congregation' (the coming together of believers) were to be denoted by the word 'church' and the literal 'covering with water' (used to mark a person's conversion to Christianity) was to be translated as 'baptize'. Those who had been described as 'elders' in an earlier translation (known as The Great Bible) became 'priests', 'love' was rendered as 'charity', and 'acknowledge' became 'confess' (see Edgar, 2011).

James also stipulated that the English text of the Bishops' Bible was to be used as the primary guide for the new translation, thus reducing the influence of the Geneva Bible, which had been produced by expatriate English religious reformers and which did not reflect the Church of England's beliefs about ordained clergy.

The text of the new Bible was based on translations from Greek, Hebrew, Aramaic, and Latin texts. The translators drew on Greek or Latin versions of Hebrew text where the latter did not reflect existing Christological interpretations. For example, the Hebrew text 'like lions they maul my hands and feet' was rendered as 'they pierced my hands and feet' in Psalm 22:16 (see Wikipedia, undated: 12).

The translators did not make much use of ancient manuscript sources, although these were available to them. Instead, they consulted existing translations of the Bible into a wide range of languages when they wanted to shed further light on possible renderings of terms and expressions.

Even the physical presentation of the finished printed version (published in 1611) can be understood in terms of its political and religious orientation. The new Bible was intended to be read in churches. It was a large folio volume using black letter typeface instead of roman typeface. It was heavy and looked authoritative and it was clearly meant for public use rather than private devotion (see Wikipedia, undated: 7). This brief case study of the production of what became known as the King James Bible demonstrates that to translate a text also means to interpret it. The translation of the Bible by a committee of scholars handpicked by the king himself and instigated during the first year of his reign was part of a wider political context. The project of translation was motivated by the desire to produce a particular kind of Bible – a Bible that was unifying in that it addressed concerns voiced by religious reformers yet reaffirming the existing organization and structure of the Church of England. James' aim was to produce a Bible that would be 'read in the whole Church' (Vance, 2011: 1) and that was authoritative enough to eventually replace the influence of competing versions such as the Geneva Bible.

Translation, however carefully and scholarly it is carried out, always takes place within a particular social context and as such it has a rhetorical function. Translation can never simply involve the reproduction of meaning contained in the words of one language in those of another. The choices a translator makes about which words to use to re-create the meaning contained in the original text are always also choices about how to position the text within contemporary social and cultural realities.

Part 2

Applications:
'doing interpretation'

5 Interpreting qualitative data: two interview extracts

In Part 1 of this book, we have been reflecting on the nature and purpose of interpretative activity. We have identified different approaches to interpretation, ranging from the 'suspicious' to the 'empathic', and we have explored the ethical dimensions of the process of interpretation. We have also considered the relationship between language and interpretation. Throughout these discussions, it has been argued that to interpret something is to change it and thus interpretation needs to be conducted responsibly. This means that the researcher needs to carefully consider her own role in making meaning and to reflect on the theoretical, practical, and ethical implications of the particular sense that she has made of the data. Our discussion so far has been largely conceptual, albeit with the support of examples and illustrations drawn from relevant literature.

The aim of Part 2 is to integrate and apply the ideas introduced in Part 1 by illustrating the dilemmas, challenges, and opportunities inherent in the process of interpretation in a more concrete fashion. Data from a study of the experience of taking part in extreme sport (Willig, 2005, 2007b, 2008b) will be examined through the lens of three different interpretative frameworks: *phenomenological analysis, discourse analysis*, and *psychosocial analysis*. Chapters 6, 7, and 8 will present three different interpretations of the same data generated by these three approaches to data analysis, thus demonstrating the differences in understanding of the same dataset that can be produced as a result. Theoretical, practical, and ethical implications of the three different interpretations will also be examined.

The aim of Part 2 is *not* to provide a step-by-step guide to data analysis for each of the three approaches. The reader is referred to relevant texts for such guidance (e.g. Frosh and Young, 2008; Smith et al., 2009; Willig, 2008a). Rather, the aim here is to demonstrate how different interpretative frameworks can shape the way in which the researcher makes sense of the data. The emphasis is on how methods of analysis offer different perspectives on the data and how such differing perspectives generate different interpretations. The aim is to show how particular readings of the data are produced through the lens provided by each of the three approaches. Each of the three approaches is based on different assumptions about what the data represents and about what the analysis of the data seeks to establish. Each of them asks different questions of the data and each one provides the researcher with a different role to play. Irrespective of the technicalities involved in the line-by-line analysis of the data required by each of the approaches, it is their general orientation to the data and their conceptualization of the researcher's role which differentiates them and which provides the researcher with a particular perspective on the data.

The discussion presented in Chapters 6, 7, and 8 is based on my own analysis of the data using each of the three approaches in turn. It is important to acknowledge that another researcher's analyses may well have generated quite different insights and no claim is made here regarding the general validity of my interpretations. However, I would argue that the types of insights generated by the analyses are very much a function of the approaches used to generate them and that other researchers using the same approach would produce similar types of insights. In other words, while the specific contents of claims made on the basis of the analysis may well vary between researchers, the types of claim made would not. Thus, for instance, a phenomenological analysis will always (seek to) generate insights into the phenomenon under investigation, its meanings, significance, and functions. A discursive analysis will always (seek to) generate an understanding of how language is implicated in producing the social and psychological processes and events depicted in the data, and a psychosocial analysis will always (seek to) answer questions about the individual's emotional investments in what they say or do.

The remainder of this chapter will introduce and contextualize the data to be analysed in Chapters 6, 7, and 8.

Introduction to the data

The data were originally collected as part of a phenomenological study of the experience of taking part in extreme sport. The aim of the original study was to gain a better understanding of the meanings that people attribute to the experience of taking part in extreme sport. It was motivated by a desire to find out what such an experience may mean to people and what it may add to people's lives. Colaizzi's (1978) guide to phenomenological analysis of qualitative data informed the procedures for data collection and analysis. Only individuals who had practised extreme sport repeatedly were eligible to participate in the research. Recruitment took place through word of mouth. Eight participants (two women and six men) took part in the study. Participants were interviewed at a location of their choice. All interviews were carried out one-to-one with no-one else present and without any interruptions. The interviews were tape-recorded on a Walkman®-sized portable Sony tape-recorder. Interviews lasted for about one hour. At the beginning of their interview, participants were reminded of the purpose of the research. In line with the British Psychological Society's guidelines for ethical research practice, they were informed of their right to withdraw from the research at any point, including their right to withdraw, retrospectively, their consent to allow me to use their data. They were assured that their names or any other identifying details would not appear in any reports of the study. All interviews were transcribed verbatim.

Participants' accounts of their experiences with extreme sport were produced in response to the following questions, which were put to them during the interview:

1. I am interested in exploring with you your experience of taking part in a form of extreme sport. To start with, can you please recall one particular occasion. Can you describe what you experienced?
2. How did you feel before you actually embarked upon the activity?
3. How did you feel afterwards?
4. What makes it different from other forms of physical activity?
5. What makes it feel good/bad/difficult/easy?
6. What makes the experience special?
7. What would be different for you if you had not done it?
8. What were you looking for when you first decided to try it?
9. What was your best/worst time?
10. Is there anything else you would like to add?

Questions 2–10 were used to prompt participants once they had had the opportunity to describe their experience of extreme sport in detail in response to Question 1. Questions were not necessarily used in the same sequence and the wording was adapted to suit the specific context within which they were used. The style of interviewing was designed to allow participants as much freedom as possible in their description of their experiences.

Reflexivity: my relationship with the data

The original data was collected almost ten years ago. To select suitable extracts from the interviews for inclusion in this book, I re-read all eight interview transcripts. Although I remembered much of what my research participants had told me about their experiences when I first interviewed them almost ten years ago, re-reading their accounts made me realize how much I myself had changed in the meantime. This awareness came about as a result of my realization that I was responding quite differently to my research participants' descriptions of their experiences. In my original encounter with the data, I had noticed that I was experiencing a sense of surprise and also some disappointment about the prominence of a competitive element and a strong achievement orientation that characterized many of the accounts. Never having engaged in extreme sport myself, I had harboured a somewhat romantic view of extreme sport expecting the experience to involve feelings of euphoria and joy, a sense of transformation, spiritual elevation even. These expectations were only partially met, and my original response to the data was very much shaped by this sense of surprise and disappointment. Re-reading the interview transcripts ten years on, I responded by feeling concerned about some of the things my participants were saying about their relationship with extreme sport. I asked myself whether some of what was said could qualify as a 'cry for help' or an expression of distress or anxiety about the need to take risks. The fact that some of the participants described themselves as 'addicted' to extreme sport had not alarmed me ten years ago but was a concern now. Similarly, references to how their friends thought they were 'crazy' and had expressed concern for their welfare suddenly seemed important and made me wonder whether such references might be understood as a deflected expression of concern on the part of the participants themselves. I began to wonder whether some participants might have been looking for reassurance from me, or whether they might have been trying to shock me. Re-reading the transcripts made me realize just how much my orientation to the accounts had changed and I reflected that this may well be the result of having trained and practised as a counselling psychologist in the intervening period.

It seemed that, in my original engagement with the data, I had approached my research participants' accounts with some expectations (for example, the expectation that extreme sport has a spiritual dimension) but without suspicion; in other words, I was taking my participants' accounts at face value. The second time around, I was more inclined to read between the lines. I now allowed for the possibility that what participants said about their experiences may not necessarily be all there was to it. I allowed for the possibility that their experiences might include thoughts and feelings that they did not explicitly acknowledge within the context of the research interview. I also noticed how in my original encounter with the data I had attempted to step into my participants' shoes and look at the world from their perspective, without adding my own commentary to this, other than to acknowledge the difference between my initial expectations and (what I assumed was) their own reality. My perspectival position was very much one of being alongside my participants and my interpretative stance was 'empathic'. The second time around I engaged with the accounts from the position of 'the other'; that is to say, someone sitting opposite the participant, who is addressed by the participant as a conversational partner. This meant that I asked myself questions about the kinds of responses participants might have wanted to provoke in me by saying what they were saying. I was paying more attention to the relational dynamics between myself and the participants during the interviews, and what this might tell me about the nature of their experiences with extreme sport. In other words, I was adopting a more 'suspicious' approach to interpreting my participants' accounts. It seems that with my changing professional identity had come a change in how I approached accounts of experience. These observations underline the importance of reflexivity when we embark upon interpretation.

The two extracts

We will be working with extracts from two of the eight interviews conducted in the original extreme sport study. They are taken from interviews with two participants whom, for the purposes of our discussion here, we shall call Ben and Anna. The two extracts have been selected because they constitute rich material with which to illustrate the three different approaches to qualitative analysis we will be concerned with in Chapters 6, 7, and 8. To ensure that the data was reasonably suitable for phenomenological, discursive as well as psychosocial analyses, I chose extracts that included detailed descriptions of experience, some conversational back-and-forth between myself as the interviewer and the participant, and some biographical material. The extracts are not necessarily taken from the beginning of an interview, and they do not represent Ben's and Anna's responses to the same interview questions.

To protect the participants' identities, all identifying details have been changed or removed from the transcripts. In fact, the changes I have made to the social demographics referred to in the extracts are so extensive that the social identities of 'Ben' and 'Anna' as they emerge from the accounts presented here do not actually exist in the real world. As a result, while the descriptions of experience are based on 'real' data, the social actors who are constructed through and within these accounts do not correspond to any real living individuals.

The two extracts we will be working with in Chapters 6, 7, and 8 are reproduced below, beginning with Ben's account of his experience of rock climbing, which is followed by Anna's description of her experience of a variety of extreme sports. Pauses longer than about two seconds are indicated by (pause) and where parts of the text have been removed from the transcript this is indicated thus (...). Laughter and other non-linguistic forms of expression are also identified by being placed in parentheses, for example (laughter) and (intake of breath).

Ben's Interview Extract

[Carla (C.) is the interviewer and Ben (B.) is the participant]

C: So you're very focused then on what you're doing during the climbing, you're focusing on where you put your feet and do you think about anything else or is it very much focusing on what you're doing?

B: No, I mean thinking on it now, you don't think about anything else. You think about where you're putting your feet, you look for where you're gonna go next. Above all, you feel it. You feel every footprint, you feel every handhold, you feel the security in it and that's what you spend, or that's what I spend all my time doing (pause) is I suppose attempting to feel secure at that precise moment and that's the only thing you think about. It's not what you're gonna do when you get to the top, it's not what you're gonna have when you get into the pub, it's not what happened twenty minutes ago, it's only that (. . .)

C: (. . .) you wouldn't be thinking about yourself, you wouldn't be aware of I am here now and you'd be more focusing on your environment, so the rocks and the next thing to hold on to?

B: Yeah.

C: You're not sort of reflecting on or maybe aware of you being there?

B: No, it's totally all about mountain.

C: Yeah, yeah.

B: I think. Totally all about the rock, particularly because I mean the steepy bits tend to be on really precipitous rock faces and it does tend to be all about rock, it does tend to be all about mountain.

C: Yeah.

B: Which is great (laughs) it's just, you lose yourself.

C: It sounds like that.

B: I suppose.

C: Yes, like you lose your sense of being separate, you're almost like part of this world, and you're just in there.

B: Mmh.

C: So when does it come, when do you kind of remember yourself and, when you finish, do you suddenly think, gosh, here I am I'm still alive, or how does it work?

B: Yeah, it's when you get to the top of that section and then you look down and (laughs) you realize what you've done.

C: It's almost like being so absorbed in what you're doing that you just focus on the immediate thing rather than the bigger picture and you in it, and then you come to the end of that section and you kind of almost realize that the bigger picture is there and you look at what's there and what's ahead and you in it.

B: Mmh.

C: So does it feel, is it a pleasant feeling?

B: Yeah.

C: Or a scary feeling or how is it?

B: It's a really pleasant feeling. Erm, sometimes, I don't know, I don't think it's scary, it's adrenaline fuelled (pause) but it's a really pleasant feeling of being, you feel, I feel, I feel my insignificance in that landscape but it's a nice feeling 'cos I find that quite comforting, you know, it's almost like (pause) nothing really matters (laughs) not so much nothing really matters as you go (puts on high-pitched voice) 'modern life is so full of stress' and yeah you've just done that thing that could've had you killed and really I mean all these piddly little things that you worry about really don't matter in the big scale of things it's, everything is cool, everything is fine so it's a feeling of comfort but it's an adrenaline-fuelled feeling of comfort (laughing)

C: Yes. Yeah, so it sounds almost like it gives you a very different perspective from the everyday life when you're here for example, it suddenly allows you to look at things from a very different place.

B: Yeah.

C: Not just physically from a different place but almost.

B: Mentally.

C: Mentally as well, and it's a good place to be to look at life. It makes things much more (pause) simple.

B: Easy.

C: In a way.

B: Yeah.

C: Easy, yeah.

B: There are no problems in the mountains other than where you stick your hand next and that's why I love it. It's the same with skiing. There are no problems skiing except how you ski next (laughing). You know, if you ski stupid, well then, but if you ski well, it's fine.

C: So how long, I'm just wondering now, how long this lasts, you know, having this perspective and looking at life, or almost, it's feeling life in a different way and it sounds like it's a really good experience, really good way of feeling alive like this, and then how long does it last afterwards?

B: Erm (pause) it's quite funny because now we're talking about it I'm re, I'm almost reliving it because speaking about it I can picture where I was when I was feeling that way and I can almost go yeah it really doesn't matter.

C: So you have it now, now is almost talking.

B: Talking about it you feel it. It's not quite as (pause) good, it's not as good a feeling as when I'm actually doing it but certainly as long as I'm in the mountains, as long as I can see the mountains then, you know, I start getting excited about it (...) I get excited when I actually see the mountains and it lasts (pause) until I suppose something trivial happens here and I've got to pay a bill or, I mean, not that I get stressed out about paying a bill but until (laughs) until I get dragged kicking and screaming back to real life. But I do kind of pick it up when I talk about it again or when (pause) (...) but I don't get that wonderful adrenaline buzz and sense of how wonderful the world actually is until I'm in the mountains or on the sea. Until I'm facing wilderness, you know, it has to, when you're actually doing the deed outside, the feeling is just pha! magic (...)

[A little later on in the interview]:

B: (...) with the sports that I've got into they look fun and they look adrenaline, they look like they've got an adrenaline buzz, they look silly (laughs)

C: How do you mean, silly?

B: Erm (long pause) partly dangerous but not dangerous. You know, something that looks like you could get roughed up pretty badly, or roughed up slightly, like mountain biking, you know, you can quite easily fall off your bike and tumble down a bank but I've done that before and you lie at the bottom (laughing) of the bank, one time was a beauty because I landed in a holly bush and I just sat there laughing because it was so funny (laughs) and yeah and my brother's favourite habit when we go sailing if I'm sailing with him, is we sail hobie cats which are little 16 foot catamarans, very very fast, a lot of fun, but really easy to tip over so there's two of you on it, there's a helm and there's crew and you have to stand out there with this harness strapped to the mast and when you're going you're all sitting there bracing 'cos it's really fast but Andy has a habit of getting me out on a line in the trapeze, and it's really windy and everyone is whohoo and then he'll drop the mainsail so the boat stops dead, the hull will come back into the water, I'll go in the drink and he thinks this is hilarious, and it is funny (laughs) it hurts when you hit the water and there's also times when we've been honking along and the hull has buried into a wave so the boat actually goes, it turns right over on itself and you go flying forward 'cos you're still trapped on this trapeze and that can be quite scary but it's really quite funny because it's a lot of fun, I suppose, it's like going to the fair and being in one of those like bungee cages where they haul it back and then ping it and you phung! and it's exactly the same thing except you're in charge of it (laughs)

Anna's Interview Extract

[Carla (C.) is the interviewer and Anna (A.) is the participant]

C: Can you describe one occasion when you took part in a form of extreme sport?

A: Sure. Okay the first one that I can think of is when I went white water rafting. This is a number of years ago and I was on a holiday for a few weeks (...) at (name of place). And I went with, I was on my own, so I joined a group of people and we went on this rafting trip. And there are two ways that you can raft, that we could raft. We could have a raft with a big oar at the back where a guy basically controls the way you go down the whole river, or we could all have pedals and we would have control over the trip down the river. The first time I went down the river, the group of people that I was with wanted to have the guide controlling it. And it was good. It was a bit of a rush and I had a great time and everything but by the time I got to the bottom I didn't get enough of an adrenaline rush. So the next time I went down, I decided to go again even though it had cost me a fortune but I was gonna do it again 'cos I didn't get the rush that I wanted from the first one. So I went down with pedals, steering ourselves down and it was probably the most terrifying thing I've ever done in my whole life (laughs) I actually thought I was gonna die but we went down, we were completely out of control the whole way and one of the guys very nearly drowned (laughs) yeah it was a bit hairy. We basically had no control until the guys in the boat just stopped pedalling so there was only me and another girl pedalling, and the guide. And we just fell out the whole way down. We just went down the whole way this rapid. But I mean I just loved it. I had to. The first time I did it I basically didn't get enough of a rush and I do these things for that, thrill and excitement so and whatever so which is why I did it the second time and absolutely loved it although having said that after getting to the end of the second trip, my nerves were pretty frayed and I haven't been again, but I would go again, yeah.

C: Right. So if we look at it in terms of just before you did it and then during it and then after, the feelings, if you can try and remember how you felt just before you actually got into this raft?

A: Before I got in I had, it was just that, I was really excited 'cos I'd never done it before. I didn't know what to expect. I didn't know (...) if it was gonna be life-threatening or not life-threatening although I had spoken to a, while we were getting prepared, one of the guys had said a little bit about (breakdowns) and things like that but that made it all the more exciting, you know, that element of danger which was great.

C: Right. Yeah?

A: I do like the fact that you might almost hurt yourself but there is also that thing that it will never happen to me. It'll happen to somebody else. I'll be fine, I'll be fine. So that's, but then through it, particularly the second run that we did, the first time we fell out that was great, I mean it was a real buzz, I was like oh we got thrown out of the boat, I was sucked down there and (intake of breath) yeah okay I lost my breath for a bit and I couldn't breathe but I came up and it was alright. It's like wow we get back in and do it again. But as we went down we fell out more and more times. It started to get a little bit scary after that. Yeah.

C: So the feelings during it were like a mixture of excitement and fear? Or how would you describe it?

A: Initially absolutely, well the whole way was exciting but yes there was definitely an element of fear. Particularly, there was one bit in particular that was incredibly frightening because there was just a giant whirlpool and we could tell from the look of this guy who was taking us down there that if we went anywhere near there we may never get out. That was almost, I mean it was a rush, it was great but it was a little bit too scary because you could see the fear in his face and it lost a little bit of, I think when I do these things I put incredible faith in the people who organize it and I don't even blink, don't think twice and then if they look a bit nervous that's when I get a little bit shaky. If you don't see that element of fear in these other people, I don't worry so much.

C: And that happened? The guy looked a little bit

A: He did. When we got to those couple of spots because he knew that we were out of control and the key, I think, was he lost faith in us being able to get out. Which was good. I mean that was another challenge in itself because it's like, you know, this is pretty serious now, there's no mucking around 'cos I sort of treat a lot of these things as a big joke, as great fun, as a huge amount of fun. So that's yeah (. . .)

C: Right. So when the guy looked a little bit worried, it kind of made it more, less fun and more of a real danger?

A: Yes. It was like, this is a little bit more serious now than what I first contemplated. 'Cos when I started, it was just fun. I mean it was just, this is gonna be great, you know. The fear, the danger factor, that you might really really hurt yourself is just not a, it's not a factor, and when it actually becomes a reality that you might really really hurt yourself, then (intake of breath) you know, it sort of takes your breath away.

C: Right. And then afterwards, when you got out, how did you feel?

A: Absolutely exhilarated. It was like, you know, not only did you have the fun factor and the fact that you very nearly died. 'Cos we did get sucked down under the water for, you know, 45 seconds under water which is a lot of time under water, in rapids and, you know, getting sucked down and to get to the end and go wow. That was just awesome. It's a great feeling and so it's like, oh yeah I'd do it again.

C: So was it a sort of sense of having done it is important? Looking back, so afterwards you felt, the idea that you've done that.

A: Yeah. I think so. I think the feeling, the rush that you get is just so, it takes a good day to come down, at least for me it does. Even longer, actually, 'cos I'm just thinking of when I first went on a big hike that lasted over a week and for about a month and a half after the walk, I was just bouncing off the walls. I just had such a great great time. This made everything in my body was just going, I just loved it. My sister thought I was completely nuts when I got back because I just couldn't sit still. So when I finish things like this it's just (intake of breath) you know.

C: So it lasts longer than, than

A: Oh it lasts much longer than the actual event itself.

C: And can you describe the, I know it's difficult to describe feelings, the quality of the feelings, but so maybe thinking about after the hike when you feel so excited, you know, what kind of thoughts and feelings do you have then?

A: It's like (long pause) I just feel like I can do anything and I just don't wanna be still and time's too short and I've just got lots of energy. Huge amounts of energy. It's just a real buzz and I'm really excited, I think, really excitable. Easy to, everything entertains me, everything's a giggle and then I sort of come off it and I, I'm not explaining myself very well but it's (pause) yeah literally bouncing off the walls, like I might sleep for four hours a night 'cos I'm just so wide awake and wanting to talk to people and stuff. I feel particularly social and wanna get out of the house and do stuff.

C: So it almost gives you an influx of energy? It gives you something additional to what

A: Yeah. I think so. That's probably why like when I think of times when I felt the urge to do things like this, like when I first, I went in an acrobatic plane and I jumped, I started to learn to sky-dive and I think about the times when I wanted to do those things, it's times when everything else in my life is boring and dull, nothing is going on and I just needed a big lift. And doing something like this gives me a big lift at the time I do it but afterwards I'm regenerated and I feel motivated to do other things.

C: Yes, right, that makes sense (. . .) and when you say about the adrenaline rush, is that a very physical thing then? Is it very physical or is it more in your head?

A: It's both, I think. I'm just thinking of bungee-jumping and standing at the edge of a platform, looking 300 feet down, I mean, that's definitely a physical, you just feel everything is, your heart's going at a million miles per hour and looking down, God, and it's a mental thing, too. It's a challenge, like to mentally make yourself jump off a bridge. Actually, it's funny when you think about it 'cos I don't know what makes me do that. When I went bungee-jumping and I was standing there, I was the first person to go and I didn't see anyone jump before me and I didn't know, I hadn't even seen it on TV, I'd never seen anybody bungee-jump before. And standing on the edge of this platform and the guy just said, I'm gonna count down from ten and then you just jump, alright? And then he counted down and I just jumped and I can't tell you what made me jump. I don't know what went through my head. It was sort of not an option. I was there, I made myself get to the edge of the platform and I just was gone. I did it. He told me to do it. And again, that's faith in the people who are organizing it. Complete faith.

C: So when he was counting down from ten, were you thinking I could stop now?

A: No.

C: Or the whole time you knew you were going to jump?

A: I was gonna jump. It was almost like the countdown from ten, the build of the rush just got bigger and bigger and bigger and my body was going (intake of breath)

C: Right. And would you say that was enjoyable or a mixture of enjoyable and not enjoyable?

A: No, a complete enjoyment. It's an incredible feeling to feel like that. To feel that you're about to risk your life doing something (pause) but you'll be alright. Pretty amazing feeling.

C: But there's sort of confidence that it will be okay? You say there's trust in the equipment and in the people? That it will be okay?

A: Yeah. I don't think (pause) Yeah, there's complete confidence in them. And faith. There's never truly a stage that I think that I'm gonna really really hurt myself. Never. It's just an incredible rush to think that I'm gonna drop 300 feet or 100 feet or whatever, and what's that gonna feel like 'cos I don't know what it's gonna feel like. I've not done it before. Yeah, but I'm just thinking, it's interesting 'cos I wonder if the events, the sports that I've done I've always got that faith in somebody else? I'm just wondering, maybe when I stopped doing things like my sky-diving, when it's just me. I have to rely on myself. I don't have that much confidence in myself to keep on going. You know, when you get to a stage, 'cos when I started sky-diving I was doing (partnered jumps) (. . .) so I was completely relying on somebody else to hook me up to the plane and everything. But when it got to the stage where I could jump on my own, I just stopped going. I mean there were a lot of reasons for that but I just wonder. I do hold a lot of faith in the people who I go with, like when I went acrobatic flying, I went

C: What's acrobatic flying?

A: It was a plane that does loops.

C: Okay.

A: You know all this (moves hand up and down) I had complete faith in the pilot. That kind of thing. But I would never consider wanting to fly the plane myself (laughs) you know, it's not something I want to pursue kind of thing. Yeah. I've got a lot of faith. And I just don't think I could be bothered. Once you've had the rush.

C: Maybe would you say that the dimension of it where you are putting yourself, your life, into the hands of someone else, in a way, is that part of the enjoyment?

A: Yeah, I think so.

C: Letting yourself fall, literally?

A: (pause) Yeah, 'cos I don't question it. I just completely think that they know what they're doing so I'll be fine.

C: Right.

[And a little later in the interview, in response to a question about what made her start being interested in extreme sport]:

A: Yeah. And I think it's part of growing up when I did all of these, you know, I'd do anything that was quite dangerous. I'd do it because I was told that I shouldn't do it. Oh and the other thing is that my stepdad used to tell me, I remember mum would, you know, don't do that, you'll hurt yourself so I'd just do it. And my stepdad on the other hand would be like yeah you can do that, you can do that. So and I was always really close to my stepdad. And if he says I can do it, then I can. And I think that's part of that faith thing again it's like, you know, dad says I can do it. Dad says I can jump off that 3-metre diving board when I was five years of age. I can do it then. So I'd go and do it. And mum would be saying, you don't (...) she can't do that, and I'd say yes I can. So it's a bit of a challenge there.

C: And it also makes me think about the sense of self as well that (pause) if you could sort of think about how, if you didn't do any of these things, you know, if you'd never done them, how would you feel differently about yourself? Or how would you see yourself differently?

A: I'd be disappointed 'cos I don't think that I'd pushed myself very hard. I think my life would be pretty boring.

C: Yeah?

A: Yeah. I need to do these things. It's something I just have to do. I know it. I feel it in myself. I get to a stage where I'm just bored or there's just something, I just feel it, there's something wrong. I can't quite put my finger on what's wrong. And if I get out and I do something like this, I've just lifted myself another level, you know. I feel like it's like you sort of sit down to this little rut and you don't know that you're in it before you get to the bottom and then it's like (intake of breath) gotta lift yourself up again and then keep on going.

6   A phenomenological reading

This chapter presents a phenomenological reading of the two interview extracts introduced in the previous chapter. The aims of this chapter are to offer an interpretation of the data that is informed by a phenomenological perspective, to reflect on such an interpretation, and to explore its various (theoretical, ethical, and practical) implications. I hope to be able to demonstrate how my analysis of the two interview extracts is underpinned by the concerns of phenomenological enquiry and how the phenomenological method's epistemological basis shapes the analysis of the data. There is a discussion of the scope of a phenomenological analysis, of what it can and cannot tell us. The chapter concludes with an appraisal of the phenomenological method, including its strengths and its limitations, and some advice on the types of data that are (and are not) suitable for phenomenological analysis.

Aims of the analysis

Before we look at the results of my phenomenological analysis, let us remind ourselves of what a phenomenological perspective involves and what the purpose of a phenomenological analysis is. As outlined in Chapter 2, phenomenological research is primarily concerned with what presents itself. It stays with and engages with the data available without dismissing any part of it and without deciding beforehand which part of the data may be more or less important, relevant or significant.

Phenomenological research seeks to engage with the research participant's account of their experience to obtain a better understanding of the quality, meaning, and significance of that experience for the person him- or herself. This means that the researcher tries to approach the data with an open mind and attempts to bracket her own assumptions about the phenomenon under investigation. At the same time, a phenomenological perspective requires that we acknowledge the importance of intersubjectivity, which means that the researcher acknowledges (and explores) the ways in which she is implicated in the process of making sense and constructing meaning. 'Bracketing' assumptions, however, does not mean erasing them; rather, it involves a process of recognizing their effects, of interrogating them, of being suspicious of them and, as a result, being able to hold them more lightly and more flexibly.

It is also important to remember that phenomenological research is concerned with experiential *phenomena* rather than with the individuals who are describing them. In other words, as phenomenological researchers we are interested in types of experiences rather than types of people. Our research participants are seen as witnesses who can tell us about the experiences we want to study; they are not themselves the focus of the research. This means that questions about *why* a particular individual experiences something in a particular way are not relevant. Phenomenological enquiry is concerned with *how* something is experienced and how such an experience is interpreted by the individual who is having the experience, of what it means to them, and what this, in turn, can tell us about the nature of the phenomenon under investigation; it is not concerned with the structure and dynamics of an individual's psyche or their personality or even their history (unless, of course, the participants themselves foreground such notions and make them part of their current experience of the phenomenon under investigation).

Process of analysis

To prepare for a phenomenological analysis of the two interview extracts, I began by reminding myself of the aims of such an analysis, as outlined in the previous paragraph. I established that the purpose of my analysis was to gain a better understanding of the nature, meaning, and significance of taking part in extreme sport activities, and that both Ben's and Anna's accounts could (potentially and if analysed well) provide me with access to such an understanding. Not having engaged in any extreme sports myself, I did not have any personal experience of the phenomenon under investigation and this meant that I was approaching the data as an 'outsider'. Thinking some more about my relationship with the data, I also realized that I was now less intrigued by the phenomenon of extreme sport than I had been when I first collected the data almost ten years ago. While back then I really wanted to know what my research participants were getting out of their extreme sport activities, I now approached the data with less eagerness to obtain answers to my questions; it also mattered less to me what the analysis would throw up. As such, I was aware that I was less emotionally invested in the process of analysis than I had been when I first collected the data. I was also aware that this time around I did not hold the same expectations regarding a possible spiritual dimension of the experience of extreme sport.

I decided to begin my phenomenological analysis by reading and re-reading the first interview extract to gain a holistic impression of the account. Given the significance of the hermeneutic circle in phenomenological interpretation, it is important to be mindful of the relationship between the parts (such as individual words, sentences or phrases that describe particular aspects of the experience) and the whole (i.e. the entire account of the experience), and this can be facilitated by gaining an impression of the extract as a whole before beginning a line-by-line analysis of it. Having read the extract a number of times, trying to really imagine what it might have been like to experience what was being described there, I returned to the beginning of the extract to examine each line of the text more closely. I thought of this stage of the analysis as a *descriptive* stage, as my aim was to capture the meaning communicated in each line of the text as carefully and accurately as possible. I did this by writing short descriptive phrases in the margins of the text, phrases that summarized and crystallized the meaning contained in the relevant lines of text without, however, transcending it in any way. For example, where Ben says 'it's totally all about mountain (...) totally all about the rock (...) Which is great (...) you lose yourself', my notes in the margins read 'loss of self experienced as positive', 'loss of sense of self through intense focusing on the external environment (rock and mountain)', and 'foregrounding of the immediate situation to the exclusion of all else including the self'. Having worked through the entire extract in this way, I then drew on my descriptive notes in the margins of the text to compose a descriptive summary statement that aims to capture the texture of the experience described in the extract, its quality, meaning, and significance from the point of view of the participant. In the summary statement, I use direct quotations from the participant's account, as this helps to bring to life my own more matter-of-fact descriptions of the experience. It also serves as a check so that readers can see for themselves whether my descriptive summary bears a close (enough) relationship to the original account.

My phenomenological analysis could have ended here; however, I chose to take it one step further by drawing on ideas and concepts from relevant literature to further illuminate the meanings invoked by the accounts and to produce a more explicitly interpretative reading. Again, it is important to sustain a phenomeno-logical perspective here, which means that the ideas and concepts from the lit-erature are not used to explain *why* my participants describe their experiences in the way that they do; rather, they are used to shed more light on *what* it is that participants are experiencing. For example, in the case of Ben's description of the pleasure of the experience of a loss of self, extant literature on the phenomenon of 'flow' (found in extreme sports as well as other intensely embodied experiences) is drawn upon to further illuminate Ben's experience of losing himself in the world. Although this second (more overtly interpretative) stage of analysis moves further away from the original accounts, I would expect my participants to still be able to recognize this part of the analysis as being relevant to their experience. I would expect them to feel comfortable reading it as it does not pathologize them or their experiences, attempting to stay within their own frame of reference without importing psychological concepts and categories with which to transform their experience into something they are unlikely to recognize. As such, I would argue, it is not a 'suspicious' interpretation.

Let us now take a look at the two sets of summary statements that I have produced on the basis of my analysis of Ben's and Anna's interview extracts. To form an opinion about the extent to which the summary statements capture the meanings communicated through the original extracts, the reader is advised to re-read the original extracts reproduced in the previous chapter before reading the summaries below.

Descriptive summary of Ben's extract

Ben's account of his experience of rock climbing emphasizes the importance of the experience of focusing on the immediate challenges presented by the present moment ('where you're putting your feet (...) where you're gonna go next'). He describes an embodied experience of interacting with the physical environment ('You feel every footprint, you feel every handhold') that allows him to stay entirely in the present with no thought for past or future, or indeed for himself ('it's totally all about mountain', 'totally all about the rock'). Ben describes the pleasure he derives from losing a sense of himself ('you lose yourself') through his absorption in his task and his environment as he foregrounds the immediate situation and its demands to the exclusion of all else. Ben's response to my question about what happens when he regains his sense of self (C: '... when do you kind of remember yourself...?') indicates that he experiences something like surprise when during a moment of reflection he registers his own actions ('... you look down and (laughs) you realize what you've done').

Ben describes the 'adrenaline-fuelled feeling of comfort' that he derives from distancing himself from the concerns of everyday life ('all these piddly little things that you worry about') by focusing on the bigger picture ('the big scale of things'). A sense of his own 'insignificance' gives him a feeling of comfort as he contemplates this 'big scale of things' where 'everything is cool, everything is fine'. Being confronted with the challenge of having to secure his survival in difficult terrain ('you've just done that thing that could've had you killed') allows Ben to put everyday concerns (such as 'paying a bill') in perspective. Going back to basics and concerning himself with his immediate survival makes life 'easy' and its demands straightforward, which is something Ben values very highly ('There are no problems in the mountains other than where you stick your hand next and that's why I love it'). Ben contrasts 'real life' and its mundane demands with the 'magic' of outdoor pursuits, which provide him with 'that wonderful adrenaline buzz and sense of how wonderful the world actually is'. He experiences extreme sport as a welcome opportunity to escape from 'real life'.

In the second part of the extract, Ben identifies a further dimension of extreme sport that he experiences as 'fun'. He describes how he enjoys being knocked about, his body being the plaything of physical forces. In this extract, he laughs a lot, invoking scenes reminiscent of comic strips such as 'Tom and Jerry'. Here, he looks at himself from the outside, reflecting on how he must have looked as he fell, tumbled, bounced, and flew forward. Although he describes these experiences as playful fun and compares them with fairground rides, he also acknowledges the discomfort and fear that are involved. At the same time, he emphasizes that he still experiences himself as 'in charge' of what happens to his body during these episodes ('you're in charge of it').

Further illumination of meanings with reference to existing literature

Ben's account indicates that during rock climbing he experiences something like 'flow', a state of mind and body that has been described in the literature as involving the experience of a unity of self, world, and activity that is represented by, and experienced through, the present moment (Csikszentmihalyi, 1975; Le Breton, 2000). It has been suggested that this is experienced as highly satisfying and fulfilling because during moments of 'flow' our customary dualistic experience of self versus world is dissolved: 'there is a melting of self into action' (Le Breton, 2000: 3) and 'homunculus, the voice within, has been silenced' (Celsi et al., 1993: 12). Everyday worries and concerns lose their significance, and we are not aware of any gap between what is and what ought to be. In this way, moments of 'flow' are akin to meditative states. 'Flow' has been identified by other researchers as being a key dimension of the experience of extreme sport (e.g. Celsi et al., 1993). By providing an opportunity to experience 'flow', rock climbing allows Ben to escape from the demands of everyday life and to get in touch with something bigger than himself. Some may describe this as the spiritual dimension of the experience.

Ben also uses extreme sport to experiment with control, allowing his body to become the plaything of external forces without, however, abandoning control altogether. In a similar way, through these activities, Ben plays with the boundaries between risk and safety, pleasure and pain, fear and fun. It could be argued that extreme sport provides Ben with an opportunity to negotiate what Spinelli (2001) describes as the various 'existence tensions' that characterize being human. These include tensions between our sense of self as a separate and self-contained entity and our close relations with others, between our sense of isolation and our sense of belonging. They also include tensions between our experience of the mental and the physical aspects of our being, as well as between our active and our more passive positioning in the world, between our sense of freedom and our experience of determinism. Spinelli (2001: 149) argues that these tensions cannot be resolved as 'each requires the other, and, indeed, exists only via its relation to the other'. So, for example, our sense of self, of being a unique, bounded entity that can be distinguished from other and different selves, is only conceivable on the basis of our relations with these other selves which can respond to our own self as such a distinct entity. Existence tensions, therefore, contain complementary elements that operate in a dialectical fashion, allowing one another to appear, to be perceived and experienced, precisely because they provide a contrast and a background against which the opposing element can stand out, as a figure against a background. From this perspective, Ben's involvement in extreme sport could be understood as his way of managing existence tensions in a creative and purposeful way as he, consciously and deliberately, negotiates the tensions between control and loss of control, between being an object and being a subject, between being manipulated and being in charge.

Descriptive summary of Anna's extract

In her account of her experiences of taking part in extreme sports activities, Anna describes how these activities enable her to achieve a high level of arousal. She is seeking excitement, the 'rush' and the 'buzz' ('I do these things for that, thrill and excitement') that she experiences when she takes risks ('To feel that you're about to risk your life doing something (pause) but you'll be alright'). Anna emphasizes the importance of generating excitement, which she communicates both in words (there are nine references to 'rush', for example) and through a sharp intake of breath which she repeats five times in the extract. She also puts this sensation into words: 'it sort of takes your breath away'. Anna explains that the effects of this arousal outlast the experience of taking part in extreme sport itself; the 'buzz', the sense of exhilaration, stays with Anna as she returns to her everyday life. Anna describes how she continues to feel aroused and stimulated after the event; she is buzzing ('I was just bouncing off the walls (...) everything in my body was just going (...) I just couldn't sit still'); she feels energized and intensely alive ('I just feel like I can do anything and I just don't wanna be still and time's too short and I've just got lots of energy. Huge amounts of energy'), wide awake and sociable ('I might sleep for four hours a night 'cos I'm so wide awake and wanting to talk to people and stuff').

Anna describes how she deliberately and purposefully seeks out opportunities for creating this 'rush' of intense and almost overwhelming sensations that she describes as both 'mental' and 'physical' in nature. She describes how she uses extreme sport to alleviate boredom and to give herself 'a big lift', recharging herself with new energy and motivation at times when life has become 'boring and dull'. She explains how the desired effect is only achieved if there is an element of real danger involved, albeit always within an envelope of ultimate security ('I do like the fact that you might almost hurt yourself but there is also that thing that it will never happen to me'). When real doubts about the latter emerge, Anna feels that it gets 'a little bit too scary', although she also acknowledges that it is precisely this sense of real danger that raises the excitement to the desired level ('when it actually becomes a reality that you might really really hurt yourself, then (intake of breath) you know, it sort of takes your breath away'). In Anna's account, the boundary between real mortal danger and ultimate safety is both important and uncertain; she welcomes a reminder that her activities are 'serious' and not just 'great fun', but at the same time she acknowledges that 'There's never truly a stage that I think that I'm gonna really really hurt myself'. In a similar way, Anna also describes how she plays with control – she seeks out situations where she has little or no control over what happens to her body (for example, in her second experience of white water rafting and also with reference to her bungee jump) and yet at the same time she ensures that there is a secure framework within which her experiences take place (for example, through the control exercised by expert organizers of the activities). Anna emphasizes the importance of her faith in the organizers of extreme sport activities ('when I do these things I put incredible faith in the people who organize it') and she reflects on the effect of this on her choice of activities ('Yeah, but I'm just thinking, it's interesting 'cos I wonder if the events, the sports that I've done I've always got that faith in somebody else?'). The presence of an envelope of ultimate security (provided by the expert organizers) is identified as a necessary condition for Anna to enjoy the thrill of the risk-taking involved in extreme sport.

In the second extract, Anna interprets her commitment to extreme sport as being connected with childhood rebellion against her mother and her closeness to her stepfather. She describes how risk-taking was a way of allying herself with her stepfather against her mother ('mum would, you know, don't do that, you'll hurt yourself so I'd just do it, and my stepdad on the other hand would be like yeah you can do that, you can do that'). Anna links this with her faith in extreme sport organizers today ('that's part of that faith thing again it's like, you know, dad says I can do it (...) I can do it then. So I'd go and do it').

Further illumination of meanings with reference to existing literature

Anna's account suggests that she is using extreme sport as a way of managing her mood. She knows what kind of an experience she is looking for (the 'buzz') and she knows what having this experience will do for her (give her 'a big lift'). Anna is active and purposive in her approach to extreme sport. Through practising particular types of extreme sport, Anna creates a space for herself to experience high levels of arousal that are generated by taking risks within an envelope of ultimate security. As such, she makes use of what Celsi et al. (1993: 12) describe as the 'set piece' whereby extreme sports practitioners 'carefully create a context of controlled uncertainty as a stage within which they can act'. Thus, what may appear, from an outside observer's viewpoint, as a reckless, perhaps impulsive act (whereby caution is thrown to the wind in the pursuit of thrills) is actually a carefully staged scenario that produces just the right kind of balance between challenge and comfort (what Celsi et al. call 'controlled uncertainty'). This scenario is created deliberately and purposefully to allow a certain kind of experience to become possible.

As in Ben's account, there is evidence of a dynamic engagement with boundaries in Anna's narrative. Anna plays with the boundary between risk and safety, moving between the conviction that nothing seriously harmful can happen to her and the acknowledgement that she may actually die or 'really really hurt' herself. Like Ben, through taking part in extreme sport activities, Anna plays with the boundaries between risk and safety, control and loss of control, fear and fun. Thus, she, too, may be using extreme sport to negotiate and manage 'existence tensions' (Spinelli, 2001).

Reflections on the analysis

My phenomenological analyses of Ben's and Anna's accounts of their experiences of extreme sport activities have generated an interpretation of the experience of extreme sport that invokes the importance of the loss of a sense of self (Ben), and of generating excitement (Anna), of the opportunity to escape from everyday life with its responsibilities (Ben) and its tedium (Anna), and of playing with boundaries between risk and safety, fear and joy, control and loss of control, as a way of managing existence tensions (Ben and Anna). My phenomenological interpretation of Ben's and Anna's accounts of their experience has sought to find meaning in their experiences without digging beneath their accounts to find hidden dynamics or mechanisms that might explain their choices, their thoughts and feelings. However, an interpretation motivated by 'empathy' (as opposed to 'suspicion') is still an interpretation in that it is a product of the relationship between the text (the data) and the interpreter (the researcher). This means that it is important to be aware of the nature of this relationship and to reflect on how it has shaped the interpretation of the data. To help me explore the intersubjective aspects of my analysis, I asked myself a number of questions. For example, I asked myself what allowed me to see what I saw in the data? What kinds of questions about the experience of extreme sport did I have in mind as I approached the data? How did my background knowledge and interests influence my initial reading of the accounts? What sort of literature did I consult as I began to try to illuminate the meanings identified by my analysis? To begin with, we need to remember that my decision to approach the data from a phenomenological perspective meant that my analysis of the text would be guided by questions about the nature and quality of experience, and that questions about cause-and-effect, about the relationship between Ben's and Anna's developmental history and their current experience, about their psychological traits or personality structure, or indeed questions about the wider social construction of extreme sport had to be put aside. However, it can be difficult to keep such questions in their place and out of the analysis; for example, I noticed how, as I read Anna's first extract, I kept wondering why it was that Anna had such a strong desire to experience 'a lift' and I began to wonder whether she was depressed and whether extreme sport might have been her way of self-medicating by generating endorphins. However, I was aware that such ideas were not compatible with a phenomenological perspective and I attempted to bracket them throughout the analysis, focusing instead on the nature and quality of Anna's experience itself.

Asking myself what allowed me to see what I saw in the data, I began to think about my background in existential counselling psychology and my immersion in existential-phenomenological literature, which has sensitized me to questions and concerns about our 'being in the world' and our relationship with time, with our bodies, the physical environment and with other people. The literature that came to my mind as I reflected on the descriptive summaries chimes with this, and it is no coincidence that I made connections between Ben's and Anna's experience and Spinelli's (2001) discussion of 'existence tensions'.

Another way in which intersubjectivity enters my interpretation is through my contributions to the conversation (i.e. the interview), which provide the context within which Ben and Anna produced their accounts of their experience. Frost (2009a) acknowledges that it can feel uncomfortable to focus on one's own contributions to an interview; however, the researcher's presence and interventions do play an important role in the direction the interview takes and are, therefore, worth taking a closer look at. Looking at my contributions to the interview with Ben, we can see that I make two types of contributions. One of these consists of my attempts to summarize and reflect back to Ben what I have understood him to have communicated in the previous turn. Summarizing and reflecting back are a way of checking with the interviewee that one has understood them correctly and it is also a way of communicating that one is listening and maintaining interest in what the interviewee is saying. The second type of contribution I make to the interview with Ben takes the form of questions that encourage Ben to take his re-flections further. These contributions build on what Ben himself has said but they also introduce new elements. For example, in my contribution at the beginning of the extract, I begin by summarizing and reflecting back,

> So you're very focused then on what you're doing during the climbing, you're focusing on where you put your feet (…)

but then move on to invite Ben to reflect further:

> (…) and do you think about anything else or is it very much focusing on what you're doing?

Interestingly, Ben explicitly acknowledges that the second part of my contribution constitutes an invitation to take his reflections further when he refers to how he is 'thinking on it now' in response to my question:

> No, I mean thinking on it now, you don't think about anything else.

There are, in fact, a number of times in the extract when Ben refers to his own process (of thinking, feeling, and reflecting) in the interview, thus indicating that my questions are encouraging him to reflect on his experience during the interview itself rather than simply to tell a story he may have told many times before. For example, at one point he says:

> Erm (pause) it's quite funny because now we're talking about it (…) I'm almost reliving it because speaking about it I can picture where I was when I was feeling that way

Overall, then, my contributions to the interview with Ben presuppose that Ben is willing and able to reflect on his experience, to engage with it right there in the interview, and that he is open to a process of meaning-making in collaboration with another person (i.e. myself). My questions presuppose that Ben can be curious about his own experience and that he is willing to scrutinize it, to interrogate it, and to explore how it is constituted. There is no doubt that my questions (and the attitude towards Ben's experience as something to be curious about, to be thought about, and examined that my questions conveyed) will have had an influence on the type of account that Ben was able to produce within the context of our interview. And this, in turn, has implications for the kinds of insights that my analysis of the data was able to generate.

Looking at my contributions to the interview with Anna, we can see that here I seem to be keen to obtain detailed descriptions of Anna's feelings before exploring the meaning of her experience. I invite her to 'try and remember how you felt just before you actually got into [the] raft', to describe 'the feelings during it', and to think about 'afterwards, when you got out, how did you feel?' At one point I acknowledge that it is 'difficult to describe feelings, the quality of the feelings' only to then invite her, again, to do just that ('what kind of thoughts and feelings do you have then?'). In addition to asking Anna to describe her feelings, I also ask for clarification of the nature of her feelings once she has described them.

For example, following her account of white water rafting I ask, 'So the feelings during it were like a mixture of excitement and fear? Or how would you describe it?', and following her description of her sky-dive I ask, 'And would you say that was enjoyable or a mixture of enjoyable and not enjoyable?' It is only after I have asked Anna five questions inviting her to describe her feelings in detail that I move on to a question that is concerned with the meaning of her experience: 'So it almost gives you an influx of energy? It gives you something additional (…)?' It is interesting to see how this question allows Anna to offer a reflection on the meaning and purpose of her activities (to give herself 'a big lift' and to make herself feel 'regenerated and (…) motivated to do other things'), a reflection that my more descriptive questions did not provoke. Looking back at the interview with Anna, I think that I found it quite difficult to relate to Anna's experience, to 'step into her shoes', and to imagine what it might have been like for her to engage with extreme sport. My descriptive questions at the beginning of the interview reflect my attempt to gain a better understanding of her experience, its quality and texture, before moving on to try to make sense of it. In retrospect, I believe that this was a helpful strategy, since premature questions about possible meanings may have resulted in me bringing ideas and concepts to Anna's experience that would not have been meaningful to her, or, worse, that might have interfered with my ability to really hear what Anna was attempting to communicate about her experience.

Phenomenological research is concerned primarily with the content of participants' accounts, with the meanings participants give to their experience, and, as discussed in Chapter 4, this means that here language is seen as a medium for expressing meanings that belong to the participants. However, in Chapter 4 it was also acknowledged that language and meaning are inextricably linked and that paying attention to the use of language can provide us with a more differentiated understanding of the meaning that is made of experience. In fact, the impression created by the initial reading of an interview transcript as a whole and its impact on the reader is inevitably a product of both the overt content (i.e. *what* is being described) and the language used to describe this (i.e. *how* something is being described). For example, an interviewee may describe what appears to be a fairly mundane, everyday event in such strong and colourful language that the impression left after reading the account is that of an extraordinary event having taken place. From a phenomenological point of view, both of these aspects of the data are significant; in fact, it is likely that the phenomenon of interest here would be that of something like 'the ordinary made extraordinary'.

Let us take a look at the use of language in Ben's and Anna's interview extracts and consider its contribution to the meanings made and represented in my analysis of the extracts. A striking feature of Ben's account is that he is using a rhetorical structure sometimes referred to as the 'three-part-list' (e.g. Edwards and Potter, 1992), which involves the repetition of a similar phrase three times in succession. The three-part-list is a rhetorical strategy that is widely used in political speeches and writings; Julius Caesar's 'Veni, Vidi, Vici' ('I came, I saw, I conquered') is a classic example. The effect of the three-part-list is to convey a message with more emphasis and thus to persuade the listener or reader of its significance. I felt that Ben's use of this construction lent a poetic, rhythmic air to his account, which also meant that his description of his encounter with the mountain acquired an almost mystic quality, as he repeated his descriptions in a mantra-like fashion. Ben uses the full three-part-list twice ('You feel every footprint, you feel every handhold, you feel the security in it', and 'It's not what you're gonna do when you get to the top, it's not what you're gonna have when you get into the pub, it's not what happened twenty minutes ago'), and an abbreviated (two-part) version ('You think about where you're putting your feet, you look for where you're gonna go next'; 'it does tend to be all about rock, it does tend to be all about mountain'; 'everything is cool, everything is fine') three times in his account of mountaineering. Ben's use of language here reinforces his description of his experience of mountaineering as somehow other-wordly, as taking him away from everyday life and its mundane demands, reminding him of the bigger picture, the beauty of the world and his own insignificance, which is something that could be described as spiritual (although Ben uses the word 'magic' to capture this quality instead). Interestingly, in the second part of the extract in his description of the rough-and-tumble of mountain-biking and sailing, Ben does not use repetition in the same way and it is noticeable that this latter account has a much speedier, staccato feel to it, thus reflecting the rapid and jolting sequence of events described in this part of the extract. Here, frequent laughter accompanies Ben's description, which supports and reinforces the slap-stick quality of this part of his account.

Moving on to Anna's use of language, perhaps the most striking feature of her style of presentation is the inclusion of a series of sharp intakes of breath that punctuate her account of her experience of extreme sport. On five occasions, Anna underlines her verbal descriptions with a sharp intake of breath. On two occasions, she does this in support of a verbal reference to losing her breath:

> I was sucked down there and (intake of breath) yeah okay I lost my breath for a bit and I couldn't breathe (. . .)

> and when it actually becomes a reality that you might really really hurt yourself, then (intake of breath) you know, it sort of takes your breath away.

In these two examples, Anna both verbally refers to and literally enacts the loss of breath. On another two occasions, however, Anna uses the intake of breath in place of a verbal description of her experience:

> So when I finish things like this it's just (intake of breath) you know.

> the build of the rush just got bigger and bigger and bigger and my body was going (intake of breath).

It is as though, here, Anna is lost for words, feeling unable to capture the intensely physical quality of her experience in words; in place of words she deploys a sharp intake of breath, thus giving expression to the sense of excitement and arousal that characterizes her experience. Interestingly, Anna's intake of breath in the final paragraph of the interview extract appears to signify something different again. In this paragraph, Anna talks about how she engages in extreme sport activities to 'lift' herself to 'another level' when she finds herself feeling bored and perhaps stuck (although she does not use this term) in the routine of everyday life; she associates the routines of everyday life with a downward movement ('you sort of sit down to this little rut'; 'you don't know that you're in it before you get to the bottom'), which she contrasts with the upward movement provided by the experience of extreme sport ('I've just lifted myself another level'; 'gotta lift yourself up again and then keep on going'). It is within this context that Anna deploys the intake of breath:

> And then it's like (intake of breath) gotta lift yourself up again and then keep on going.

Looking across these three different ways in which Anna deploys the sharp intake of breath, we can surmise that for Anna extreme sport provides access to an intensely physical experience that is very powerful yet difficult to put into words and which lifts her out of the viscous monotony of everyday life's routines and onto a higher plane where she can feel more energized again. Anna's use of a sharp intake of breath in three different contexts reinforces the connection between Anna's experience of physical excitement during extreme sport, the influx of energy she experiences as a result, and the effects of this on her mood for considerable periods of time afterwards.

In my discussion of my phenomenological analyses of Ben's and Anna's interview extracts, I have concentrated largely on each participant's interview extract separately, only occasionally making links between them. My descriptive summaries for Ben and Anna are entirely self-contained and specific to Ben's and Anna's respective accounts. However, the illumination of their experiences in the light of existing literature began to identify a shared theme around the use of extreme sport in the negotiation of existence tensions. It is no coincidence that a more abstract, theoretically inflected interpretation of each individual's account facilitates conceptual cross-referencing between, and a potential integration of, accounts. After all, the very act of abstraction involves moving away from the concrete detail of an account; it involves an attempt to identify higher level categories that can capture the meaning contained within the detailed description of a specific, concrete experience so that we can recognize it as an instance of a more general phenomenon. So, for example, through such a process of abstraction, Ben's concrete experience of trying to maintain control while allowing his body to become the plaything of external forces becomes an instance of negotiating the existence tension between freedom and determinism. It is important to acknowledge that the move from an engagement with the concrete to a concern with the abstract involves a number of choices regarding the concepts we choose to draw on during the process of abstraction and that these choices will shape the insights we gain as a result.

Appraisal of the phenomenological reading

In this final section, I want to review and evaluate my application of a phenomenological perspective to Ben's and Anna's interview extracts, and to reflect on the nature and value of the interpretation that I have generated.

The aim of the analysis had been to gain a better understanding of the nature, meaning, and significance of taking part in extreme sport activities. To what extent has my phenomenological analysis of Ben's and Anna's accounts provided us with such an understanding? Looking back at the two descriptive summaries together with my reflections on these in the light of relevant literature, we can identify two shared meanings that underpin both accounts. Both Ben and Anna invoke an active engagement with boundaries between apparently opposing elements as being an important part of their experience of extreme sport. Taking part in extreme sport activities allows both Ben and Anna to experience and negotiate tensions between aspects of human existence in a way that brings them a sense of satisfaction. In addition, both Ben's and Anna's experience of extreme sport involves a deliberate and purposeful seeking out of situations that will generate a particular kind of experience (in Ben's case 'flow' and in Anna's case 'buzz') which is highly valued by them and which they are not able to access in everyday life. However, while my analysis has, indeed, generated some insights into the nature, meaning, and significance of the experience of extreme sport, it is also clear that Ben's and Anna's experiences of extreme sport are by no means identical. Ben's account of his experience emphasizes the loss of self, his sense of merging with something bigger than himself, and the joy associated with this. As such, Ben's account invokes a meditative, almost spiritual quality and a sense of liberation and freedom from the burden of being an individual. By contrast, Anna's account is very much concerned with excitement and with the effects of high levels of physiological arousal on her body and on her mood. Anna's experience is intense to the point of being overwhelming (after all, it 'takes her breath away') and she emphasizes the importance of feeling energized through her encounters with risk.

How does a phenomenological approach deal with such differences? It may be tempting to think of these differences in Ben's and Anna's accounts as indicators of differences between the two participants' personalities, their emotional constitutions or the content of their psyches. However, we need to remember that from a phenomenological perspective we are interested in the phenomenon under investigation (i.e. the experience of extreme sport) rather than our individual participants' psychological make-up. This means that our reflections need to concern themselves with the phenomenon itself. Are Ben and Anna really describing the same phenomenon? After all, Ben is talking about his experience of mountaineering while Anna describes what happens to her during white water rafting and bungee jumping. Perhaps there is no such thing as a phenomenology of extreme sport? Perhaps the category 'extreme sport', which is after all largely a marketing category, includes a range of activities that differ significantly in terms of the experiences they generate? Was I wrong to set out to attempt to study the 'phenomenon of extreme sport', and would it have been more productive to focus on one particular type of activity (i.e. mountaineering *or* white water rafting *or* bungee jumping) rather than lump them together on the assumption that they share something significant? Looking at the analysis of the data across the eight participants in the original study (see Willig, 2005, 2007b, 2008b) it becomes clear that there is a difference between the nature, quality, and significance of the experience of mountaineering and that of other types of extreme sport (e.g. skydiving, bungee jumping, white water rafting) with the former incorporating a spiritual dimension that appears to be absent in the latter activities. It could, therefore, be argued that the study has identified two distinct phenomena. As such, the study has indeed improved our understanding of the phenomenon of extreme sport because it has generated a more differentiated conceptualization of its structure, to the point of discerning the presence of two quite different experiential formations.

My inclusion of reflections on the descriptive summaries with reference to published literature has meant that my phenomenological analyses of Ben's and Anna's accounts have been linked to existing theories (of 'flow' and of 'existence tensions'), thus providing empirical support for them. These theories have not, in this case, been modified in the light of my data analysis; however, this is something that could happen as a result of making links between phenomenological analyses and existing theories.

Any ethical concerns that may arise as a result of my phenomenological analysis are likely to be associated with acts of omission rather than commission. In other words, it could be argued that my decision to take Ben's and Anna's accounts of their experience at face value and not to apply my psychological knowledge and expertise to dissect their thoughts, feelings, and motivations has meant that my analysis was unable to reveal any underlying psychic mechanisms and structures that generate and sustain my participants' experiences. It could be argued that a failure to look for such structures and mechanisms results in a superficial reading, which effectively colludes with my participants' disavowal of any possible problematic or destructive dimensions of their commitment to extreme sport. Indeed, some of the participants in the original study (Willig, 2005), including Ben, had described themselves as 'addicted' to extreme sport and several of them had reported that their friends thought that they were 'crazy' to be doing what they were doing. However, my analysis of Ben's and Anna's accounts does not include considerations as to what it may be about Ben and Anna (and their backgrounds, developmental histories, attachment patterns, mental states, psyches, and so on) that makes them susceptible to the attractions of extreme sport. Thus although ethical concerns are more usually expressed in relation to 'suspicious' interpretations of research participants' accounts (see Chapters 2 and 3), it is important to acknowledge that a lack of suspicion, and a commitment to a hermeneutics of empathy and meaning-recollection do have their own ethical implications. A refusal to pathologize, to look for underlying yet unacknowledged fears, desires, and motivations on the part of the participant does mean that the researcher is unable to generate insights into the psychology of extreme sport at a deeper level.

Not all researchers do, of course, believe that it is meaningful to look for such a deeper level or, indeed, that such a level exists at all.

These reflections take us on to a wider consideration of the scope of phenomenological analysis and a consideration of the types of data that are suitable for such analysis. We have established that a phenomenological perspective is concerned with the nature and quality of experience; the aim of a phenomenological analysis is to illuminate experiential phenomena. Phenomenological research is driven by questions about *how* something is experienced and *what it is like* to experience it. It seeks to understand experience rather than to discover what is 'really going on' or why something may have happened. This means that from a phenomenological perspective it is irrelevant whether a research participant's account is an accurate reflection of what happened to them, since what matters here is the participant's own interpretation of their experience, the meaning that they give to the experience.

Phenomenological knowledge, then, is knowledge about human experience, not knowledge about the material world or, indeed, the structure of the human psyche. Its scope is limited to the experiential dimension. The type of data suitable for phenomenological analysis, therefore, needs to provide the researcher with information about the nature, quality, and texture of research participants' experiences. Rich, descriptive accounts are preferable and the focus of such accounts needs to be experience itself. As we have seen within the context of our discussion of Ben's and Anna's accounts of their experiences of extreme sport, the researcher's initial research focus (i.e., in our case, the phenomenon of 'extreme sport') does not always correspond to the phenomena identified in the analysis of the data (for example, different types of extreme sport may give rise to different experiential phenomena). It is important, therefore, to remain open to revisions regarding the nature of the phenomenon under investigation, or indeed to the possibility that there is more than one phenomenon present.

7   A discursive reading

In this chapter, we re-visit Ben's and Anna's accounts of their experiences of extreme sport; this time, however, we shall view the data through a discursive lens. In this chapter, we are concerned with *the way in which* Ben and Anna talk about their experiences, with how they construct their experiences through language, and how this positions them and the interviewer. We shall pay attention to the action orientation of the accounts and to what is accomplished by constructing the experience in a particular way within a particular context. Again, it is hoped that the discursive analysis presented here will demonstrate how such an analysis is underpinned by a clear epistemological position and a set of theoretical concerns, and that these are specific to a discourse analytic perspective, generating a particular kind of interpretation of Ben's and Anna's accounts. The chapter will explore the theoretical, ethical, and practical implications of a discursive reading of the data, and it will consider the strengths and limitations of such discourse-based interpretations. As before, the chapter concludes with some guidance regarding the kinds of data that are (and are not) suitable for this type of analysis.

Aims of the analysis

Approaching data from a discursive perspective involves focusing on language. After all, the purpose of a discursive analysis is to gain a better understanding of how the use of language (that is to say, the choice of words, grammatical constructions, and various rhetorical strategies) is implicated in the construction of particular versions of events. Discourse analytic research is concerned with the *effects* of discourse and, as such, its primary objects of interest are talk and text. Thus, in the same way that phenomenological research is primarily concerned with understanding experiential phenomena (rather than the particular individuals who have experienced such phenomena and are able to describe them), discursive research is primarily concerned with discourse (rather than the individuals who use discourse and whose speech or writing constitutes the data to be analysed). In other words, the research questions that drive discourse analytic research are about the (social, institutional, psychological) effects of discourse, and not about the thoughts and feelings within the individual speakers that may give rise to the words they utter. A discursive analysis always *starts with* discourse. Some versions of the discourse analytic method do go on to ask questions about how discourses may shape individual subjectivity; however, here subjectivity is conceptualized as the *product* of internalized discursive constructions and positionings, never as an entity that pre-exists discourse.

A discursive perspective is grounded in a social constructionist position, which means that the kind of knowledge a discourse analyst seeks to produce is knowledge about the processes by which particular kinds of 'knowledge' and 'understanding' are produced. The aim of discourse analytic research is, therefore, *not* to find out more about how things 'really' are (as in realist approaches to research) or even how something is experienced (as in phenomenological research). It is essential that a focus on language as constructive and performative is maintained throughout the analysis, and that the researcher does not get side-tracked by questions about the nature of the events described or about the inner worlds of the participants who describe them.

It is important to remember that a discourse analytic approach to research is based upon the assumption that *all* accounts of human experience are mediated by language, which means that *all* social and psychological phenomena are constructed in one way or another, and that all knowledge about the world and experience of the world are very much socially mediated. From this point of view, individual experiences are the product of internalized social constructions. In other words, when participants are telling the researcher about their experiences, they are not seen to be giving voice to an inner reality (as in *phenomenological* research) or to be providing information about social/psychological processes (as in *realist* research); instead, the researcher is interested in how socially available ways of talking actually construct the phenomenon of interest and how these are deployed by the participant within the context of the conversation which constitutes the data to be analysed. Here, the role of the researcher is to draw attention to the constructed nature of social reality, to trace the specific ways in which particular phenomena are constructed through discourse, and to reflect upon the consequences of this for those who are affected (that is to say, who are 'positioned') by these social constructions.

Process of analysis

I began my discursive analysis of Ben's and Anna's interviews by reading and rereading the transcripts, paying particular attention to the use of language. As I did this I noticed that on occasion I would lose myself in the content of what was being said and forget about my focus on discourse. Other times I would pay attention to the choice of words and grammatical constructions, only to find that I struggled to notice anything interesting about them. To help me adopt and sustain a discursive perspective in relation to the texts, I asked myself a number of questions about what I was reading as I was reading it. These included questions about what sorts of assumptions (about the world, about people, about extreme sport) appeared to underpin what was being said and how it was being said. I also asked myself whether (and if so, how) what was being said could have been said differently without fundamentally changing the meaning of what was being said. For example, my opening question to Anna (C: 'Can you describe one occasion when you took part in a form of extreme sport?') presumes that both Anna and myself share an understanding of what 'extreme sport' is and that the term designates a type of activity that can take different forms. My question also presumes that such activities take place on particular, distinct, and clearly identifiable occasions and that the experience of taking part in them can be described in words. As such, my opening question to Anna constructs extreme sport in a particular way and it invites a particular kind of account of it. Just think of how different an opening would have been offered to Anna had I said, 'So, Anna, tell me, you and extreme sport – what's that all about then?'

During my initial readings and re-readings, I was struck by some of the rhetorical features of the transcripts. These included Ben's use of repetition (including his three-part-lists already referred to in Chapter 6), and his use of laughter and pauses, as well as Anna's breathlessness and the speed and fluency of her delivery. I made a note of these and decided to explore their meaning and function further within the context of the detailed line-by-line analysis that would constitute the next stage of analysis.

I started with Ben's transcript, reading each line of text (this could be a phrase, a sentence, a question or a short paragraph), thinking about what was being said and how it was being said. I wrote notes on my reflections in the margins of the transcript. As I worked through the transcript I was able to identify patterns such as Ben's use of three-part-lists within the context of describing the other-worldy nature of being in the mountains, or the appearance of pauses in conjunction with Ben's use of the first person singular ('I'), which positioned Ben as someone who is actively reflecting there and then, within the context of the interview. This stage of the analysis allowed me to tentatively identify discursive constructions and positionings used in Ben's account of extreme sport, and to begin to see how the rhetorical strategies he deployed supported such constructions and positionings. I also explored the ways in which my own questions and contributions to the interview constructed meaning and how they positioned Ben and myself, and how this may have shaped Ben's account. Having completed the line-by-line analysis, I reviewed my notes and attempted to integrate my observations in such a way as to produce a coherent discursive reading of Ben's interview extract. I then repeated the same procedure with Anna's transcript, producing a second discursive reading. Each of these is presented separately below.

As a final stage in my discursive analysis, I offer some reflections on the availability of discursive resources with which to construct experiences of 'extreme sport' and their implications for subjectivity and practice. Here, I consider the potential consequences of the discourses that are used for those who are positioned by them, both in terms of their subjective experience and their ability to act in the world.

A discursive reading of Ben's extract

It is interesting to note how my questions, from the very beginning of the extract, position Ben as the expert on an experiential process that can be dissected and scrutinized. My questions invite Ben to explain to me exactly what is happening in his mind and body when he practises extreme sport. I ask him repeatedly what he is thinking and feeling when he is climbing and how he relates to himself during the climb. My questions construct extreme sport as an experience that is composed of distinct elements (thoughts, feelings, sensations) that can be identified and described in detail. My questions presuppose that Ben, as a practitioner of extreme sport, is in a position to provide an insider account of this experience, and that I do not have the same expert knowledge that Ben has. However, at the same time, my questions assume that there is a characteristic pattern, an identifiable sequence of thoughts, feelings, and sensations that can be identified and understood, even by the uninitiated like myself. This becomes particularly clear when I ask Ben, 'how does it work?'

Taking a closer look at my questions, we can also see that although I position Ben as the expert on his experience, I do not follow his lead when he talks extensively about 'feelings' ('Above all, you feel it') and about 'losing himself' ('you lose yourself'); instead I continue with my questions about what he is or is not 'thinking', 'focusing', and 'reflecting' on. In this way, I continually reintroduce the reflective self, thus constructing myself and Ben as always potentially self-aware and self-monitoring. Ben does not seem to resist this positioning and, in turn, constructs himself as self-reflexive when he says, 'Yeah, it's when you get to the top of that section and then you look down and (laughs) you realize what you've done'. Together, Ben and I continue to construct him as the object of our scrutiny, with me emphasizing my outsider status by asking questions which indicate that I have no idea what the experience of extreme sport might involve (for example, when I ask 'So (…) is it a pleasant feeling (…) or a scary feeling or how is it?'), while Ben positions himself as being curious about himself in a new way within the context of the interview (for example, when he observes 'it's quite funny because now we're talking about it I'm (…) almost reliving it because speaking about it I can picture where I was when I was feeling that way'). Thus, although I position myself as a reflective subject who wants to acquire knowledge about the world (after all, I am the researcher who is seeking to answer her research question), Ben adopts a more complex dual position as both subject (in his capacity as a reflexive self seeking to understand his experiences) and object (after all, it is his experience that we are both puzzling over) of the research.

In his responses to my questions, Ben uses two distinct styles of talking about his experiences. One of these is characterized by a frequent use of the generic 'you' (as in 'you lose yourself'), and it is often punctuated by laughter. It also contains few or only very brief pauses; here, Ben speaks fluently and without hesitation, making categorical statements without qualifying them (e.g. 'that's why I love it'). Here is an example:

> B: There are no problems in the mountains other than where you stick your hand next and that's why I love it. It's the same with skiing. There are no problems skiing except how you ski next (laughing). You know, if you ski stupid, well then, but if you ski well, it's fine.

This style of talking creates the impression that what is being described here is straight-forward and that the speaker is very clear about the message he wants to convey; the laughter reinforces this impression by suggesting that what is being said here is so obvious that to spell it out is perhaps unnecessary and, therefore, somewhat ridiculous.

The second style of talking is characterized by the use of 'I' (as in 'I feel my insignificance'), by frequent and relatively long pauses, as well as hesitations and changes in direction. It also involves the use of qualifiers and hedges (such as the expression 'I suppose' and adverbs such as 'almost') whose function is to weaken the speaker's commitment to the claims and assertions contained in what he is saying. This second style of talking allows Ben to appear to be giving expression to his reflections as they unfold, without a clear sense of where he may be going with them. The following extract illustrates this style of talking:

> B: Talking about it you feel it. It's not quite as (pause) good, it's not as good a feeling as when I'm actually doing it but certainly as long as (...) I can see the mountains then, you know, I start getting excited about it (...) I get excited when I actually see the mountains and it lasts (pause) until I suppose something trivial happens here (...)

Below is an example of where Ben moves from one style to the other, so that an initial phase of reflection (ending with the first 'nothing really matters') is seen to precede a more confident assertion of a position that Ben appears to feel comfortable with:

> C: So does it feel, is it a pleasant feeling?
>
> B: Yeah.
>
> C: Or a scary feeling or how is it?
>
> B: It's a really pleasant feeling. Erm, sometimes, I don't know, I don't think it's scary, it's adrenaline fuelled (pause) but it's a really pleasant feeling of being, you feel, I feel, I feel my insignificance in that landscape but it's a nice feeling 'cos I find that quite comforting, you know, it's almost like (pause) nothing really matters (laughs) not so much nothing really matters as you go (puts on high-pitched voice) 'modern life is so full of stress' and yeah you've just done that thing that could've had you killed and really I mean all these piddly little things that you worry about really don't matter in the big scale of things it's, everything is cool, everything is fine so it's a feeling of comfort but it's an adrenaline-fuelled feeling of comfort.

It seemed to me that Ben's use of the two styles in conjunction makes his account more persuasive, as his conclusion (that he experiences 'an adrenaline-fuelled feeling of comfort') is presented as the product of a process of careful and deliberate reflection rather than coming across as a throw-away comment or an assertion based on prejudice.

In my discussion of the use of language in the interview extracts within the context of my phenomenological reading in Chapter 6, I had already drawn attention to Ben's utilization of repetition in general, and his deployment of three-part-lists in particular. I observed that Ben's use of repetition gave a poetic, rhythmic quality to his account that chimed with his description of mountaineering as taking him away from 'the real world' with its mundane demands and pressures. The use of repetition was seen as reinforcing the meaning given to the experience of extreme sport by Ben. Revisiting Ben's use of the three-part-list from a discursive point of view allows us to ask questions about its rhetorical function. To do this, we need to examine carefully the context within which it is deployed. Ben produces two three-part-lists in quick succession in his response to my question about whether he thinks about anything else while he is focusing on climbing. Here is the relevant section of the transcript:

> C: So you're very focused then on what you're doing during the climbing, you're focusing on where you put your feet and do you think about anything else or is it very much focusing on what you're doing?
>
> B: No, I mean thinking on it now, you don't think about anything else. You think about where you're putting your feet, you look for where you're gonna go next. Above all, you feel it. You feel every footprint, you feel every handhold, you feel the security in it and that's what you spend, or that's what I spend all my time doing (pause) is I suppose attempting to feel secure at that precise moment and that's the only thing you think about. It's not what you're gonna do when you get to the top, it's not what you're gonna have when you get into the pub, it's not what happened twenty minutes ago, it's only that (...)

In his response to my question, Ben goes to some lengths to elucidate how during the climbing he remains focused on the present moment. Rather than simply answering my question with a straightforward 'Yes' (as in 'Yes, it is very much about focusing on what I'm doing'), Ben produces a descriptive account that emphasizes the connectedness of his mind and body with the present moment. He deploys a three-part-list to draw attention to the importance of 'feelings' ('Above all, you feel it. You feel every footprint, you feel every handhold, you feel the security in it'), and then another three-part-list to stress how thoughts about even the immediate past or future do not feature when he is in the moment ('It's not what you're gonna do when you get to the top, it's not what you're gonna have when you get into the pub, it's not what happened twenty minutes ago'). As a result, Ben has done much more than simply answered my question; he has produced a persuasive argument in support of his claim that when climbing he does not think about anything else. Also note Ben's move from using the generic 'you' to the specific and personal 'I' half-way through his response before returning to the generic 'you' again ('and that's what you spend, or that's what I spend all my time doing (pause) is I suppose attempting to feel secure at that precise moment and that's the only thing you think about'). Here, Ben is switching between the two styles of talking identified earlier and, as suggested before, it could be argued that this serves to make his account more convincing, as it implies that his reflections involve a process of genuine soul-searching. From a discursive point of view, then, both the use of three-part-lists and the deployment of the two styles of talking in conjunction constitute rhetorical strategies whose deployment help to make Ben's account more compelling and, therefore, more persuasive.

Interestingly, neither of these two rhetorical strategies feature in the second part of Ben's extract. Here, Ben responds to my request for clarification regarding sports which in the previous turn he had described as looking 'silly':

B: (...) with the sports that I've got into they look fun and they look adrenaline, they look like they've got an adrenaline buzz, they look silly (laughs)

C: How do you mean, silly?

After a long pause, Ben goes on to characterize such sports as 'partly danger-ous but not dangerous', and then offers a fast-paced account of examples of minor sporting accidents. Its fast pace and the complete absence of hesitations and repeti-tions gives Ben's account a hard-hitting quality, thus echoing the events described therein. The fluency of the account also implies that Ben is very familiar with the kinds of experiences he is describing and that he is untroubled by them. How-ever, at the same time Ben takes care to ensure that the listener appreciates the physical and mental challenges involved in these experiences by describing their challenging nature in detail and in evocative terms; for example, he reminds me that when mountain biking 'you can quite easily fall off your bike and tumble down a bank' and when sailing hobie cats it is 'really easy to tip over', and he acknowledges that 'it hurts when you hit the water' and that it 'can be quite scary' to fly forward trapped on a trapeze. In his account, Ben keeps returning to his assertion that these experiences are 'fun' or 'funny' while also describing them as involving pain and fear. There is a further contrast between the comic strip quality of the descriptions evoked by terms such as 'whohoo', 'ping', and 'phung' and sup-ported by Ben's frequent laughter, and Ben's references to being 'roughed up' and his description of being knocked about in various ways. The rhetorical effect of juxtaposing his descriptions of mentally and physically challenging and arguably rather dangerous activities with a light-hearted, trivializing attitude towards them is to position Ben as someone who is tough enough not to be unsettled by a brush with physical danger. It is interesting to note that this part of the extract is pre-ceded by an exchange during which Ben acknowledges that as he is getting older he is 'getting a little bit wary because there's been a few people that I've known that have died doing things', and when I reflect this back to him, he expresses some self-consciousness about his cautious attitude:

C: (...) you're saying with age you feel a bit more aware or more concerned about the risks

B: Yeah (laughs)

C: Than you used to?

B: Isn't that silly?

So putting the second part of Ben's extract in context, we could speculate that Ben's construction of himself as tough enough to handle the cut and thrust involved in extreme sport, to the point of being amused by it, is in fact a way of distancing himself from his earlier positioning as someone who is becoming increasingly cautious with age. A discursive perspective requires that we approach talk and text as a form of action, which means that we pay attention to what a speaker is *doing* when she or he is saying something. In this case, we have attempted to understand what Ben is doing when he constructs himself as 'tough enough'. We have done this by looking at the discursive context within which he has done this, which has allowed us to formulate a hypothesis regarding the interactive business Ben may have been attending to.

A discursive reading of Anna's extract

In response to my opening question (C: 'Can you describe one occasion when you took part in a form of extreme sport?'), Anna produces a lengthy account of not one but two such occasions. Anna's account takes the form of a conventional narrative that begins with the identification of a place ('I was on holiday for a few weeks (...) at [name of place]') and a point in time ('a number of years ago'), and goes on to tell the story of how she came to take part in two white water rafting expeditions. What is interesting about Anna's narrative from a discursive point of view is the fact that she describes the first trip (where the guide controlled the raft) only to contrast it with the second one (where she and the other holiday makers in the raft controlled the pedals), which she then identifies as her preferred experience. By juxtaposing the two trips Anna foregrounds the one quality of the experience that attracts her to extreme sport, namely the 'adrenaline rush'. In her story she positions herself as an active seeker of 'thrill and excitement', somebody who goes to great lengths ('even though it had cost me a fortune but I was gonna do it again') to generate a sufficiently powerful 'rush'. In Anna's opening narrative we can already begin to identify her construction of herself as someone who is strongly drawn to experiences that provide her with an 'adrenaline rush'; in fact, she is so strongly drawn to them that her ability to resist this 'urge', as she calls it later on in the extract, is compromised. For example, having described the second trip as involving a complete loss of control over the raft and as being 'probably the most terrifying thing I've ever done in my whole life', Anna concludes that she 'had to love' the experience ('I just loved it. I had to'). In her construction of herself as someone who is so powerfully attracted to courting danger as to discard any cautionary impulse, Anna uses a series of extreme case formulations (Pomerantz, 1986):

> A: So I went down with pedals, steering ourselves down and it was prob-
> ably the *most* terrifying thing I've *ever* done in my *whole* life (laughs) I
> *actually thought I was going to die* but we went down, we were *completely*
> out of control the *whole* way and one of the guys *very nearly drowned*
> (laughs) (...)

Extreme case formulations (italicized in the quote above for easy identification) are formulations that take claims or evaluations to their extremes to provide an effective warrant for them and thus to legitimize them. In this case, Anna's claim (that she is irresistibly drawn to extreme sport) is supported by the extreme nature of the risks and dangers she exposed herself to, which she evokes very powerfully with the help of the extreme case formulations deployed in the quote. This compulsive aspect of Anna's relationship with extreme sport is affirmed at the end of the extract when Anna concludes, 'I need to do these things. It's something I just have to do'.

Anna's construction of herself as irresistibly drawn to extreme sport together with her frequent references to the impact of the extreme sport experience on her physiology (e.g. the 'adrenaline rush', 'frayed nerves', the 'buzz', 'huge amounts of energy', 'your heart's going a million miles per hour') invokes a discourse of addiction whereby the compulsion to engage in a behaviour is attributed to its powerfully rewarding physiological effects, which in turn have a positive impact on mood. Anna's use of a discourse of addiction is particularly evident in her account of the after-effects of an episode of extreme sport. She begins with a description of the physiological effects of the activity:

> A: (...) the feeling, the rush that you get is just so, it takes a good day to come down, at least for me it does. Even longer, actually, 'cos I'm just thinking of when I first went on a big hike that lasted over a week and for about a month and a half after the walk, I was just bouncing off the walls. I just had such a great great time. This made everything in my body was just going, I just loved it. My sister thought I was completely nuts when I got back because I just couldn't sit still. So when I finish things like this it's just (intake of breath) you know.

When I ask her about her 'thoughts and feelings' when she is aroused in this way, Anna goes on to portray what can only be described as a euphoric state of mind that she links to her physiological state of arousal:

> C: And can you describe (...) what kind of thoughts and feelings (...) you have then?
>
> A: It's like (long pause) I just feel like I can do anything and I just don't wanna be still and time's too short and I've just got lots of energy. Huge amounts of energy. It's just a real buzz and I'm really excited, I think, really excitable. Easy to, everything entertains me, everything's a giggle and then I sort of come off it and I, I'm not explaining myself very well but it's (pause) yeah literally bouncing off the walls, like I might sleep for four hours a night 'cos I'm just so wide awake and wanting to talk to people and stuff. I feel particularly social and wanna get out of the house and do stuff.

Some of Anna's terminology in these extracts, such as her references to 'coming off it' and 'coming down', is identical to that used to capture drug users' experiences; the terms 'rush' and 'buzz' are also familiar from accounts that drug users may give of their experience. These commonalities confirm that Anna does indeed position herself within a discourse of drug addiction when she talks about her experiences of extreme sport.

Note also Anna's reference to 'not explaining [herself] very well' in the second quote, and her incomplete sentence ('it's just (...)') followed by a sharp intake of breath in the first quote. Both of these can be read as a way of emphasizing the embodied quality of an experience that cannot be adequately captured in words. In this way, Anna is reinforcing her construction of her experience as akin to an addiction, which is, after all, also something that is seen as irrational and overwhelming and that tends to escape the addict's own ability to understand and make sense of.

Interestingly, at the same time as she is positioning herself as something of an extreme sport addict, and thus not fully in control of her actions and choices, Anna also ensures that the listener is aware of her courage and competence, both qualities that require self-discipline and willpower. Such qualities are in contrast with, and therefore distance Anna from, the common stereotype of the drug addict, which is associated with a lack of self-control and emotional instability. Note how she draws attention to the fact that it was 'the group of people that I was with [who] wanted to have the guide controlling it', thus indicating that it was not her who opted for the less challenging version of white water rafting. A little later on when she describes the second expedition (with pedals) Anna explains that, 'We basically had no control until the guys in the boat just stopped pedalling so there was only me and another girl pedalling, and the guide'. Both of these comments do not actually add anything to the storyline of what Anna is describing when she introduces them; in fact, the second comment (about only her, the other girl, and the guide pedalling) does not actually fit with the account within which it is embedded, since the point of her narrative here is to emphasize how little control the occupants of the raft had, irrespective of who was or was not pedalling at the time. This indicates that the function of these two comments is to manage the impression the listener may obtain of Anna's personal attributes rather than to provide information about the sequence of events described in the narrative. Again, we can see how a discursive analysis involves paying attention to context and how important it is to look at the meaning and function of what is being said in context.

Discourse analytic research is concerned with the ways in which language is used to construct particular versions of reality within particular contexts. As a result, there is no expectation that speakers should construct the subjects and objects of which they speak in consistent and uniform ways throughout an account. On the contrary, discourse analysts expect and look for variability in the accounts they study. It should, therefore, come as no surprise to find that Anna constructs herself in more ways than the one we have already identified when we came across Anna's use of a discourse of addiction and her positioning of herself as an extreme sport 'addict'.

Anna also constructs herself as somewhat naïve and childlike, as possessing a quality that made me think of the expression 'bright-eyed-and-bushy-tailed'. Anna repeatedly describes herself as 'really excited' and she confesses that 'I sort of treat a lot of these things as a big joke'. She draws attention to her inexperience ('I didn't know what to expect'), her sense of invulnerability ('It will never happen to me, it'll happen to somebody else. I'll be fine, I'll be fine'), and her faith in being looked after by those in charge of the extreme sport event ('I put incredible faith in the people who organize it'). This attitude is clearly demonstrated by her account of her initial innocent enjoyment of what was clearly a very dangerous situation:

> A: (...) the first time we fell out that was great, I mean it was a real buzz, I was like oh we got thrown out of the boat, I was sucked down there and (intake of breath) yeah okay I lost my breath for a bit and I couldn't breathe but I came up and I was alright. It's like wow we get back in and do it again.

A closer inspection of the context within which Anna deploys such a discourse of innocent enjoyment reveals, however, that her construction of herself as naïvely optimistic and trusting precedes an account of her realization that her childlike faith in that things will 'be fine' was in fact misplaced. In other words, Anna's positioning of herself as 'bright-eyed-and-bushy-tailed' constitutes the opening sequence of a tale of a loss of innocence. Here is the full account:

> A: Before I got in, it was just that, I was really excited 'cos I'd never done it before. I didn't know what to expect. I didn't know (...) if it was gonna be life-threatening or not life-threatening although I had spoken to a, while we were getting prepared, one of the guys had said a little bit about (breakdowns) and things like that but that made it all the more exciting, you know, that element of danger which was great.
>
> C: Right. Yeah?
>
> A: I do like the fact that you might almost hurt yourself but there is also that thing that it will never happen to me. It'll happen to somebody else. I'll be fine, I'll be fine. So that's, but then through it, particularly the second run that we did, the first time we fell out that was great, I mean it was a real buzz, I was like oh we got thrown out of the boat, I was sucked down there and (intake of breath) yeah okay I lost my breath for a bit and I couldn't breathe but I came up and I was alright. It's like wow we get back in and do it again. But as we went down we fell out more and more times. It started to get a little bit scary after that. Yeah.

Note how in this extract Anna cites herself ('I was like oh we got thrown out of the boat, I was sucked down there and (intake of breath) yeah okay I lost my breath for a bit and I couldn't breathe but I came up and I was alright. It's like wow we get back in and do it again'). The use of the active voice of a witness is a rhetorical device that serves to animate an account and to make it more believable. It is an instance of 'footing' (see Clayman, 1992; Goffman, 1981), a rhetorical strategy that involves the deployment of voices and perspectives in an account in a way that makes it more persuasive to the listener. Anna's use of this strategy invokes her 'innocent' voice by quoting her thoughts at an earlier point in time, before she realized how dangerous her situation really was. We literally 'hear' the 'innocent Anna' speak to us through the verbatim quote, thus reinforcing the contrast between her initial naïve nonchalance and her subsequent fearful concern. As Anna's account of her experiences of white water rafting unfolds, 'an element of fear' is introduced that quickly grows in significance (references to fear are italicized for easy identification):

> A: (...) It started to get *a little bit scary* after that. Yeah.
>
> C: So the feelings during it were like a mixture of excitement and fear? Or how would you describe it ?
>
> A: Initially absolutely, well the whole way was exciting but yes there was definitely *an element of fear*. Particularly, there was one bit in particular that was *incredibly frightening* because there was just a giant whirlpool and we could tell from the look of this guy who was taking us down there that if we went anywhere near there we may never get out. That was almost, I mean it was a rush, it was great but it was *a little bit too scary* ...

Anna's construction of herself as naïvely expecting her encounter with extreme sport to be 'a big joke, (...) great fun, (...) a huge amount of fun' only to be confronted with the sobering experience of acute fear positions Anna as someone for whom fear was not on the agenda when she embarked upon white water rafting. In this version of events, Anna was taken by surprise by the 'terrifying' nature of the experience – she was quite literally swept away, physically and emotionally. At the same time, Anna reminds the listener that it is precisely the intensity of the experience which attracts her and which makes her seek out similar experiences:

> C: Right. So when the guy looked a little bit worried, it kind of made it more, less fun and more of a real danger?
>
> A: Yes. It was like, this is a little bit more serious now than what I first contemplated. 'Cos when I started, it was just fun. I mean it was just, this is gonna be great, you know. The fear, the danger factor, that you might really really hurt yourself is just not a, it's not a factor, and when it actually becomes a reality that you might really really hurt yourself, then (intake of breath) you know, it sort of takes your breath away.
>
> C: Right. And then afterwards, when you got out, how did you feel?
>
> A: Absolutely exhilarated. It was like, you know, not only did you have the fun factor and the fact that you very nearly died. 'Cos we did get sucked down under the water for, you know, 45 seconds under water which is a lot of time under water, in rapids and, you know, getting sucked down and to get to the end and go wow. That was just awesome. It's a great feeling and so it's like, oh yeah I'd do it again.

Here, Anna suggests that it is precisely the unexpected nature of the 'reality that you might really really hurt yourself' that has such a strong impact ('it sort of takes your breath away'). In the second part of the above extract, Anna's reminder to the listener of the extremely challenging nature of her experience ('Cos we did get sucked down under the water for, you know, 45 seconds under water which is a lot of time under water, in rapids ...') suggests that she expects the listener not to have fully grasped the extent of the danger that she had exposed herself to, thus mirroring her own incredulity at what she has done. One of the effects of this construction is to position the listener alongside Anna in a state of amazed wonder ('wow') at what Anna is describing. Anna's construction of herself as split (into a part that innocently expects to be safe and a part that seeks out real danger) and her presentation of herself as struggling to fully grasp what she has done position her as not fully responsible for her actions.

In fact, Anna's account is shot through with dualistic constructions of the self that reinforce her construction of herself as not fully in charge of her actions (e.g. when she is unable to resist the 'urge' to take risks) and feelings (e.g. when she is taken by surprise by fear). Dualistic constructions of the self involve references to different parts of the self and/or to a lack of unity or integration of parts of the self. For example, Anna's description of her experience of 'the rush' uses dualistic discourse. Let's take another look at her account of the after-effects of taking part in a big hike:

> A: (...) the feeling, the rush that you get is just so, it takes a good day to come down, at least for me it does. Even longer, actually, 'cos I'm just thinking of when I first went on a big hike that lasted over a week and for about a month and a half after the walk, I was just bouncing off the walls. I just had such a great great time. This made everything in my body was just going, I just loved it. My sister thought I was completely nuts when I got back because I just couldn't sit still. So when I finish things like this it's just (intake of breath) you know.

Note how Anna conceptually separates 'the rush' from herself when she says 'the rush that you get'. She does not say 'the rush that you are', for example, or even 'the rush that you experience'. 'The rush that you get' suggests that 'the rush' is a distinct entity that somehow attaches itself to her person. A little later in this quote she refers to her body and what is happening within it ('everything in my body was just going'). Here, Anna also invokes a dualistic conception as Anna's body is presented as distinct from herself, something which belongs to her ('*my* body') but which is also distinct from her (after all, Anna did not say 'everything in me was just going'). It is worth pointing out that a dualistic construction of the self, drawing on a biochemical discourse that constructs the material body (with its powerful urges and desires) as being in conflict with the moral self (which attempts to overrule the material body), is, of course, part and parcel of the discourse of addiction that Anna invokes earlier on in her account.

Later on in the interview, Anna takes up a position of an outside observer of herself, reflecting on what she does and why. Here, she creates a dualism between herself as the observer and herself as the object of her observations. In this way, she disavows an insider perspective and finds herself speculating about her motives in much the same way that I or anyone else may speculate. For example, in the following quote Anna disclaims any knowledge of why she does what she does:

> A: (...) Actually, it's funny when you think about it 'cos I don't know what makes me do that. When I went bungee-jumping and I was standing

there, I was the first person to go and I didn't see anyone jump before me and I didn't know, I hadn't even seen it on TV, I'd never seen anybody bungee-jump before. And standing on the edge of this platform and the guy just said, I'm gonna count down from 10 and then you just jump, alright? And then he counted down and I just jumped and I can't tell you what made me jump. I don't know what went through my head. It was sort of not an option. I was there, I made myself get to the edge of the platform and I just was gone.

Here, dualistic constructions of the self ('I don't know *what makes me* do that'; 'I can't tell you *what made me* jump'; 'I don't know *what went through my head*'; '*I made myself* get to the edge of the platform') allow Anna to disclaim knowledge of her motives. A little later, she goes on to develop a hypothesis about her motives for giving up sky-diving:

A: (. . .) Yeah, but I'm just thinking, it's interesting 'cos I wonder if the events, the sports that I've done I've always got that faith in somebody else? I'm just wondering, maybe when I stopped doing things like my sky-diving, when it's just me. I have to rely on myself. I don't have that much confidence in myself to keep on going. You know, when you get to a stage, 'cos when I started sky-diving I was doing (partnered jumps) (. . .) so I was completely relying on somebody else to hook me up to the plane and everything. But when it got to the stage where I could jump on my own, I just stopped going. I mean there were a lot of reasons for that but I just wonder.

Again, although she identifies a possible motive ('I don't have that much confidence in myself to keep on going'), Anna presents this as a hypothesis that she has arrived at through observation and reflection rather than an insight based on direct self-knowledge ('it's interesting 'cos I wonder . . .'; 'I'm just wondering, maybe . . .'; 'I mean there were a lot of reasons for that but I just wonder'). In the second part of her account, in response to my question about what made her take up extreme sport in the first place, Anna takes her speculations further and offers a psychodynamic reading of her attraction to extreme sport:

A: Yeah. And I think it's part of growing up when I did all of these, you know, I'd do anything that was quite dangerous. I'd do it because I was told that I shouldn't do it. Oh and the other thing is that my stepdad used to tell me, I remember my mum would, you know, don't do that, you'll hurt yourself so I'd just do it. And my stepdad on the other hand would be like yeah you can do that, you can do that. So and I was always really close to my stepdad. And if he says I can do it, then I can. And I think that's part of that faith thing again it's like, you know, dad says I can do it. Dad says I can jump off that 3-metre diving board when I was five years of age. I can do it then. So I'd go and do it. And mum would be saying, you don't (. . .) she can't do that, and I'd say yes I can. So it's a bit of a challenge there.

Here, Anna takes up the position of a grown-up who is looking back at her child-hood experiences and finds new meaning in them. She makes a connection between her faith in the organizers of extreme sport and her relationship with her stepfather, and she offers an interpretation that links her attraction to extreme sport with rebellion. Such connections subtly invoke psychodynamic discourse by accounting for adult behaviour with reference to childhood experiences. Again, Anna constructs her insights as the product of a dualistic scrutiny of herself as an object of interest (in this case, herself as a rebellious child), thus distancing herself from their content and problematizing their truth-value. After all, if Anna herself does not know why she does what she does, how can anyone be sure about her motives? And if Anna has no ownership of her motives, how can she be expected to take responsibility for her actions? Thus, from a discursive point of view, Anna's use of dualistic discourse allows her to disclaim responsibility for her actions and their consequences.

Reflections on the analysis

A discursive reading of Ben's and Anna's interview extracts has allowed us to focus on Ben's and Anna's use of discursive resources to construct particular versions of their experiences of extreme sport. We have identified a number of rhetorical features, including different *styles of talking*, *three-part-lists*, the *use of contrasts* (e.g. between style and content), *extreme case formulations* and *footing*, all of which were interpreted as constituting strategies that, in one way or another, served a persuasive function. In other words, our discursive analysis has approached Ben's and Anna's accounts of their experiences as a form of social action and throughout our analysis we have asked what Ben and Anna were *doing* when they said what they said. To enable us to do this, we have paid attention to the discursive context within which their various comments were made. This, in turn, involved looking at the interviewer's contributions to the interview and trying to obtain an understanding of the interactive business Ben and Anna may have been attending to when they said what they said.

My style of questioning constructed extreme sport as an experience that is composed of distinct elements (thoughts, feelings, sensations) that occur in a characteristic pattern that can be described and understood; it also positioned my interviewees as self-aware, reflective selves who are willing and able to scrutinize themselves. In fact, on occasion my style of questioning seems to imply that the purpose of the interview was to subject my interviewees' experiences to something akin to scientific scrutiny, for example when I invite Anna to dissect the feelings she has during a particular episode of extreme sport (C: 'So the feelings during it were like a mixture of excitement and fear? Or how would you describe it?'). It could be argued that this style of questioning foregrounded agency and account-ability, and that Ben and Anna responded to this by providing accounts that either disclaimed responsibility for their actions (e.g. Anna's use of a discourse of addiction and dualistic constructions of the self) and/or that deployed rhetorical devices designed to make their accounts more persuasive (e.g. Ben's use of three-part-lists or Anna's use of extreme case formulations and footing). It could be argued that my style of questioning, and indeed the entire interview situation itself, positioned Ben and Anna as having to account for their actions (in this case, their engagement with extreme sport) and that such a positioning provokes accounts that, in one way or another, rhetorically manage responsibility. In other words, Ben and Anna were invited to account for themselves and it should come as no surprise that, in response to this, they deployed discursive devices and rhetorical strategies that would help them manage their own stake in the conversation. Thus, from a discursive point of view, Ben's and Anna's accounts tell us more about the type of situation they found themselves in (i.e. an interview in which they were invited to account for their actions) than about Ben and Anna as unique individuals or, indeed, about the nature of their experiences of extreme sport.

In addition, of course, our analysis tells us something about the discursive resources available in our culture that can be used to talk about, and thus to construct, 'extreme sport'. For example, Anna's use of a discourse of addiction was interesting in that it demonstrated how the same discourse can be used to frame extreme sport and drug use. It was also interesting to see how dualist discourse was invoked in the construction of pleasure, and how a separation of mind and body was presented by both Ben and Anna as a precondition for the achievement of a truly joyful experience. Such observations can lead us to speculate about our culture's construction of the body as the primary site for pleasure and enjoyment, and the assumption that thinking interferes with feeling. This chimes with a strict separation between 'work' and 'leisure' where 'leisure' is increasingly associated with physical gratification (eating, drinking, the use of recreational drugs, sex) and where the purpose of leisure activities is to help the individual to 'switch off' from work. A Foucauldian discourse analysis would be concerned with such issues and would require us to examine wider discourses and practices that help us to understand how such a mind–body separation functions in our culture, how it arose historically, and how it is maintained through various institutional practices.

Another discourse worth commenting on is a psychological discourse that underpins my questions and some of Ben's and Anna's responses to them. As indicated earlier, my questions presuppose that there is something going on inside of Ben and Anna (thoughts, feelings, etc.) which can be brought to awareness and which can be talked about and understood; it is also implied that a better understanding of Ben's and Anna's thoughts and feelings will allow us to better understand why they do what they do. These assumptions are, of course, part and parcel of a psychological discourse; a discourse that presupposes the existence of individual subjects with an interior (a psyche) that contains cognitions and emotions. Anna takes this construction further when she constructs a split self which contains unconscious motivations ('I don't know what made me do that') and which has its origin in childhood ('And I think that's part of that faith thing again it's like, you know, dad says I can do it'). Here, psychodynamic discourse makes an appearance. Again, from a Foucauldian point of view, we would be interested in the historical origins of available ways of talking about, and thus constructing, experiences. For example, we would be looking at the historical emergence of individualism, and the ways in which the arrival of psychoanalysis shaped discourses about human experience.

A final stage in a Foucauldian style discourse analysis would involve asking questions about how the discourses used to construct the experience of extreme sport position their users and how this may shape their actual experiences of themselves in the world. For example, we may speculate that, by positioning herself within a discourse of addiction, Anna accepts that there are powerful forces at work within her over which she has little or no control. This may mean that Anna begins to feel powerless and that it may be difficult for her to stop engaging in extreme sport should she wish to do so (see Eiser, 1984; Gillies and Willig, 1997). Similarly, positioning oneself within a dualist discourse may discourage attempts to integrate experiences that seem to originate in different parts of the self, leading to an increasingly fragmented sense of self. Finally, embracing a psychoanalytic construction of the self may feed the belief that, to truly understand oneself, one needs to first seek expert help from a psychotherapist.

Appraisal of the discursive reading

In this chapter, we have been concerned with identifying the discursive resources and strategies used by Ben, Anna, and myself in our talk about extreme sport. The aim of the analysis has been to better understand how Ben and Anna construct their experiences of extreme sport through language, how this positions them, and what may be some of the consequences of these constructions and positionings. In line with the aims of discursive analysis and in accordance with its epistemological position, our analysis has taught us something about the use of rhetorical devices and the availability of discourses; however, it does not allow us to draw any conclusions about Ben's or Anna's personalities or motivations, or indeed about the nature or meaning of the experience of extreme sport itself. Let us remember that social constructionist research adopts a profoundly sceptical position in relation to 'knowledge'. What is of interest here is not so much what is really going on or how something is actually experienced by participants, but rather how people talk about the world and, therefore, how they construct versions of reality through the use of language. This means that questions about the inner world of research participants, their motivations, desires, and intentions are suspended and instead the researcher is concerned with how they deploy discursive resources within particular contexts. However, it could be argued that although discourse analysts do not show any overt interest in the inner world of the speakers whose words they analyse, implicitly they do attribute intentions to them when they trace the action orientation of their talk. For example, when we observe that a particular rhetorical strategy is used to disclaim responsibility for an action or to make an argument more believable and, therefore, more persuasive, are we not implying that the speaker seeks to disclaim responsibility or to persuade? If not, why would they be deploying the strategy in the first place? So although discourse analysts do not attribute enduring traits or dispositions to their research participants in the way that some psychologists may do (e.g. when they account for a person's behaviour with reference to traits such as extroversion or impulsivity), discourse analysts do assume that a person's contributions to a conversation are motivated by their desire to achieve particular interactional objectives such as to save face, to persuade or to disclaim undesirable attributions. There is an assumption that speakers are motivated by a desire to manage their stake in the conversation, and that nothing is said without consideration of its possible effects upon the listener. This means that a discursive approach to the analysis of accounts can come across as somewhat 'suspicious' of what interviewees are saying; interviewees are constructed as being concerned with managing the impression they make upon the interviewer rather than, say, with sharing their true feelings or with getting something difficult and painful 'off their chest'. In other words, discourse analysts never take anyone's words at face value.

From an ethical standpoint, one could question the acceptability of analysing Ben's and Anna's accounts through a discursive lens when these accounts were provided in good faith and with the belief that the interviewer was genuinely interested in the nature of their experiences (rather than in how they deployed discursive strategies to manage their stake in the conversation). A Foucauldian approach to discourse analysis is, in my view, less problematic in this regard because its focus is not so much on the action orientation of talk as on the availability of discursive resources within a socio-cultural context. Here, research participants are not seen as strategic users of discourse but rather as historical subjects who are themselves constructed through and positioned within discourse. Either way, it is important to remember that discourse analysis is primarily concerned with discourse and not with people.

From an epistemological point of view, any text constitutes suitable data for a discourse analysis. However, I would argue that for ethical reasons very personal accounts of experience, and particularly accounts concerned with suffering and distress that were provided by participants who believed that the interviewer was genuinely interested in the experiential aspects of their account (rather than the discursive ones), should probably not be subjected to discursive analysis (see also Willig, 2004).

Finally, discourse analysis does not provide answers to questions about individual differences. For example, we are not able to account for the differences between Ben's and Anna's use of discursive resources in their construction of 'extreme sport' other than with reference to the discursive contexts within which they spoke. From a discursive point of view, Ben and Anna said what they said because of the requirements of the discursive contexts within which they found themselves; they were simply attending to the interactive business at hand. In other words, discourse analysts do not look 'outside the text' to find answers to question about the text. This means that if we were curious about why a particular research participant appears to display a preference for a particular way of constructing meaning or why she tends to position herself in a particular way, we would need to look for a methodology other than discourse analysis to find answers to these questions. The psychosocial approach (to be discussed in the next chapter) is one method that can help us to address such concerns.

8   A psychosocial reading

In this chapter, we return for a third and final time to Ben's and Anna's accounts of their experiences of extreme sport. This time we approach the data by asking questions about Ben's and Anna's emotional investment in what they are saying. This time around we are curious about *why* Ben and Anna speak about extreme sport in the way that they do; we want to know what motivates them, as unique psychological subjects, to act in just the way that they do. To find answers to these questions we shall adopt a perspective that could be described as psychosocial. It is important to remember at this point that there are a number of quite different ways in which psychosocial research can be approached, and that there are currently a number of rather different versions of a psychosocial perspective available to researchers. These differ, among other things, in terms of their commitment to a particular theory of the psychological subject (e.g. Kleinian or Lacanian), as well as in terms of their understanding of the social dimension of human subjectivity (see Frosh, 2010, chapter 7, for a detailed discussion of such differences). My description of the analysis presented in this chapter as 'psychosocial' seeks to indicate that here we are dealing with an approach to interpretation that attempts to address questions about our participants' accounts of their experiences in such a way as to ensure that 'emotion and irrationality are included in the relevant discussions of subjectivity' (Frosh, 2010: 219). In this chapter I do not, therefore, propose to represent the new discipline of psychosocial studies (if, indeed, there is such a discipline given the many and extensive differences in perspective that are included under its umbrella); rather, I aim to illustrate the application of an approach to interpretation that is concerned with the dynamics of psychic formations and psychological processes, and to discuss its implications for qualitative analysis.

As in the previous two chapters, in my discussion of my interpretation of the data, I aim to demonstrate how the adoption of a particular interpretative framework with its associated epistemological position and theoretical concerns shapes the way in which the researcher makes sense of the data. Again, theoretical, ethical, and practical implications of the reading will be discussed, as will be its particular strengths and limitations. The chapter concludes with some recommendations concerning the types of data that are (and are not) suitable for psychosocial analysis.

Aims of the analysis

My psychosocial analysis will be concerned with making links between what my research participants are saying and doing, and their emotional investments in this. My psychosocial perspective involves making the assumption that people are motivated by emotional dynamics that have their origin in childhood. Such an approach is committed to the use of resources drawn from psychodynamic theorizing in an attempt to identify underlying psychic structures and processes that motivate research participants' overt behaviours, including their verbal accounts and ways of interacting with an interviewer. This means that although a psychosocial analysis starts with an exploration of the text (i.e. *what* is being said and *how*), it then moves on to look beyond the text itself (e.g. at the participant's personal biography, or at the interviewer's emotional response to the participant's account and presentation) to account for what is being said (i.e. to find out *why* a participant may have said what they said). Thus, a psychosocial perspective encourages us ask the sorts of questions, which both phenomenological researchers and discourse analysts would normally set aside.

The aim of my psychosocial analysis is to identify psychic structures and/or processes that can account for the data. This means that this version of the psychosocial approach could be described as adopting a *realist* position in relation to knowledge generation (see Willig, 2012). From such a position, the researcher seeks to obtain a rich, accurate, detailed, and comprehensive picture of (some aspects of) human psychology. The assumption that underpins this type of research is that there are certain processes or patterns of a social and/or psychological nature that inform the behaviour and the thinking of research participants, and that these can be identified by the researcher. As such, this type of research is characterized by a *discovery orientation* (see Madill et al., 2000). The role of the researcher in this situation is akin to that of a *detective* who uses their skills, knowledge, and experience to uncover hitherto hidden processes and who can make sense of people's behaviour by identifying their underlying motives and intentions. However, while subscribing to the belief that there is something 'real' and enduring (such as psychic structures or emotional investments) that can be identified by the researcher, a psychosocial perspective also holds that the relationship between what presents itself (e.g. the participant's words and demeanour) and the structures and mechanisms that underpin this (e.g. the participant's desires, intentions, and motivations) is by no means straightforward. Rather, the assumption is that the data needs to be interpreted to provide access to the underlying structures that generate the manifestations that constitute our data. Therefore, a psychosocial approach requires that we adopt a *critical realist* position. Critical realist research can vary in the extent to which it asserts the existence of underlying structures and mechanisms with anything approaching certainty. Some researchers present their analyses with caution and the proviso that the interpretations offered represent possibilities rather than certainties (e.g. Frosh and Young, 2008). Others take a much more 'knowing' stance and present their analyses as insights into how things (actually, really) are (e.g. how people function psychologically) (e.g. Hollway and Jefferson, 2000).

Process of analysis

As I had already carried out phenomenological and discursive analyses of Ben's and Anna's transcripts, I felt quite familiar with their accounts before embarking upon the psychosocial analysis. In fact, while I was conducting the two earlier analyses I had already written some notes on ideas and observations that I thought might become relevant later when I was going to re-examine the accounts from a psychosocial perspective. For example, Ben's expression of a desire for things to be clear and simple, and his enjoyment of being alone in the wilderness made me wonder whether there may be some unresolved tensions or uncomfortable complexities in his social relationships. This idea resonated with Ben's description of his interactions with his brother, which sounded like that of sparring partners who are close but who feel somewhat antagonistic towards one another at the same time. Similarly, having identified Anna's construction of herself as childlike, I wondered whether there might be a connection between this and Anna's relationship with her stepfather, whom she describes as having validated and encouraged her when she was growing up. Before I returned to the transcripts for my psychosocial analysis, I read through these notes and reflected on them. I also reflected on the findings from the phenomenological and the discursive analyses, and realized that in a sense these two analyses had already provided me with answers to questions about *what* it was Ben and Anna were experiencing (after all, this had been the focus of my phenomenological analysis) and *how* they talked about it (this had been addressed by my discursive analysis). It was now left to the psychosocial analysis to attempt to answer questions about *why* this might have been the case. So, unlike a psychosocial researcher who approaches a text without having conducted other types of analysis first, I decided that I could skip the first, more descriptive, stage of psychosocial analysis (which seeks to establish what participants are saying and doing within a social context), and move straight to the theoretically driven interpretation of the material. In other words, I could use my earlier analyses to provide me with the themes and phenomena that my psychosocial interpretation would, hopefully, help to explain, or at least shed further light on.

Although I felt reasonably confident that this approach was justified, I decided to return to the unmarked, 'clean' (i.e. unanalysed) copies of Ben's and Anna's transcripts one more time, and re-read them with an open mind. The aim of this exercise was to provide myself with an opportunity to pick up any themes, constructions or patterns that had not been captured during the two earlier rounds of line-by-line analysis. This was important because each of the two earlier readings had been conducted with particular over-arching research questions in mind, which had been consonant with the respective methods of analysis applied. Although psychosocial analysis does tend to utilize some aspects of a discursive perspective during the first stage of analysis (when it seeks to identify discursive constructions and positionings preferred by the research participants), I allowed for the possibility that other aspects of the text might strike me as relevant to a psychosocial analysis. This meant that, in the end, the psychosocial phenomena to be accounted for during the second stage of analysis included a collection of themes arising from careful and repeated reading of the two transcripts including but also moving beyond the earlier two types of analyses. The second stage of the analysis involved an attempt to account for these themes by formulating a convincing account of the emotional and psychological dynamics that may underpin Ben's and Anna's accounts of their experiences of extreme sport.

A psychosocial analysis of Ben's account

My psychosocial interpretation of Ben's account starts with a brief sketch of the most salient themes that emerge from Ben's description of his experience of extreme sport. Some of these themes will be familiar from our earlier analyses. I then draw on information about Ben's relationship with his brother, which he refers to in the second part of the extract, to shed further light on the themes that structure Ben's account. Here, I offer a psychodynamic reading of Ben's account that attempts to explain Ben's commitment to extreme sport with reference to his emotional life and his relationship with members of his family of origin.

Let us start with a reminder of how Ben characterizes his relationship with extreme sport. At the beginning of the extract, Ben describes how much he appreciates the experience of focusing so intently on the task of climbing that he has no thoughts for the past or the future, to the point of losing himself and of merging with his physical environment. Our phenomenological analysis described this experience as akin to states of 'flow' (Csikszentmihalyi, 1975). A little later on in the extract, Ben acknowledges that he enjoys the feeling of losing himself, which results from focusing only on the mountain ('Which is great [laughs] it's just, you lose yourself'), and that he finds it comforting to feel his own insignificance ('I feel my insignificance in that landscape but it's a nice feeling 'cos I find that quite comforting'). Ben describes how much he appreciates this sense of merging with something larger than himself ('it's totally all about mountain') and how he feels reassured by an awareness of 'the big scale of things' where his everyday worries do not matter.

From a psychosocial perspective, we may want to know why it is that Ben is so attracted to the experience of 'flow', and what it is about Ben that makes him derive comfort from feeling that he has lost himself in something bigger, more significant than himself. A clue is provided by Ben's references to his search for security and the part this plays in bringing about the conditions that generate the state of 'flow'. Here is how Ben describes the process:

> B: No, I mean thinking on it now, you don't think about anything else. You think about where you're putting your feet, you look for where you're gonna go next. Above all, you feel it. You feel every footprint, you feel every handhold, you feel the security in it and that's what you spend, or that's what I spend all my time doing (pause) is I suppose attempting to feel secure at that precise moment and that's the only thing you think about.

It seems that Ben's search for (physical) security leads him to focus so intensely upon his physical environment and the task at hand that he forgets about himself, his memories (the past), and his desires (the future) to the point of not experiencing himself as being there at all. And this, in turn, results in a feeling of comfort, a feeling that 'nothing really matters' and that 'everything is cool, everything is fine' – in other words, a feeling of having obtained (psychological) security.

We have established that Ben desires security and that he is able to achieve a sense of security when he is in the mountains where he can lose himself in the bigger picture and experience a sense of his own insignificance. It is noteworthy that Ben's experience of security does not involve other people. On the contrary, the pleasure that he experiences when 'facing wilderness' is all about not having to relate to anyone else. He is happiest when he can forget even about himself. Ben appreciates the fact that in the mountains, things are straightforward and simple; all that matters is 'where you stick your hand next'. Why is it that Ben seeks a feeling of security and harmony in solitude? Are Ben's experiences with other people perhaps less easy and straightforward than his experience of the mountains? The second part of Ben's extract suggests that Ben's relationship with his brother Andy is complex. On the one hand, Ben suggests that he and his brother regularly play sports together, which indicates that they enjoy spending time together. On the other hand, Ben describes how Andy enjoys tripping him up when they go sailing together and that Ben regularly finds himself at the receiving end of practical jokes which Andy finds 'hilarious' and which leave Ben feeling hurt and scared, and possibly also humiliated. The second part of Ben's extract makes disturbing reading in that some of the content of what Ben is describing (for example, the fear and pain that Ben experiences when he is being 'roughed up') does not seem to fit with Ben's style of narration (for example, the cartoonish quality of his descriptions, his frequent laughter and references to how much 'fun' it all was). The tension within his account could be understood as an indication that Ben himself finds it difficult to fully accept the emotional implications of what he is describing. Perhaps it is difficult for Ben to accept that there is some hostility in his brother's behaviour towards him? Perhaps Ben's presentation of his interactions with Andy as nothing more that rough-and-tumble play protects Ben from having to acknowledge deeper tensions between the two of them? From a psychosocial point of view, we would want to know much more about the nature and quality of the relationship between Ben and Andy, the two brothers' relationships with their mother and father, and any history of sibling rivalry because this may help us account for the way in which Ben talks about his relationship with his brother in the interview. Further information about Ben's early life would help us answer the sorts of question a psychosocial analysis would want to address. For example, could it be that Ben's desire to experience 'flow' and his enjoyment of merging with a bigger picture may be a reaction to his experience of being bullied by his brother Andy? After all, a desire for 'flow' is also a desire to not stand out, to not be noticed (even by oneself); in a way, it is a desire to not really be there at all, to not exist as a separate entity in the world. Being bullied, on the other hand, is about being picked on, being singled out as a suitable victim, and then feeling unable to hide from the unwanted attention. Could it perhaps be that Andy picked on Ben because Ben, as the younger of the two brothers, received more attention from his mother or father? Could an intense sibling rivalry be at the bottom of the tense relationship between the brothers? To answer these questions we would need to have access to much more information about Ben's personal biography than our interview extract contains. However, there is further evidence within the extract itself that could be read as providing tentative support for our developing formulation. Let's take another look at Ben's emphatic proclamation that:

> B: There are no problems in the mountains other than where you stick your hand next and that's why I love it. It's the same with skiing. There are no problems skiing except how you ski next (laughing). You know, if you ski stupid, well then, but if you ski well, it's fine.

Here, Ben praises the simplicity and consistency of how the mountains allow him to operate. There is a clear and simple logic at work that dictates that if one climbs or skis well, one will succeed, whereas if one does not climb or ski well, one will be in trouble. In the mountains, there is a clear and logical relationship between what Ben does and what the outcome will be. This contrasts with what happens in Ben's social relations. Here, Ben can try as hard as he might to sail well, but Andy will still ensure that Ben falls into the water and hurts himself. Perhaps this extends into their interactions outside of the sporting environment. Perhaps Ben feels that however much he tries to please and placate Andy, Andy will still want to fight with him.

Another bit of evidence in support of our interpretation can be found in Ben's attempts to minimize the significance of the events he is describing. For example, about half-way through the extract he refers to how 'all these piddly little things that you worry about really don't matter in the big scale of things', and a little later on he describes how the magical feeling of having been in the mountains lasts until 'something trivial happens here and I've got to pay a bill'. It is interesting that Ben describes the very things that he escapes from when he goes to the mountains as 'piddly' and 'trivial'; however, if they really were as insignificant as Ben suggests here, would they really have the power to drive him into the mountains? Would he really need to take such drastic steps to escape from them? Ben's minimization here mirrors his trivialization of the impact of Andy's behaviour in the final part of the extract, where his description of what happens to him as a result of Andy's actions constructs a version of events resembling a Tom-and-Jerry comic strip.

As Ben puts the 'trivial' demands of everyday life on a par, at least linguistically, with his brother's bullying, could it be that the one can stand in for the other? In other words, could it be that when Ben talks about the 'piddly little things that you worry about' he is actually thinking of his problems with Andy? Could it be his complex and unresolved relationships with members of his family, including Andy, that drive him into the mountains? Is Ben perhaps seeking to escape from the challenges of these relationships when he merges with the mountain and loses his sense of self? Does he wish he were part of something bigger and therefore unidentifiable as 'Ben', so that Andy would not pick on him any more? One supportive piece of evidence for this interpretation can be found when Ben acknowledges that he does not actually 'get stressed out about paying a bill' just after he has invoked 'paying a bill' as representing the demands of everyday life which put an end to his feeling that 'nothing really matters'. A little earlier in the extract I ask Ben how long his feeling that 'nothing really matters' lasts when he comes back from the mountains. Ben replies:

> B: I get excited when I actually see the mountains and it lasts (pause) until I suppose something trivial happens here and I've got to pay a bill or, I mean, not that I get stressed out about paying a bill but until (laughs) until I get dragged kicking and screaming back to real life.

So, if it is not actually paying a bill that forces Ben to face up to what he calls 'real life', then what might it be? It could be argued that in the light of the graphic descriptions of what happens to Ben when his brother plays sports with him, the expression 'until I get dragged kicking and screaming back to real life' takes on a more ominous meaning. It could be argued that Ben's choice of words here, albeit unintentionally, invoke a connection between Ben's conceptualization of 'real life' and his difficult relationship with his brother. Finally, we may wonder whether Ben's reference to having to 'pay a bill' carries symbolic meaning whereby in Ben's experience reality demands that bills are paid including the price he has to pay for being his mother's (or father's) favourite. This price may take the form of being the target of Andy's anger and resentment. Again, here we would probably need to presume that Ben did not make these connections consciously and that our identification of any potential symbolic linkages and associations cannot be anything more than speculative, especially given our lack of knowledge about what actually happened when Ben was growing up.

A psychosocial analysis of Anna's account

Again, before embarking upon a psychosocial interpretation of Anna's account, we need to remind ourselves of the central themes that structure Anna's description of her experience of extreme sport. Most of these themes will be familiar from our earlier analyses. To shed further light on Anna's deeper motivations, we then revisit the themes, this time making links between Anna's thoughts and feelings about extreme sport, and her comments about her relationship with her mother and stepfather. Again, the aim of making such links here is to develop a psychodynamic formulation that attempts to make psychological sense of Anna's commitment to extreme sport with reference to her emotional life and her relationship with members of her family of origin.

Careful reading of Anna's account suggests that Anna's relationship with ex-treme sport revolves around the achievement of a high level of arousal, of gen-erating excitement, of producing a 'buzz' and a 'rush'. She values extreme sport for making her feel excited and aroused, and for allowing her to continue to feel energized long after the extreme sport event itself has come to an end. For an episode of extreme sport to produce the desired effect, Anna needs to experience real fear alongside a sense of ultimate safety. This is achieved by the presence of an experienced event organizer. Throughout her account, Anna invokes a discourse of addiction whereby she constructs herself as needing to engage in extreme sport in much the same way that a drug addict needs their 'fix' ('I need to do these things'). Alongside taking up the position of the 'extreme sport addict', Anna also constructs herself as being childlike by displaying innocent enthusiasm and naïve faith in being looked after by those more knowledgeable and experienced than herself (i.e. the event organizers).

From a psychosocial point of view, we want to know more about the emotional investments that underpin Anna's relationship with extreme sport. We want to understand what motivates Anna's construction of extreme sport as an addiction and her adoption of the positions of 'addict' and 'child'. What is Anna trying to gain, psychologically, by positioning herself as she does? Again, as with Ben's account, some clues are provided when Anna talks about her relationship with her mother and stepfather in the second part of the transcript. Anna tells me that when she was growing up she would 'do anything that was quite dangerous' and that she would 'do it because I was told that I shouldn't do it'. Anna then specifies that it was her mother who was telling her not to take risks ('I remember mum would, you know, don't do that, you'll hurt yourself') while her stepfather would encourage Anna to go ahead and try to master physical challenges ('And my stepdad on the other hand would be like, yeah, you can do that, you can do that'). Anna explains that she followed her stepfather's advice because she was close to him ('I was always really close to my stepdad. And if he says I can do it, then I can'). Although Anna does not spell this out, the implication here is that her relationship with her mother was perhaps less close, or at least less straightforwardly so, than that with her stepfather; after all, Anna did not follow her mother's advice and she does not state that she was close to her mother. In the light of this piece of biographical information, Anna's construction of herself as childlike begins to make sense. In our discursive analysis we observed that Anna juxtaposes a construction of herself as somewhat naïve and innocent when she embarks upon extreme sport activities ('I'd never done it before. I didn't know what to expect'; 'when I started, it was just fun'; 'I'll be fine, I'll be fine') with a construction of her activities as being extremely dangerous and unsettling ('it was probably the most terrifying thing I've ever done in my whole life [laughs] I actually thought I was gonna to die'; 'we did get sucked down under the water for, you know, 45 seconds under water which is a lot of time under water, in rapids'). The effect of this was to produce a narrative that pointed to a loss of innocence on Anna's part.

Re-reading these sections of the transcript through a psychosocial lens, I was beginning to wonder whether Anna's (probably unconscious) intention here would have been to produce alarm and concern in the listener. Was Anna presenting herself as a naïve and unsuspecting child walking right into a life-threatening scenario to evoke the kind of response she received from her mother when, as a five-year-old, she approached the 3-metre diving-board? Was she deploying extreme case formulations ('most terrifying thing I've ever done'; 'completely out of control'; 'one of the guys very nearly drowned') to shock me into trying to discourage her from continuing to put her life at risk? Is Anna, in fact, issuing what amounts to a threat when on two separate occasions she concludes her account of a particularly dangerous and unsettling episode of extreme sport by saying 'I would do it again'? From a psychosocial perspective, taking what we know about Anna's relationship with her mother and stepfather into account, we can begin to think about the possibility that Anna's relationship with extreme sport constitutes an attempt to be noticed in a particular kind of way. It can be understood as Anna's way of trying to recreate a childhood scenario where her mother's attention was captured when Anna threatened to embark upon activities that her mother considered too risky for her. At the same time, engaging in extreme sport provides Anna with a sense of closeness to her stepfather, who approves of Anna taking up physical challenges. Thus, by engaging in extreme sport, Anna is symbolically addressing both her parents – her mother through causing her to worry, and her stepfather by seeking his approval. We do not know how Anna's mother's relationship with Anna's stepfather developed and how this might have been experienced by Anna. Further information about this could help us to gain a deeper understanding of the emotional dynamics that underpin Anna's relationship with extreme sport. For example, it may be that little Anna experienced the relationship between her mother and her stepfather as threatening because it excluded her and that she derived satisfaction from acting in a way that led to a conflict between her mother and stepfather. Perhaps taking risks had become Anna's way of having her needs met in a number of ways – by attracting attention, by gaining approval, and by interfering with what she perceived as an unwelcome symbiosis between her mother and the new man in her mother's life? We could go as far as to speculate that Anna's actions constitute something like a cry for help. Such an interpretation is supported by Anna's references to how she engages in extreme sport when life has become 'dull and boring' and when she feels the need to 'lift herself up'. It could be that Anna has deep-seated feelings of not being important to her mother, of not mattering enough, of not being loved. These are getting her down to the point where she feels depressed and in need of 'a big lift'. Here is how Anna describes the sense of unease and discomfort that leads her to engage in extreme sport:

> A: Yeah. I need to do these things. It's something I just have to do. I know it. I feel it in myself. I get to a stage where I'm just bored or there's just something, I just feel it, there's something wrong. I can't quite put my finger on what's wrong. And if I get out and I do something like this, I've just lifted myself another level, you know. I feel like it's you sort of sit down to this little rut and you don't know that you're in it before you get to the bottom and then it's like (intake of breath) gotta lift yourself up again and then keep on going.

I have suggested that one way of making psychological sense of Anna's strong attraction to extreme sport is to propose that by engaging in extreme sport Anna recreates a childhood scenario that used to allow her to have some of her needs met. Within this, she also ensures that there is always a parental figure present, namely the experienced event organizer who takes ultimate responsibility for Anna's safety and who makes Anna feel secure and cared for. In this way, it could be argued,

extreme sport provides Anna with an opportunity to address some of her unconscious desires and to feel better as a result, albeit only temporarily.

The concept of the 'secure base' (Ainsworth, 1967; Bowlby, 1988) and its role in
the emotional development of the child can shed further light on Anna's references
to the importance of the presence of event organizers. Anna emphasizes repeatedly that she has 'faith' in the people who organize extreme sports events. She tells
me that 'when I do these things I put incredible faith in the people who organize
it', and she repeats this assertion several times throughout the extract ('And again,
that's faith in the people who are organizing it. Complete faith'; 'Yeah, there's
complete confidence in them. And faith. There's never truly a stage that I think
that I'm gonna really really hurt myself. Never'; 'I had complete faith in the pilot';
'I just completely think that they know what they're doing so I'll be fine').

Anna acknowledges that when she has to rely on herself to ensure that she is
safe, she feels less secure and less comfortable with extreme sport. She recognizes
that her confidence comes from her faith in the expertise of the event organizers
rather than her own competence and skill; she says, 'I don't have that much
confidence in myself to keep on going'. Towards the end of the extract, Anna
makes a connection between her reliance on event organizers and her relationship
with her stepfather when she was growing up:

> A: And I think that's part of that faith thing again it's like, you know, dad
> says I can do it. Dad says I can jump off that 3-metre diving board when I
> was five years of age. I can do it then. So I'd go and do it.

Bowlby (1988) argues that one of the central features of parenting is to offer a
secure base for the child. Bowlby (1988: 12) explains that this involves

> the provision by both parents of a secure base from which a child or
> adolescent can make sorties into the outside world and to which he can
> return knowing for sure that he will be welcomed when he gets there,
> nourished physically and emotionally, comforted if distressed, reassured
> if frightened.

The secure base allows the child to explore her environment and to learn as a
result. As long as the child knows that she can return to the secure base whenever
she feels the need for reassurance, the child is able to test her limits and to take
risks. The child is able to gain skills and confidence through her interactions with
her social and physical environment while deriving a sense of security and safety
from knowing that there is a secure base in the background. Eventually, as the
child grows up, she experiences less and less of a need to physically return to the
secure base for reassurance. Her excursions become increasingly extensive and her
confidence grows as she becomes more independent and competent.

Anna's description of her relationship with the event organizers of extreme
sport and the way in which she likens this to her childhood relationship with
her stepfather suggests that for Anna the secure base is an issue. It seems that she
derives satisfaction from creating a scenario that allows her to re-experience the
presence of a secure base when she takes risks. It is as though Anna's engagement

in extreme sport in the presence of an experienced event organizer allows her to experience a very particular sense of safety, one that depends upon the physical presence and encouragement of the 'secure base' to the point of placing Anna in the position of an obedient child. She does what she is told. Note the similarity between Anna's description of her bungee jump ('the guy just said, I'm gonna count down from ten and then you just jump, alright? And then he counted down and I just jumped and I can't tell you what made me jump') and her account of her response to her stepfather's encouragement to jump off the diving board ('Dad says I can jump off that 3-metre diving board when I was five years of age. I can do it then. So I'd go and do it'). It seems as though Anna has not developed an internalized sense of security; she requires the presence, and indeed the instructions, of the parental figure to take the risk. She derives great pleasure from the feeling of ultimate security that is provided through the presence of someone in whom she has 'complete faith' and who will ensure that she is 'alright' no matter how dangerous her behaviour is ('It's an incredible feeling to feel like that. To feel that you're about to risk your life doing something (pause) but you'll be alright. Pretty amazing feeling'). Again, we do not know enough about Anna's biography to draw conclusions about her attachment history; however, it is possible that Anna's desire for experiences that allow her to feel safe in the way that she does has its origin in an insecure attachment to her mother and/or father.

Reflections on the analysis

My psychosocial reading of Ben's and Anna's interview transcripts has identified a concern with emotional security in both accounts. Both Ben and Anna describe how their particular ways of engaging with extreme sport allow them to create experiences that provide them with a sense of containment and a feeling of safety. For Ben, this happens when he loses his sense of self as he merges with the mountain during 'flow'; for Anna, it happens when she takes risks within an envelope of ultimate security provided by the event organizer. In both cases, my psychosocial interpretation has drawn on biographical information about their relationships with members of their families of origin to better understand what motivates Ben's and Anna's search for a sense of safety. I suggested that it could be Ben's experiences of tensions, and perhaps even bullying, in his relationship with his brother that underpin his emotional investment in extreme sport. And I proposed that Anna may be motivated by the desire to recreate a childhood scenario that allows her to feel both important and safe, and that this desire itself could perhaps be explained with reference to Anna's insecure attachment to one or both of her parents. In both cases, I have suggested that these deeper motivations may not be something that Ben and Anna are necessarily consciously aware of, and I have shown how some evidence in support of my interpretations could be found in Ben's and Anna's use of language, metaphors, symbolic linkages, and associations between people and events. In addition, I have drawn on psychological theory (such as attachment theory) to enrich my interpretations.

My psychosocial reading is based on the premise that it is possible, and indeed likely, that people are not necessarily aware of what really motivates them. This means that initial impressions or appearances can be misleading. Thus while Ben and Anna outwardly appear to be incredibly brave and confident individuals who take up challenges that most of us would baulk at, my psychosocial analysis has identified a strong need for security at the root of Ben's and Anna's dedication to extreme sport. My psychosocial reading focused on the possible psychological and emotional functions that engagement with extreme sport may fulfil for Ben and Anna respectively, and this perspective led me to look beyond appearances. This meant that once I had identified a particular meaning in Ben's or Anna's experience (e.g. Ben's sense of losing himself in 'flow', Anna's excitement at risking her life and feeling safe at the same time), I would ask myself why they might want or need that meaning in their life. What did they gain from it, and which unmet needs and desires might this point to? In this way, I produced a reading of Ben's and Anna's transcripts that foregrounds their unmet needs, their childhood wounds, their dissatisfactions, disappointments, and frustrations. In other words, it is a reading that focuses on what may have gone wrong as Ben and Anna were growing up, and what may be missing from Ben's and Anna's emotional lives as a result. However, it is also a reading that is concerned with Ben's and Anna's strategies for addressing such problems; it positions them as active agents in the pursuit of happiness, as it interprets their actions as an attempt to address unmet emotional needs and/or to provide themselves with opportunities for emotional repair. In this case, both Ben and Anna seem to be using extreme sport activities to access experiences that provide them with a sense of ultimate safety and security that does not depend upon their relationships with either members of their families of origin or, indeed, any other intimate or close relationships. Both Ben and Anna seem to have found a way of meeting some of their emotional needs for containment and security while maintaining a high level of independence and self-sufficiency.

Appraisal of the psychosocial reading

My psychosocial analysis of Ben's and Anna's accounts of their experiences of extreme sport has generated some insights into the emotional dynamics that may underpin these experiences. The analysis has drawn on biographical information provided in the accounts to make connections between Ben's and Anna's childhood experiences, including their relationships with members of their families of origin, and their present-day commitment to extreme sport. The analysis has attempted to develop an understanding of how the practice of extreme sport may provide Ben and Anna with experiences that meet some of their emotional needs. As such, a psychosocial reading of Ben's and Anna's interview extracts aspires to provide us with answers to questions about what motivates these two individuals to repeatedly engage in a practice which constitutes a considerable challenge to them (both physically and emotionally) and which carries a real risk of loss of life or serious injury. Our psychosocial analysis, therefore, presumes that there is something that needs to be explained; that there is something that is puzzling and that requires further investigation. After all, we would not be conducting a psychosocial enquiry into why it is that Mr Smith goes to the supermarket on his way home from work, or why Ms Jones feeds the cat in the morning (although, of course, there may be fascinating psychosocial aspects to what Mr Smith chooses to buy once he has arrived at the supermarket, or why Ms Jones chooses to share her home with a cat). The starting point of any psychosocial analysis is the belief that what presents itself (i.e. the phenomenon of interest) is a manifestation of underlying, possibly unconscious, emotional dynamics that give rise to the thoughts and behaviours that constitute the phenomenon of interest. The assumption here is that behaviour can be explained, and that valid explanations for adult behaviour can be found by taking a closer look at people's childhood experiences and relationships, and the impact these may have had upon the child as she or he was growing up. It is important to acknowledge that while the aims of such an analysis are extremely ambitious – after all, we seek to explain why a person does what they do in just the way that they do it – the actual insights generated can only ever be suggestions. In other words, our psychosocial analysis cannot provide us with any certainty about why Ben and Anna engage in extreme sport; rather, our analysis has allowed us to generate a series of hypotheses regarding their motivations. If we were working therapeutically with Ben and Anna, and if Ben and Anna had chosen to come to therapy to better understand themselves and their way of life, we could take these hypotheses back to our clients and invite them to reflect on their validity. However, as we only have access to two relatively brief extracts from one-off interviews with Ben and Anna as research participants, we are unable to pursue any further explorations of our hypotheses or indeed to test their validity.

We have established that our psychosocial analysis is based upon the premise that Ben's and Anna's choices and actions (i.e. their commitment to extreme sport) require an explanation, and that their accounts need to be interpreted to provide us with meaningful answers to our questions about Ben's and Anna's motives for their behaviour. Our analysis has generated tentative explanations that locate Ben's and Anna's motives in unmet childhood needs for containment and security. As such, our analysis implies that Ben and Anna, driven by unconscious motives as they are, do not themselves have full access to an understanding of why they do what they do. This is particularly pertinent given that both Ben's and Anna's actions regularly lead them to put their lives at risk. Does the analysis suggest, then, that it is, in fact, Ben's and Anna's unconscious that is making decisions with potentially disastrous consequences? Does it suggest that Ben and Anna quite literally do not know what they are doing, and that they cannot fully appreciate the danger they are putting themselves in because the true source of their motivation is unknown to them? It could be argued that our psychosocial analysis leads us to pathologize Ben's and Anna's behaviour because we see it as an expression of an underlying problem. We assume that there is some unresolved issue that interferes with their ability to function without having to resort to taking risks to feel okay. The perspective we adopt when we examine our data through a psychosocial lens constructs extreme sport as a solution to an emotional problem, thus presupposing that there is an emotional problem to be solved.

It is quite common for psychosocial-style analyses to come to the conclusion that research participants' words and actions can be understood as ways of managing difficult emotions. Here, participants' words and actions are interpreted as ways of avoiding, denying, defending against, compensating or substituting for deep-seated feelings that cannot be accessed and expressed directly within the context of the research interview. This means that this type of analysis tends to assume two things: there is an assumption, first, that some psychological fault lines exist in research participants' psyches; and, second, that research participants are motivated to cover these up in some way. These are powerful assumptions to make, and, even though there is a rich tradition in psychological theorizing and practice (e.g. see Grant and Crawley, 2002; Jacobs, 1998) that builds upon these assumptions, they remain theory-based presuppositions and remain somewhat controversial. This raises ethical issues regarding the way in which research participants are positioned within a psychosocial interpretation. To presume that our research participants do not actually know why they act the way they do (even if they themselves think they know) means that we deny them the right to give meaning to their own actions. We as researchers claim the right to make sense of our research participants' experiences, and as a result we deprive our research participants of agency within, responsibility for, and ownership of their own life story. This could be regarded as unethical. Also, the presumption that our participants must be damaged in some way and that their choice of leisure activity constitutes an attempt to repair such damage or to compensate for it views our participants' experiences through the lens of pathology and fails to recognize, appreciate, and respect the intrinsic meaning and value of their activities for the participants themselves. It amounts to a commitment on the part of the researcher to 'psychologize' all aspects of experience, including the spiritual (cf. Fingarette, 1963, in Simmonds, 2006a), and it could be argued that this means that we as researchers are not really willing to hear what our participants themselves have to say about their experiences, and this again could raise ethical concerns. Finally, we need to consider the potential impact of a psychosocial interpretation on our research participants. My sense is that the impact would be quite strong, as a psychosocial interpretation is concerned with very personal aspects of experience. Irrespective of whether the participant's response was one of amusement, anger or curiosity, I would expect it to be of some emotional intensity. If in addition their original account of their experience seemed to the research participant to be relatively unproblematic and straightforward, we could expect their exposure to a psychosocial reading of it to also raise further questions and concerns regarding the 'true' meaning of their experience and perhaps also concerns about their mental and emotional health. This is especially likely to be the case if the interpretation is produced by someone that the research participant considers to be an expert in the field of psychological analysis. Reading the researcher's psychosocial interpretation may, therefore, lead a research participant to question their own thoughts and feelings, choices and way of life in a way that they have not done before. While this may well be constructive in the long term, there is no guarantee that this will be the case; in addition, from an ethical point of view, research participants who have not consented to being confronted with potentially challenging interpretations of their thoughts and feelings should not be exposed to such material within the context of the research.

The quality and scope of a psychosocial analysis depends, of course, on the skill and experience of the researcher. However, the suitability of the data is equally important. To produce a rich and convincing psychosocial reading, the researcher needs to have access to biographical information about the participant. It is impossible to make the sorts of links and connections required by psychosocial research without sufficient information about the participants' early life and their relationships with members of their family of origin. The more information of this nature is available to the researcher, the better. My psychosocial analysis of Ben's and Anna's interview extracts was limited in scope because the biographical information I was using was very limited. This meant that much of what I suggested in my psychosocial reading remained highly speculative. If richer information about Ben's and Anna's early life had been available, I would have been able to base my conclusions on stronger evidence as further details about Ben's and Anna's childhood experiences would have either supported or undermined my emerging interpretations. The thinner the evidence in support of a psychosocial reading, the less grounded the interpretation will be. Such interpretations can be likened to what Freud referred to as 'wild analysis' (Freud, 1957, in Simmonds, 2006b), whereby psychoanalytic interpretations are generated but not then tested within the clinical situation with the resulting danger of producing meaningless or inappropriate readings of the material (see also Frosh, 2010).

It could, of course, also be argued that even where rich biographical information is available and the researcher produces a psychosocial reading that is grounded in the detail of a particular research participant's unique life history, interpretations generated by such an analysis will always be somewhat predictable. This is because the theoretical perspective that informs the analysis directs the researcher to look for possible connections between the participant's words and conduct, and any emotional investments and psychodynamics that may underpin them. As Frosh (2010: 202) argues, the 'deeply-rooted infant-centredness of psychoanalysis ... often produces rather predictable motivational accounts and interpretive strategies'. This, however, is perhaps not so different from other theoretical approaches where the theoretical constructs with which the researcher approaches the data will inevitably shape what kinds of insights can be generated. After all, we are not surprised when discourse analysts extract discursive constructions from a text, or when phenomenologists produce descriptions of experiential phenomena.

In general terms, I would argue that, to conduct ethically sound, high-quality psychosocial analyses, researchers need to maintain a critically reflexive distance from their emerging interpretations so as to ensure that they do not pursue a line of reasoning that loses contact with what has been presented in the actual interview session. I conclude by endorsing Frosh and Young's (2008: 117–18) recommendation that any use of psychodynamic understanding in qualitative research 'must be tentative, rooted both in biographical information and in dynamic contact with research participants that allows space for emotional connectedness and the observation and thoughtful reflection on the relationship that arises'.

9 Conclusion

We are coming to the end of our reflections on interpretation. In this final chapter, we return to some of the themes that were of concern in earlier chapters in an attempt to draw some conclusions about how to meet the challenge of interpretation in qualitative psychology. The chapter begins with an appraisal of the insights gained on the basis of the three interpretations of the experience of extreme sport presented in Chapters 6, 7 and 8, and a brief discussion of how other methods of qualitative analysis (including grounded theory, ethnography, action research, narrative, and thematic analysis) are positioned in relation to these. The chapter goes on to address the question of how to evaluate interpretative research. It introduces a pluralistic approach to interpretation and discusses its implications for qualitative research practice. The chapter concludes by recommending responsible, reflexive, and flexible interpretation as a form of ethical research practice.

Three interpretations: review and appraisal

Our three interpretations of Ben's and Anna's accounts of their experience of extreme sport presented in Chapters 6, 7, and 8 have generated rather different insights into the phenomenon of interest. The phenomenological interpretation has provided us with a better understanding of what taking part in extreme sport means to our research participants, and on the basis of this understanding we have been able to gain an insight into the nature, meaning, and significance of the phenomenon of extreme sport itself. As a result, we have a clearer understanding of what extreme sport may offer, experientially and perhaps also existentially, to those who take part in it. The discursive interpretation, on the other hand, has provided us with insights into the ways in which our research participants, and myself as the interviewer, use discursive resources and strategies to construct meaning around 'extreme sport' and how such constructions position us as speakers. We have gained an understanding of what talk about 'extreme sport' can do, both to us and for us as participants in a conversation. Finally, the psychosocial interpretation has generated insights into the possible psychodynamics underpinning our research participants' accounts of their experiences of extreme sport. As a result, we have developed an understanding of what it might be that motivates our participants to engage with extreme sport in just the way that they do; we now have some ideas about what their emotional investments in their commitment to extreme sport may be, and we have a sense of how and why extreme sports activities may meet some of our participants' emotional needs.

Reflecting on my experience of producing the three readings of the data, I was struck by how different the process of engaging with the data in each case had felt. There had not just been a difference in the analytic procedures I applied, the steps I took to find (different types of) meaning in the texts; there had also been a marked difference in the nature and quality of my experience of working with the data.

Reading and re-reading the accounts through a phenomenological lens had felt like reading in the dark. I remember the feeling of straining and struggling to really 'see' what my participants' accounts were describing. There was a sense of not wanting to miss anything, however small or apparently insignificant, which might constitute an essential dimension of their experience. Approaching the data from a phenomenological perspective meant that I assumed that I did not know what my research participants were experiencing and that to gain access to their experience I needed to make a sustained effort to 'hear' what they were saying. My experience of conducting a phenomenological analysis of the accounts involved focusing, peering, scrutinizing; it involved listening carefully, revisiting the material repeatedly, always assuming that there may be something I had not picked up. Reflecting on my experience of working with the data phenomenologically, I became aware of just how much of what I did felt like trying to heighten the accuracy of my perception. I imagined myself as someone creeping along a barely visible path at night, in the dark, straining to hear and see, periodically stopping in my tracks to pick up subtle messages from my environment. It is interesting to note how my description of my subjective experience of working phenomenologically invokes images and metaphors that resonate with phenomenology's concern with the nature of what 'appears' to us and its commitment to creating the conditions in which phenomena can 'show themselves'. Here is how Heidegger (1962: 59; in Mulhall, 1996: 26) defines what constitutes a phenomenon:

> Manifestly, it is something that proximally and for the most part does not show itself at all: it is something that lies hidden, in contrast to that which proximally and for the most part does show itself; but at the same time it is something that belongs to what thus shows itself, and it belongs to it so essentially as to constitute its meaning and its ground.

In addition, for a phenomenon to be able to show itself, there needs to be a clearing, a space within which such disclosure can happen. In our case, the researcher is that space. The phenomenon discloses itself through its interaction with the researcher who, therefore, allows it to appear. Again, this resonates with my perceptual analogy whereby a sound or an image can be said to appear, to be made into a particular sound or image, only through being heard or seen by someone. Within the context of my analysis, I was the person straining to hear the sound, to see the image, and, thereby, allowing it to show itself, to appear as a phenomenon that can be described and reflected upon.

My experience of producing a discursive reading of the two accounts had been rather different. Here I experienced myself as more in control, as more active and purposive in my approach to the data. I was quite clear in my own mind as to what I was looking for in the data. In fact, upon my first reading, I was struck by a number of places in the transcripts where something discursively interesting was clearly happening. My relationship with the text was, therefore, one whereby it felt as though the text was offering me a series of analytic tasks whose general nature was familiar to me. In other words, I knew what was expected of me and I approached the text as someone who was setting out to tackle a clearly defined challenge. Initially, there was a certain freedom and playfulness in my engagement with the data as I began by analysing those sections of the texts that stood out as the most obvious and fruitful targets for discursive scrutiny. Having explored those sections and having made connections between them and the surrounding material, I revisited the transcripts, reading through them again and again, looking for textual evidence that would shed further light on the interactional business that the participants in the conversation may have been attending to. It felt as though I was combing through a head of tangled hair, going over and over the same places to make sure that no knots, no tangles were left behind. Wherever I came across a little bit of resistance, a subtle obstruction, a minor blockage, I would return to that place and run my analytic comb through it again. Wherever I still had unanswered questions about a particular discursive construction or a rhetorical strategy, I would return to that section in the text and attempt to answer them. There was something very satisfying about this process, and although it required a lot of concentration, effort and patience I also felt as though I was being carried along by the process itself. I felt myself responding to the text, and I sensed that I could, and would, continue with this analytic process until the text had nothing left to offer me. As a result, I did not feel myself struggle to maintain motivation and I did not lose momentum prematurely. Reflecting on this experience, I wonder whether it was the theoretical frame that supports discourse analytic research that allowed me to feel guided by the text itself. After all, discourse analytic research starts with the assumption that the text itself is active in that it constructs versions of reality, it positions speakers, and it achieves effects. Discourse analysts are extremely respectful of the text that is ascribed with considerable power and importance in discourse analytic work. My experience of working with the text as though it was a co-researcher, a partner in the analytic process, reflects and embodies this theoretical stance.

Finally, my encounter with the data from a psychosocial position generated yet another subjective experience of qualitative analysis for me. Now my engagement with my research participants' accounts engendered a sense of being pulled quite strongly in a particular direction, along a narrative path that made sense to me and yet felt somewhat precarious at the same time. There was a sense of things falling into place easily, perhaps too easily, and of my thinking, the way in which I was making connections and forming hypotheses about my participants' psycho-dynamics, moving forward very quickly. I remember feeling rather 'speedy', with a sense of exhilaration and excitement about how my psychosocial narrative was taking shape. I was aware of how easy it would be to get carried away by my own psychosocial formulations, and I felt the need to make an effort to rein myself in, to slow down, and to become more suspicious of my own emerging narrative.

I thought of the sensation one experiences on a fairground ride where it feels as though one's body is ahead of where it ought to be, and one leans back in one's seat in an attempt to slow things down. Within this context, Freud's choice of label to describe interpretation that has lost the connection with its empirical base as 'wild interpretation' (Freud, 1957) resonated strongly with me. There was indeed something 'wild' about the way in which I felt pulled along by the alchemy of data and theory. There was something exciting and enjoyable about being able to 'make things fit together' in a way that explained the research participants' actions, and I became aware of the seductive potential of theory-driven interpretation. Again, as with my discursive interpretation, there was a sense of ease and a momentum that was generated by the availability of a theory that could 'make sense' of the data with some elegance and relative ease. Frosh (2010) acknowledges that while a psychoanalytic perspective offers helpful ways of connecting social phenomena with psychic formations, it also harbours the danger of silencing alternative readings. He describes this as one of the regressive tendencies in psychoanalysis, which include:

> the powerful sense that once one has developed a psychoanalytic per-spective one has been transformed through a procedure that has often been compared with mystical conversion (Gellner, 1985), after which it becomes impossible to see things in any other way but through a psycho-analytic lens.
>
> (Frosh, 2010: 194)

This conversion effect is, of course, not unique to psychoanalysis, and can come into play in relation to any macro (or 'grand') theory that offers a set of concepts with which to explain global phenomena such as 'human experience' or 'social change' (cf. Popper, 1945). My experience of a mixture of exhilaration and appre-hension when engaging in psychosocial analysis can perhaps be understood as a manifestation of my ambivalence about how to relate to such a powerful theory.

In the light of my reflections on the experiential quality of conducting different types of qualitative analysis, it appears that to generate different kinds of inter-pretation requires not just the application of different analytic strategies but also the adoption of a different stance towards the data. It requires an entirely differ-ent engagement with the material to be analysed and it generates a very different relationship with the data. How might other qualitative methods of analysis fit with the three different orientations identified above? And how do they relate to the distinction between 'suspicious' and 'empathic' approaches to interpretation introduced in Chapter 1? In the next section, we shall attempt to locate a range of qualitative analytic approaches on a continuum ranging from 'tentative' (open, explorative) to 'prescriptive' (closed, certain) styles of interpretation.

Styles of interpretation: a continuum

The first thing to note is that I am aware that my choice of descriptors (*tentative*, *open*, *explorative* as opposed to *prescriptive*, *closed*, *certain*) may appear to imply some value judgements regarding the desirability of the orientations labelled thus. Certainly within our general cultural context of early twenty-first century liberal democracies, the term 'open' is likely to be evaluated more positively than the term 'closed'. It could also be argued that within the context of contemporary academic qualitative psychology the term 'prescriptive' can be heard as implying rigidity, while 'explorative' may sound more attractive. Indeed, as discussed in Chapter 4, our choice of terminology constitutes an interpretative act and will have consequences for how our messages are read. Having said this, I want to emphasize that in my view all approaches to interpretation have something to offer and that what matters most is that the researcher is fully aware of exactly what their chosen style of interpretation can and cannot deliver, its parameters and limitations, including the ethical challenges inherent in it. This is, of course, the motivation behind writing this book. My aim is to encourage self-conscious, reflexive, and ethical interpretation in qualitative psychology, and it is my hope that the reflections contained in this book will help to encourage this.

The idea of a continuum of orientations to interpretation may help us locate our own approach more clearly and to think through the theoretical, practical, and ethical implications of adopting our chosen style. It should also help us to evaluate our research more effectively, as the criteria for evaluating interpretative research will differ depending on our preferred approach to interpretation. Issues around evaluation will be discussed in the next section.

Returning to the three interpretations of our extreme sport data, I would argue that my phenomenological reading can be located at the 'tentative' end of the continuum. Here, both the insights generated by the analysis and the experiential quality of conducting the analysis were steeped in uncertainty. My approach to interpretation was based on the assumption that I did not know what the experience of extreme sport was about and that any knowledge about it would have to come from my participants. Since I also assumed that I had no direct access to their experience and that my ability to 'hear' and 'see' what their accounts described was limited as well as mediated by what I brought to the analysis, I attempted to maintain an attitude of caution and an openness to changing my mind regarding what I thought might be going on in the data throughout the analysis, and indeed afterwards. The aim of the phenomenological analysis was to offer an exploration of the meanings contained within the research participants' accounts, which would, hopefully, amplify (again, note how this term resonates with the sight/sound based perceptual analogy I used in my experiential account) them and enable third parties to gain some insight into what extreme sport means to those who practise it. Overall, then, my phenomenological analysis aspired to produce an 'empathic' reading and it adopted a 'tentative' orientation to interpretation.

My discursive reading was less tentative. I felt supported by a clearly defined theoretical framework that guided my analysis, and I produced insights that deployed theoretical constructs ('discourse', 'discursive construction', 'discursive strategy', 'positioning', etc.) drawn from this theoretical framework. While I was not always entirely confident about my analytic performance in that I was aware that another researcher might have produced a more sophisticated discursive analysis, I did not have any real doubts about the type of thing I should be looking for. The theory underpinning my method was helpful in that it provided me with a clear direction as to what was of interest to the analysis and what was not, and it equipped me with questions that I could ask of the data to drive my analysis forward. In other words, there was a prescriptive dimension to my discursive engagement with the data. The analysis, therefore, also felt somewhat less open than the phenomeno-logical work that I had done, although my continuous revisiting of the 'knots' and 'tangles' in the data meant that I was open to alternative (but always, of course, discursive) interpretations of sections of the text, particularly in the light of the surrounding discursive context. This meant that my discursive reading remains provisional because further considerations of context (both the local context of the research interview and the cultural context of talk about extreme sport) might change my understanding of what was going on in the data. The analysis does not claim to provide more than a partial understanding of the discursive dynamics at play in the two interview extracts, and the certainty with which it makes its claims is, therefore, tempered by an openness to the possibility of a widening of our understanding of what is going on in the text.

Finally, my psychosocial reading was guided by some quite specific theoretical assumptions about what sorts of things motivate people to do the things they do. This meant that my analysis did not feel tentative in the way that my phe-nomenological work had done. Although I retained some doubts as to whether I was correct in the connections I made between my research participants' manifest words and actions, and any underlying emotional investments and motivations that I proposed, for the purpose of the analysis I did assume that there were some psychological dynamics to be discovered and that these held explanatory power. As with my discursive analysis, therefore, my doubts arose from my awareness of my limitations as a researcher rather than being part and parcel of the analytic approach taken. And again, as was the case with my discursive interpretation, the availability of a strong theoretical framework meant that my psychosocial ana-lysis could draw on specific ideas and concepts (such as the notion of emotional investment, the importance of relations within the family of origin, the role of unconscious motivations, etc.) to give it direction. Since there is no consensus regarding the theoretical basis of psychosocial analysis in the literature (see Frosh, 2010), I did have some freedom in choosing my theoretical tools. However, once I had committed myself to a particular version of psychosocial analysis, the lens through which I read the data was in place and my analysis followed a predictable course, taking on a more prescriptive flavour as a result.

To sum up, then, it seems that both discourse analysis and psychosocial analysis with their theory-driven, and therefore rather more 'suspicious', approach to inter-pretation can be placed nearer the 'prescriptive' end of the continuum of styles of interpretation, while phenomenological analysis with its more 'empathic' orien-tation is closer to the 'tentative' position. Interestingly, although psychoanalytic theory has been widely criticized for the certainty with which it often makes its claims about what is 'really going on' inside the human individual, it seems that it was discourse analysis with its clear theoretical position regarding the role of language in human experience and interaction that offered the most 'prescriptive' style of interpreting the data.

Grounded theory

It seems that it is a research method's relationship with theory that determines its place on the continuum between 'tentative' and 'prescriptive' styles of interpretation. This means that grounded theory methodology (e.g. Charmaz, 2006; Glaser and Strauss, 1967; Strauss and Corbin, 1998) whose entire *raison d'être* is to facilitate a process whereby new theories can emerge from data, would need to be placed very close to the 'tentative' position. There are, of course, marked differences between grounded theorists in terms of the strategies that they recommend in support of the process of theory generation; for example, while Glaser (1992) advises against approaching the data with anything other than an open mind, Strauss and Corbin (1990, 1998) are much more prescriptive in that they recommend the use of a coding paradigm that directs the researcher's attention to particular features of the data (such as interactional strategies and their consequences). Yet other grounded theorists (e.g. Charmaz, 2006) encourage the inclusion of reflexivity and a fuller acknowledgement of the role of the researcher in constructing theoretical understanding. In addition, there are different views regarding the role of deduction in grounded theory methodology, with some (e.g. Strauss and Corbin, 1990, 1998) arguing that grounded theory research involves the formulation of something like preliminary hypotheses or theoretical claims which are then tested and developed through further data collection and analysis; others (e.g. Glaser, 1992), by contrast, prefer to stick to a purely inductive model. Despite these differences, I would argue that grounded theory methodology's relationship with theory is tentative and non-prescriptive because theory formulation is the goal of research rather than the starting point.

Ethnography

Ethnography takes a similar approach to grounded theory in that the ethnographic researcher enters the field with an open mind regarding the nature of the events she or he will encounter there. Like the grounded theorist, the ethnographer does have a research question in mind; however, this question is really little more than an acknowledgement of what motivates the researcher to commence the research in the first place rather than a theoretically derived problem statement. For example, the researcher might want to understand what car modification means to young men (Bengry-Howell, 2005; see also Griffin and Bengry-Howell, 2008) or what it is that constitutes the 'electric' atmosphere at football matches so highly valued by football fans (Marsh et al., 1978). The aim of ethnographic research is to obtain an insider view of a particular dimension of people's everyday lives by participating, overtly or covertly, in it for a sustained period of time. There is a theoretical basis to such research in that ethnographic researchers tend to be interested in specific cultural practices and their meanings rather than, for example, being concerned with the quality of individuals' subjective experiences as a phenomenologist might be. As Griffin and Bengry-Howell (2008: 16) explain, '[E]thnography focuses on cultural interpretation, and aims to understand the cultural and symbolic aspects of people's actions and the contexts in which those actions occur'. This means that ethnographic research, while being very open as to the precise nature and content of people's actions, does presume that people's actions are not devoid of cultural and symbolic meaning and that such meanings are significant. Indeed, drawing on Punch (1998) and Denscombe (2003), the authors spell out that:

> Ethnography is founded on the assumption that the shared cultural meanings of a social group are vital for understanding the activities of any social group. The task of the ethnographic researcher is to uncover those meanings.
>
> (Griffin and Bengry-Howell, 2008: 16)

Ethnography's theoretical base directs the researcher's attention to certain aspects of the data and it supplies the researcher with sensitizing concepts such as the notion of 'cultural practice' or 'cultural meaning'. However, within these broad assumptions and conceptual tools, the ethnographic researcher is encouraged to approach the data with humility and an attitude of not-knowing as they are seeking to understand what is going on from the point of view of those who are involved in the action. The ethnographer rejects the role of expert and this means that, although theoretically grounded, ethnographic research aspires to maintain a flexible and reflexive stance, remaining explorative and open to changes in perspective throughout the research. Such research is, therefore, perhaps best placed in the middle of our continuum.

Action research

Action research shares ethnography's respect for the perspectives of its research participants and its rejection of an expert role. Reason and Bradbury (2001: 1) describe action research as a 'participatory, democratic process concerned with developing practical knowing in the pursuit of worth-while human purposes'. Here, the researcher engages in collaboration with the research participants with the explicit aim of bringing about change in some parts of the latter's everyday lives. The precise nature and direction of this change is not pre-determined by the researcher; instead, it emerges from consultation with those who will be affected by it, namely the research participants. The researcher contributes their time and skills, and it is hoped that the researcher's involvement in the process of collectively identifying goals and implementing strategies to reach these goals will allow him or her to develop a better understanding of how social change comes about. Ideally, the action researcher develops a theoretical understanding of (some aspects of) social change as a result of being involved in an action research project. Again, as with grounded theory, it seems that here theory generation is the goal of the research rather than its point of departure. However, at the same time we need to acknowledge that action research does rely upon a theoretical base. This can be more or less developed, depending on the researcher's background and their theoretical and political commitments. At its most basic level, action research presupposes that the most effective way of bringing about an improvement in people's quality of life is through forms of collective action. It assumes that it is social practices that inform how people experience aspects of their lifeworld, and that it is these practices that need to be modified to enhance individuals' well-being. Most action research also presupposes that empowerment of research participants (and, indeed, of people in general) is a desirable thing. It has been acknowledged that action research is 'a value-based practice, underpinned by a commitment to positive social change' (Kagan et al., 2008). Action researchers' definition of what constitutes 'positive social change' tends to involve the redistribution of power in one way or another through empowering those who traditionally have little control over the conditions in which they live and work. At the more theoretical end of the spectrum of action research there are action researchers who are committed to a sophisticated theoretical framework that equips them with an understanding of the structure of contemporary societies and the place of various social groups within this. For example, feminist or Marxist action researchers will bring with them a fully developed theoretical tool-kit that will inform the ways in which they will understand the people and events they encounter during the action research process. The importance of the action researcher's theoretical outlook becomes very clear when we consider the potential effects of the researcher's choice of label for those she or he writes about; should they be described as 'workers', 'women workers', 'women', 'citizens', 'people' or 'individuals'? It is clear that our choice of label alone imports theoretical assumptions about what is important and what is not in relation to the social processes under investigation. While it is impossible to approach a social situation without any preconceived categories and concepts – after all, we do need to refer to the people we encounter in the course of our research as something – I would argue that there are more and less prescriptive versions of action research. As before, the more heavily theoretically based forms of action research tend to be more prescriptive and less tentative than those that are not committed to a particular macro ('grand') theory of society. This is particularly the case where researchers are deeply committed to a particular theory and there is no provision for allowing the incoming data to modify the theoretical categories that are used to make sense of the data.

Narrative

Similarly, narrative approaches to qualitative research are not easy to place. This is because there are both open and rather more prescriptive versions of narrative research. Narrative researchers share an interest in the stories people tell about their experiences, and they share a commitment to the idea that it is through constructing narratives about their lives that people organize and bring meaning to their experiences. As Murray (2003: 116) puts it, narrative allows us 'to define ourselves, to clarify the continuity in our lives and to convey this to others'. Narrative research concerns itself with the content, structure, and form of the stories people tell. However, while some narrative research is primarily concerned with the content of the story, its substance, and its gist, other styles of narrative research are particularly interested in the story's structure and form, its internal organization and use of linguistic features (see Smith and Sparkes, 2006, for a review of differences in approach and tensions within the field of narrative inquiry). The former approach is perhaps more psychological in orientation as it seeks to advance the researcher's understanding of the relationship between the stories that are told and the storytellers' subjective experiences (including their feelings and their sense of self) (e.g. Crossley, 2000; Smith and Sparkes, 2002). It could be said that this approach to narrative research is underpinned by a phenomenological curiosity. Other styles of narrative analysis, however, have a more discourse analytic flavour in that here the researcher is interested in the narrative strategies through which particular versions of human experience, and indeed of social reality more generally, are constructed. Citing Gubrium and Holstein (2000), Smith and Sparkes (2006: 184) describe this as a concern with 'the artful side of storytelling'. This type of narrative analysis would be able to make use of similar kinds of theoretically derived conceptual tools as discourse analytic research in its search for evidence of the various discursive strategies that are used in constructing a story and its characters. I would argue, therefore, that the phenomenologically inflected version of narrative research is less theory-driven and, therefore, would need to be placed closer to the 'tentative' end of our continuum than the discursively oriented version. However, it is important to acknowledge that all narrative research is based on the theoretical premise that telling stories is fundamental to human experience, and that it is through constructing narratives that people make connections between events and interpret them in a way that creates something that is meaningful (at least to them). This means that all narrative research is theory-driven, as the researcher's theoretical premise will lead them to look for stories. The difference between approaches lies in the types of questions researchers will ask about the stories they are analysing, with phenomenologically inflected research asking questions about what happens in the story (and what are the implications of this for the subjectivity of the storyteller), and discursively oriented narrative research asking questions about how the story is told (and the implications of this for what happens socially, between people) (see Denzin, 1997).

Thematic analysis

Finally, a few words about thematic analysis, which Braun and Clarke (2006: 77) describe as 'a poorly demarcated and rarely acknowledged, yet widely used qualitative analytic method'. Thematic analysis refers to the process of identifying themes in the data which capture meaning that is relevant to the research question, and perhaps also to making links between such themes. In this way, thematic analysis helps the researcher identify patterns in the data (see Braun and Clarke, 2006). It has been argued (e.g. Boyatzis, 1998; Ryan and Bernard, 2000) that thematic analysis does not, in fact, constitute a method of analysis in itself because the systematic process of extracting themes from data can form a part of a wide range of qualitative approaches to data analysis that differ significantly in terms of their epistemological orientations. This means that, having extracted themes, the researcher still needs to decide what these themes represent; for example, does a theme represent a discursive construction, a thought, a feeling, a psychological mechanism? Does the researcher take the theme at face value, as something that directly reflects the research participant's experience, or does the researcher approach the theme as something that needs to be explained in its own right? Answers to these types of questions will reveal the epistemological and theoretical positions adopted by the researcher, and it is those positions that have implications for the approach to interpretation that is adopted in the study. Thematic analysis can underpin both 'empathic' and 'suspicious' interpretations, and it can, therefore, be associated with research across our continuum, including both 'tentative' and 'prescriptive' approaches and, indeed, anything in between.

Evaluation

So what makes a 'good' interpretation? So far in this chapter we have been concerned with difference. We have been trying to develop a better understanding of what differentiates the approaches to interpretation that qualitative psychologists may adopt in their engagement with their data. These differences encompass variations in epistemological orientation as well as differences in style and in the researcher's attitude towards the results of their interpretative labour. However, despite these differences, we can assume that all researchers aim to generate interpretations that are in some way valuable. In other words, there is a shared ambition to produce 'good' interpretations, whatever that may mean. Qualitative researchers have debated the question of what constitutes 'good' qualitative research at length and for some time (e.g. Chamberlain, 2000; Forshaw, 2007; Madill et al., 2000; Reicher, 2000; Willig, 2007a; see also Willig, 2008a, Chapter 9), and we are not going to review these debates here. Instead, we shall look at available strategies for validating interpretations and try to form a view about their usefulness.

To begin, we need to remind ourselves that the criteria we use for evaluating a piece of qualitative research (or any research, for that matter) need to be congruent with the epistemological orientation of that particular piece of research (e.g. Madill et al., 2000; Rennie, 2004; Willig, 2012). This means that to assess the quality of a research study, we would need to ask to what extent it has met its own objectives. The research needs to be evaluated on its own terms. So when attempting to determine whether an interpretation is a 'good' interpretation, we need to start by establishing what the purpose of producing the interpretation had been in the first place. Was its aim to capture the quality of an experience? Was it to try to identify underlying mechanisms or dynamics that can account for the data? Was it concerned with explaining the data through the lens of existing theory? Or was its motivation to develop an entirely new theory? As discussed in earlier chapters, interpretations can have very different purposes and they can have very different relationships with theory. As we have seen, some of these differences are captured by labels such as 'empathic' versus 'suspicious', or 'tentative' versus 'prescriptive'. Once we have established the (intended) remit of the interpretation we can begin to think about evaluating it.

Williams and Morrow (2009: 577) identify what they describe as 'three major categories of trustworthiness to which all qualitative researchers must attend'; these are 'integrity of the data', 'balance between reflexivity and subjectivity', and 'clear communication and application of findings'. The following discussion of what may be involved in evaluating interpretations is structured around these three categories, although my operationalization of them differs somewhat from Williams and Morrow's (2009) original version.

Integrity of the data

Scrutinizing the 'integrity of the data' means paying attention to the relationship between the data and the claims that are made in the interpretation of it. At the end of each of the empirical chapters (Chapters 6, 7, and 8), I discussed the suitability of our two interview extracts for the type of analysis presented in each chapter. I observed that for a phenomenological reading we require data that provides the researcher with information about the nature, quality, and texture of research participants' experiences, which means that rich, descriptive accounts of subjective experiences are preferable in this case. I suggested that any type of text would be suitable for discursive analysis, although there may be ethical constraints on whether a particular text is deemed appropriate material for a discourse analysis. Finally, I argued that, to produce a convincing psychosocial reading, the researcher needs access to a good amount of biographical information about the participant. Ideally, there should also be some information about the way in which the researcher experienced the participant within the context of the research interview and the effect the participant may have had on the researcher. This demonstrates that different styles of interpretation benefit from different types of data. Thus to assess the trustworthiness of an interpretation we need to evaluate the extent to which the data upon which it is based is suitable and sufficiently rich for the interpretation to be reasonably well grounded within it. In other words, the quality of the data needs to be appropriate to and compatible with the interpretative approach and strategy the researcher has decided to adopt. In addition, the quantity of data also plays a role because, as Williams and Morrow (2009: 578) point out, 'quantity of data is key to filling out categories or themes in such a way that the reader is able to grasp the richness and complexity of the constructs under investigation'. So although an interpretation may be plausible and interesting, our confidence in its trustworthiness will be low unless the data we have available for inspection is rich and comprehensive enough to flesh it out, and to demonstrate that the interpretation can make sense of a variety of related manifestations of the phenomenon under investigation. It has also been argued (e.g. McLeod, 2001; Sullivan, 2008) that qualitative researchers' tendency to break up narrative accounts by extracting themes can mean that the structure and coherence of the account is lost and its narrative dimension (and the meanings associated with that) cannot be analysed. This means that the early stages of transformation of the data (from 'raw data' into some form of 'meaning units') already set the scene for the types of interpretation that are, and are not, then possible. Again, it is crucial that the researcher makes an informed decision about such data transformation and recognizes that data handling (including transcription; see Emerson and Frosh, 2004; Kvale, 1996) already constitutes a form of interpretation. To evaluate an interpretation's trustworthiness, then, we need to carefully examine its relationship with the data that supports it.

Balance between reflexivity and subjectivity

The 'balance between reflexivity and subjectivity' is concerned with the relationship between the data and the researcher's standpoint or perspective. In earlier chapters, we have established that interpretation is always and necessarily a joint venture in that the interpretation will contain something that belongs to the researcher as well as something that belongs to the text. We established that, to interpret an account, the researcher needs to bring some ideas, some expectations, some conceptual tools with which to approach the text. At the same time, the researcher needs to be open to being changed by the encounter with the text. This means that in any interpretation something comes from the researcher and something comes from the participants (or at least from the accounts they provide). To evaluate an interpretation we need to examine this relationship. Again, how much should come from the researcher and how much should come from the data depends on the approach to interpretation the researcher subscribes to. Clearly, 'suspicious' interpretations require (and, therefore, allow for) more input from the researcher's own conceptual framework than 'empathic' interpretations do. As a result, an interpretation that aspires to be 'empathic' but is then found to have read participants' accounts through a highly prescriptive theoretical lens would need to be evaluated less positively than an openly 'suspicious' interpretation that does the same. Schmidt (2006, Chapter 7) provides a helpful review of the very diverse positions scholars in philosophical hermeneutics have taken regarding the question of how to validate interpretations. He identifies positions ranging from the belief that methodological diligence can ensure that interpretations are valid to the belief that there is no criterion for judging the validity of an interpretation, as there is no such thing as 'truth'. Given the lack of consensus on the question of the validity of interpretations, the best we can do to evaluate interpretative research is to scrutinize the extent to which the balance between bottom-up (or participant-led) and top-down (or researcher-led) input is congruent with the researcher's declared approach to interpretation.

Depending on the approach taken, researchers may use various strategies designed to increase the trustworthiness of their interpretations. For example, some researchers advocate the use of participant validation or member checking (e.g. Colaizzi, 1978; Lincoln and Guba, 1985) to ensure that the researcher's interpretations do reflect the participants' own experiences. Williams and Morrow

(2009: 579) argue that 'participants' feedback can serve as an excellent check that the researcher has achieved the desired balance between the participants' voices (subjectivity) and the researcher's interpretation of the meaning (reflexivity)'. However, not all researchers desire such a balance. Some would argue that a participant's lack of endorsement does not mean the interpretation is misguided or, indeed, that a participant's agreement with the researcher means that the researcher has 'got it right'. Langdridge (2007) points out that even in phenomenological research, particularly if it is of a hermeneutic nature, the analysis may well present something that a participant may not recognize as being relevant to their experience. This does not necessarily mean that the insight is not valid. It may be the case that the participant does not acknowledge a particular dimension of their experience so as to avoid confronting perhaps painful or disturbing features of it. Again, it depends on what the interpretation aims to do. If it aims to capture the meaning an experience has for a participant, then the participant's endorsement does have value. However, if the aim is to identify an unconscious motivation, then we would not expect a participant to be in a position to validate the interpretation because, of course, they would not themselves be aware of any unconscious motivations (see, for example, Hollway and Jefferson, 2000).

Another strategy for increasing trustworthiness is bracketing whereby the researcher engages in reflexive scrutiny of their own assumptions and investments in particular ideas and perspectives that they then attempt to put to one side, or at least to hold lightly and flexibly, during the process of data analysis. I would argue that although the extent to which bracketing constitutes a meaningful strategy for increasing the quality of a researcher's interpretation depends on the type of interpretation they aim to produce, all qualitative researchers need to engage in some measure of reflexivity so that, as Williams and Morrow (2009: 579) put it, they can 'recognise their own experiences as separate from the participants' stories'. Similarly, maintaining an openness to alternative interpretations is another strategy that all qualitative researchers ought to adopt. However, this strategy will play out differently in relation to different approaches to interpretation. While 'tentative' approaches (such as we might see in a grounded theory study, for example) require the researcher to remain open for as long as possible so that any conceptualizations or hypotheses that emerge will be as data-driven as possible, more 'prescriptive' approaches will tend to engage in sense-making much earlier in the analytic process but will then need to demonstrate openness to alternative interpretations when assessing the validity of these early formulations in the light of the entire dataset. Here, the quality and quantity of the data available is clearly of great importance, as discussed in the preceding section on the 'integrity of the data'.

Clear communication and application of findings

Our third and final criterion for assessing the value of an interpretation is concerned with its usefulness. As Williams and Morrow (2009: 580) argue, 'clear communication and application of findings' are crucial if a study is to have any impact.

To assess a study's value, we need to reflect on the extent to which the insights generated by it contribute something useful to the field; for example, does it allow us to improve clinical practice, or does it reveal limitations in existing approaches to the subject matter? Does it identify meaningful directions for further research, or does it contribute to some form of social change? In other words, does the research have any 'social validity' (see Morrow, 2005; Williams and Morrow, 2009)? Asking such questions implies a pragmatist orientation. Here, we are not concerned with whether or not an interpretation is an accurate reflection of 'reality' or whether or not it is 'true' (whatever this may mean); rather, we are interested in the consequences of having access to the interpretation. From a pragmatist point of view, the insights generated by research are tools for action; as Cornish and Gillespie (2009: 802) put it, '[R]ather than *mirroring* reality, knowledge *mediates* our relation to the physical and social world' (italics in original). To assess the pragmatic value of an interpretation we need to think about whether it serves the purpose for which it was conceived. Does it provide an answer to the original research question? Does it allow the researcher to do what they set out to do when planning the research? Clearly, for an interpretation to have pragmatic value, the researcher needs to have thought about the purpose of generating such an interpretation before embarking upon the research. There needs to have been a wider project of which the interpretation in question forms a part. For example, a researcher may be interested in what makes people take health-related risks, and their wider goal may be to find ways of reducing the incidence of risky practices among young people. In such a case, the criterion for judging whether something is a 'good' interpretation would be whether it helps the researcher (or others) to design effective health promotion in the future. Alternatively, if the researcher's goal was to raise research participants' awareness of what motivates their behaviour, then positive feedback from participants that reading the researcher's interpretation has indeed helped them to understand themselves better would indicate that the interpretation was 'good' in that it met its own objectives and was useful in the way that it aspired to be. Of course, we could also move beyond considerations of the researcher's own objectives, and we could ask whether the interpretation is useful in ways that the researcher had perhaps not anticipated. We could consider interests over and above those of the researcher and bring our own views on what constitutes socially useful knowledge to bear upon our evaluation. After all, a pragmatist perspective does not dictate which of many possible interests our interpretation should advance; it merely advocates that any knowledge produced on the basis of our research should be evaluated in terms of its usefulness. This means that our pragmatist evaluation of an interpretation necessarily involves moral choices about which interests ought, and which ought not, to be served by it.

A pluralistic approach to qualitative research

Up until now I have been writing about different approaches to qualitative analysis and interpretation as constituting alternatives that each have something distinctive to offer to the researcher, and among which researchers will need to choose their preferred style. However, in recent years qualitative psychologists have begun to question the assumption that due to the presence of epistemological differences between qualitative methodologies researchers are compelled to choose between them, and methodological pluralism has emerged as another option. Frost (2009b: 32) argues that '[T]he mono-method approach provides detailed insight into individual experience from a particular epistemological framework but leaves the qualitative researcher open to accusations of "methodolatry" (Curt, 1994) and a pre-occupation with tensions between qualitative methods (Willig, 2000)'. As an alternative Frost (2009b) proposes that the combination of qualitative approaches within the context of one study allows for a multi-layered understanding of the data from which an audience can then select those aspects that have meaning and value to their area of interest. This means that the pragmatic value of a multi-layered reading of the data is high because it has the potential to speak to diverse interests. In addition, a pluralist approach also provides an opportunity to explore the epistemological tensions between the various methods and to reflect on the implications of this for the trustworthiness of the insights generated by them. The Pluralism in Qualitative Research project (see Frost, 2009b) has engaged with such questions by comparing different researchers' interpretations of the same data. Lyons and Coyle (2007) present a similar endeavour in their discussion of a range of readings of one and the same dataset produced by different qualitative approaches.

Although there are not many examples of fully fledged pluralistic studies in which a dataset is analysed repeatedly using a number of entirely different qualitative methods, researchers have begun to advocate forms of binocularity (see Frosh and Young, 2008) whereby data is examined through more than one lens during the course of data analysis. For example, Frosh and Young's (2008) psychosocial analysis of narratives of brotherhood involves an initial discursive reading of their interview transcripts; this reading seeks to identify constructions of brotherhood and the discourses from which such constructions are drawn. A second reading then deploys psychoanalytic interpretative strategies to 'thicken' the initial reading; here, the focus of the enquiry is emotionality, and its aim is to deepen the researchers' understanding of what motivates participants to talk about their brothers in the way that they do.

Similarly, Eatough and Smith's (2008) approach to their interpretative phenomenological analysis of subjective experiences of anger involves navigation between different levels of interpretation, starting with a detailed phenomenological reading that takes the form of a 'thick description', which is then followed by a process of interrogating the participant's sense-making in more depth. This second level of analysis involves critically probing and then theorizing the data, thus offering a deeper hermeneutic reading. Smith at al. (2009) endorse the application of several levels of interpretation in interpretative phenomenological analysis. They invoke the hermeneutic circle, which requires the phenomenological researcher to move between the parts (such as passages in an interview transcript or particular extracts from it) and the whole (the entire transcript) so that different, and arguably increasingly sophisticated, understandings can be generated by examining the whole in the light of the parts and vice versa (see Smith et al., 2009: 104–5, for an example of this).

Another example is Langdridge's (2007) critical narrative analysis, which integrates aspects of phenomenological and narrative approaches. Critical narrative analysis seeks to offer a 'synthesis of a variety of analytical tools to better enable the analyst to work critically with the data and to shed light on the phenomenon being investigated' (Langdridge, 2007: 133). Critical narrative analysis involves six stages of analysis during which the researcher re-visits the data, each time with a different analytic focus. The initial reading (stage 1) focuses on the researcher's relationship with the text; the second reading (stage 2) identifies narratives in the text, their tone, and rhetorical function; stage 3 examines the types of self that are brought into being by the narrative(s); stage 4 is concerned with the thematic priorities of the text; stage 5 interrogates the data through the lens of critical social theory; and stage 6 produces a synthesis of the insights generated during stages 1–5.

Finally, Frost (2009a) reports a study in which she used what she describes as a 'within-method pluralistic approach' in her analysis of an interview with a woman about her experience of the transition to second-time motherhood. Here, a number of different styles of narrative analysis were applied to the data, one after another, to produce several layers of understanding of the data, with each new layer adding depth and texture to the interpretation. Frost (2009a) describes how she initially approached the interview through the lens of Labov's (1972) model so as to identify the narrative structure of the account. She then drew on Gee's (1991) model to gain a deeper understanding of the meanings contained within the elements of the story told in the interview, and this in turn allowed her to think about the interviewee's beliefs and motivations. The next step in the analysis involved the use of reflexive awareness in a further reading of the text, this time with the aim of examining the effects of the interviewer's presence during the interview. This stage in the analysis allowed Frost (2009a) to find alternative meanings in her interviewee's comments, and to adjust her understanding of the account in the light of these. In a final stage of the analysis, Frost (2009a) returned to the transcript to specifically focus on her interviewee's use of metaphors and similes. This generated further insights into the emotional impact of second-time motherhood upon her interviewee.

The idea that making room for different perspectives may facilitate rather than hinder understanding is, of course, not new. For example, Gergen (1999) has written about the concept of polyvocality and its potential contribution to new ways of understanding ourselves, and our relationships with others and with the world around us. The rationale behind advocating a pluralistic approach to qualitative research is that, given that human experience is complex, multi-layered, and multi-faceted, a methodology that aims to amplify meaning, rather than seeking to pin down meanings, may be more appropriate. Holstein and Gubrium (2000) advise that instead of seeking theoretical integration of perspectives, qualitative researchers should engage in a process of shifting between perspectives as they move through a cycle of interrogation of the data, temporarily deferring one perspective only to return to it again a little later. The authors argue that they view such an 'analytics of interpretive practice as more like a skilled juggling act' (Holstein and Gubrium, 2000: 495) than an act of synthesis. They also use the metaphor of 'shifting gear' to capture the spirit of such data-driven shifts in perspective. Their account of this process is worth quoting in full, as it offers the reader an engaging take on what is involved in such varifocal analysis:

> One can liken the operation to shifting gears whilst driving a motor vehicle equipped with a manual transmission. One mode of analysis may prove quite productive, but eventually it will strain against the resistance engendered by its own temporary analytic orientation. When the analyst notes that the analytic 'engine' is labouring under, or being constrained by, the restraints of what it is currently being 'geared' to accomplish, she can decide to virtually 'shift' analytic 'gears' in order to gain further purchase on the aspects of interpretive interplay that were previously bracketed. Just as there can be no prescription for shifting gears when driving (i.e. one can never specify in advance at what speed one should shift up or down), changing analytic brackets always remains an artful enterprise, awaiting the empirical circumstances it encounters. Its timing cannot be pre-specified. Like shifts in gears whilst driving, changes are not arbitrary or undisciplined; rather they respond to the analytic challenges at hand in a principled, if not predetermined, fashion.
>
> (Holstein and Gubrium, 2000: 502)

Another way of thinking about the kind of qualitative analysis that involves the production of a series of different, but not mutually exclusive, readings is to liken the researcher's relationship with the data to that between an interviewer and an interviewee. In other words, the researcher engages with the data by asking a series of questions of the data, and these questions move the analysis forward, in the same way that questions move a conversation forward. Here, the researcher works through the text repeatedly, asking different questions of the narrative each time. The first set of questions may be concerned with the content of what is being said, with the aim of clarifying its meaning. The next set of questions may be about the style and the tone of the account, and what is communicated in this way. The next cycle of analysis could be concerned with questions about the dominant themes that emerge from the text, and how they may resonate with discourses that are available in the wider culture. The next round of questions could focus on connections that could be made between what is being said and how it is being said. Questions could also be asked about the interaction between the interviewer and the interviewee and its implication for what was talked about and how. The list of possible questions that a researcher can ask of their data is probably endless, as unanticipated questions could be generated on the basis of answers to earlier questions. The researcher's engagement with the data itself changes the researcher's perspective and this change in perspective then informs the researcher's renewed effort to make further sense of the data by looking at it from another angle, shedding light on a different dimension of the phenomenon. From this point of view, qualitative research is about attempting to discover new aspects of a totality that can never be accessed directly or captured in its entirety.

To illustrate a way of working that allows the research to be driven by emergent questions, and to draw attention to how different epistemological perspectives can be mobilized during this process, I have described a hypothetical study involving a researcher who wants to understand what happens when someone is diagnosed with a terminal illness (Willig, 2012). I have suggested that, first of all, the researcher might want to listen to first-person accounts of this experience. To this end, she may conduct semi-structured interviews with a number of participants who have had this experience. Here, her aim would be to shed light on the experience of receiving a terminal diagnosis. At this point, the researcher adopts a realist approach, taking the accounts at face value. She may produce a thematic analysis that aims to capture and systematically represent the process of being given a terminal diagnosis. She may identify a number of interesting patterns in relation to the ways in which participants were treated by medical staff and perhaps also in the ways in which the participants' loved-ones responded to the situation. Perhaps, at this point, the researcher notices that, despite their many shared experiences with medical staff and loved-ones, the participants gave quite different meanings to their illnesses. She also notices that this seemed to inform the participants' sense of themselves as a terminally ill patient and how they felt about their illness. To better understand these differences, the researcher arranges further interviews with the participants, this time using a phenomenological approach to explore their subjective experience in greater depth. This phase of the research generates a further set of themes, this time capturing the existential dimensions of the experience of being diagnosed with a terminal illness and the range of existential meanings that can be given to such an experience. However, the researcher may also be struck by the observation that all the participants included references to the question of responsibility (for the illness) and that many of them grappled with issues around blame in their accounts. She may decide that she wants to find out more about this and adopts a social constructionist approach, focusing on the use of discourses of individual responsibility within the context of terminal illness. She returns to the data (both sets of interviews) and analyses them again, this time using a discourse analytic approach. To contextualize her participants' use of discourse in their constructions of meaning around their terminal diagnosis, the researcher also analyses newspaper articles and television documentaries about terminal illness and compares the discursive constructions used there to those deployed by the participants. There is, of course, much more that could be done to shed light on the experience of being diagnosed with a terminal illness, and additional cycles of data interrogation could be undertaken. However, even the three cycles of analysis traced in our hypothetical example demonstrate how, rather than being mutually exclusive, realist, phenomenological, and social constructionist forms of knowing can be thought of as complementary in that each provides access to different aspects of the experience of being diagnosed with a terminal illness.

Ethical implications

In the previous section, we introduced an approach to qualitative research that involves the production of a series of readings of the same data, allowing the researcher to engage with different dimensions of the material. The result of such a multi-layered analysis is what Frost (2009a: 9) describes as 'a multi-dimensional interpretation', which is potentially capable of capturing many different facets of the phenomenon under investigation. Such a multi-layered interpretation can take the form of a more narrowly focused binocularity where the data is read through two pre-determined interpretative lenses, or it can be more pluralistic in that it offers a whole series of readings that are driven by a potentially unlimited number of emergent research questions. What may be the ethical implications of a turn to forms of pluralism in qualitative interpretation? Are multi-dimensional interpretations less ethically sensitive than uni-dimensional ones? And do 'suspicious' interpretations, once they form part of a pluralistic reading, lose some of their power to impose meaning on the data? It could be argued that the more interpretations we have access to, the less likely we will be to impose any one of them to the exclusion of all other possibilities. Engaging in a pluralistic style of analysis requires the researcher to hold interpretations lightly and flexibly. The switching between interpretative lenses that characterizes a multi-layered reading of the data protects the researcher against becoming too attached to any one particular perspective. As a result, even a 'suspicious' reading, while retaining its 'prescriptive' analytic style, will lose its 'closed' quality once it becomes part of a multi-dimensional interpretation. It could be argued, then, that pluralistic qualitative analysis can be placed at the 'tentative' end of our continuum of styles of interpretation, even when the various interpretative lenses that are used in the course of such an analysis are in themselves 'prescriptive'. This means that pluralistic qualitative research provides researchers with an opportunity to engage in theory-driven, 'prescriptive' styles of analysis and to generate 'suspicious' interpretations while remaining committed to the tentativeness, openness, and explorative orientation associated with a hermeneutics of meaning-recollection. Depending on the degree of compatibility between the epistemological bases underpinning the various readings contained within a multi-dimensional interpretation, the researcher may attempt to integrate the various readings in a way that allows them to tell a coherent story about the phenomenon under investigation. Alternatively, the researcher may choose to let the readings sit alongside one another, leaving it to the reader to decide which one(s) to respond to and in what way(s). Indeed, Frosh (2007) argues that the search for coherent stories that make sense of the data is a questionable goal in qualitative analysis. He develops the argument that there are dangers associated with the desire to 'make sense' and advises that '[L]imits to making sense, to making connections, have to be set' (Frosh, 2007: 638). This is because, he argues, 'the human subject is *never* a whole, is always riven with partial drives, social discourses that frame available modes of experience, ways of being that are contradictory and reflect the shifting allegiances of power as they play across the body and the mind' (Frosh, 2007: 638; italics in original). In other words, qualitative interpretations that 'make sense' of human experience do not, in fact, reflect the nature and quality of human experience that is always and necessarily (at least somewhat) fragmentary and contradictory. This means that a researcher's attempt 'to understand' what is going on may well be based on the misplaced assumption that there is something going on that 'makes sense' and that can be understood. Frosh (2007: 644) endorses Parker's (2005b) Lacanian argument that 'we should approach a text not as something we can understand, but rather as something waiting to be opened up'; this does not mean, of course, that no meaning can be found but rather that meanings surface and slip away again as new meanings emerge.

The idea that becoming less certain about what is going on may be helpful has also been advanced within the context of existential psychotherapy where a sedimented self-structure with its rigid dispositional stances is seen to limit possibilities for experience and action (e.g. Spinelli, 1994). Within this context, the process of de-sedimentation – that is, the opening up of a person to alternative interpretations of themselves and the world around them – is desirable as it enables new ways of relating to the world. However, at the same time, Spinelli (2007) argues, a degree of sedimentation is necessary for us to be able to maintain a relatively stable worldview, including a sense of ourselves and our place in the world. It seems that narrative cohesion and a grounding in what is experienced as (relatively) fixed essences seem to be necessary for people to avoid fragmentation and to find meaning in their existence. This resonates with the concluding section of Chapter 3, where I drew attention to the psychological significance of meaning-making. I argued that, particularly at times of major changes in people's life circumstances, when their sense of identity and their place in the world are disrupted, people seek to create meaningful stories about their experiences. Making sense of what is happening to us constitutes an important part of finding ways of coping with life events. So while offering multi-layered interpretations of an account may reduce the ethical risks associated with the imposition of 'closed' readings produced by an expert researcher, the promotion of multiple and potentially conflicting readings can also present ethical challenges, especially where no attempt is made to integrate the diverse readings in some way. A 'polymorphism of marginal, "disintegrated" qualitative research', to borrow Frosh's (2007: 644) terms, constitutes an interesting alternative to qualitative researchers' traditional commitment to narrative coherence, but it also interferes with what to many people, including many of our research participants, is a highly valuable and indeed necessary process, namely that of giving meaning to experience. Qualitative researchers have commented on interviewees' efforts to interpret their own experiences within the context of the research interview; indeed, interpretative phenomenological analysis explicitly engages with a 'double hermeneutic' that involves the researcher making sense of the participant's own interpretation of their experience (see Smith and Osborne, 2003; Smith et al., 2009). Sometimes interviewees will invite or even urge the interviewer to provide them with interpretations to assist them in the task of 'making sense' of what they are experiencing (e.g. Fulder-Heyd, 2011). It could be argued that an analytic strategy that seeks to 'disrupt' and 'disorganise' (see Frosh, 2007: 644) research participants' accounts and which, therefore, conflicts with the participants' own declared aim to 'make sense' of their experience, may raise ethical concerns about the effects of such a strategy upon the participant, especially where participants have access to the researcher's (multi-layered and potentially disruptive and disorganizing) readings.

Closing reflections

I would like to conclude by proposing that, whatever style of interpretation we choose to adopt within the context of a particular study, it is essential that we remember that the act of interpretation is both a responsibility and a privilege. When we analyse a text, we transform it (and ourselves) in the process. Interpretation always involves both the opening up and the closing down of possibilities, and it always has consequences. Throughout this book, I have drawn attention to the ethical implications of interpretative activity, and, although at times these considerations have perhaps raised more questions than they have answered, I would argue that putting ethics at the heart of interpretative research is vital if we are to embrace the 'turn to interpretation' in qualitative research. I would argue that the process of reflecting on the ethics of interpretation is valuable regardless of the outcome of such reflections. In other words, perhaps there is no such thing as an 'ethical interpretation'; however, there is an ethical way of engaging in the process of making interpretations. I hope that the reflections presented in this book will encourage discussion and debate around what we are doing when we are interpreting other people's accounts of their experiences, and therefore promote responsible, reflexive, and flexible interpretation as a form of ethical research practice.

Appendices

I A conversation with Professor Stephen Frosh

Stephen Frosh and Carla Willig

(CW = Carla Willig; SF = Stephen Frosh)

CW: Maybe we can start with the most predictable question I guess, which would be what in your view is 'interpretation'? Do you have a definition? Or how would you explain to an alien, for example, what it is?

SF: Gosh. Well, it's as always, it's going to be one of the most complicated questions. I mean there are some very clear answers within certain theoretical paradigms, in particular in relation to psychoanalysis. So, you know, if you are going to talk about it psychoanalytically, interpretation always refers to some unconscious meaning that's found in whatever material it is that you're observing or hearing. But I think I always use it more broadly than that, to mean an act of sense-making, in which the interpreter, perhaps the researcher in our context, imposes some kind of structure on the material that they're getting.

CW: Right.

SF: And that's variable, because it does include quite a lot of things which I think other people might consider just to be at a descriptive level rather than an interpretive level. Because the act of description itself imposes structure. And even, I don't know if you've seen the book I did with an ex PhD student of mine, Peter Emerson?

CW: Yes.

SF: It's on critical narrative analysis. You see there we argue that the act of transcribing is a very active process of interpretation. We tried to show that the different modes of transcription can produce very different readings of the material you have transcribed. You are already involved in a process of sense-making: all the decisions you make about what to select, about how to portray, how to chunk sentences, it's all interpretive. So, there's a problem with what I just said, which is that interpretation then can become much too broad as a concept. And it starts to mean anything that happens, you know, interactionally even. But I don't quite, I don't really see a way of escaping that, and I think once you've started as a researcher to structure what has been said, if we talk about interviews in particular, there are acts of interpretation going on.

CW: Right. So meaning-making in its widest sense involves interpretation?

SF: Yes it does, I'm sure it does, because it involves the act of participation of the analyst, researcher, whoever.

CW: OK. Because we bring something to it. So when you mentioned at first the definition from psychoanalysis, which is much more specific than the general one, does that mean there are levels of interpretation?

SF: No, I'm not sure that it does mean that. Because that would assume buying in totally to the idea of an unconscious and while I do adopt a psychoanalytic frame for my own thinking, I wouldn't want to constrain my understanding of interpretation from that. If I think for instance of students, PhD students that I've supervised, whose work has not been psychoanalytic, but still constantly trying to understand what the interpretive frame is that they're deploying. And how their own acts of interpretation are occurring, even if they're not using the psychoanalytical one. I would want to use psychoanalytic interpretation as an example for an especially heavily theoretically driven mode of interpretation, which is still an act of sense-making on the part of the analyst involved. It just happens to be that there are certain conditions for psychoanalytic interpretation. For example, it refers to the past, or it makes sense of breaks in discourse by reference to unconscious processes. There are conditions for calling something a psychoanalytic interpretation.

CW: Right.

SF: But that doesn't mean other things aren't interpretive.

CW: Yes.

SF: They just may not fulfil those conditions for psychoanalytical interpretation.

CW: Right. So, there's a specific theoretical base that is used to make these interpretations?

SF: Yeah. I mean, to give an example, we have quite often students who are very enthusiastic about working psychoanalytically, and I have not uncommonly dissuaded them from being too psychoanalytic in their work because it doesn't seem necessary. It doesn't mean that I don't regard what they've done as interpretive. And that would be true of many students doing narrative and discourse analytic work. They're doing interpretation, I am sure they are, it's just not psychoanalytic interpretation.

CW: So when you said sometimes it's not necessary to do this more specifically psychoanalytic interpretation, how do we decide whether or not it's necessary? Because I'm thinking, when you said that, I immediately thought about clients and, you know, sometimes one might go there, and other times decide not to go there. How would you decide?

SF: Yeah, I'm not sure that the right word is 'necessary'. OK a few things about this. First of all, are we talking about the research context here primarily?

CW: Mainly, yes.

SF: Because I think the difference between research and clinical work is really important in this. Despite there being quite a lot of apparent face similarities between the activities that might go on in a clinical situation and the kind of narrative or clinically oriented research interview, I think there are quite important differences.

And those really have to do with the relationship that evolves between the researcher or the therapist, and the participant or the client. So, if I could take that step first and then come back to your question. So the first thing, which I think really one learns from psychoanalysis and probably from all clinical work, is just how heavily contextualized any interpretation is, and how much it relates to the, how much it refers to the relationship, in which it is embedded. And psychoanalytic interpretation is really clear about that. I mean an interpretation takes place, you know, most fundamental interpretation takes place within the context of a transference relationship; it only makes sense within that context. If you're my patient and you say something to me as your therapist or analyst, my understanding of all of what you've said would be governed by my reading of what kind of relationship you're imagining you're having with me, and what kind of relationship I'm imagining I'm having with you. And the capacity to reflect on that is really important for thinking about what interpretation to put on your words; whether it's me just understanding them, or whether it's literally an interpretation of the kind where I give something back to you and hopefully it will change your view, that kind of psychoanalytic intervention or interpretation. And that's true, of course, in a research setting as well as in the therapeutic setting. The participant in research is involved in some kind of relationship with the researcher and imagines something about it. But what you'd have much less of in the research environment, almost always, is evidence that enables you to understand what that relationship is, particularly compared with a therapeutic relationship, particularly in one where you see people for a long time. But actually it doesn't even require a long time, if you'd seen them repeatedly at least, over a reasonable period of time, you can start to kind of make some reasonable judgements about what might be going on and you can test your interpretations a bit, you can try them out, see what happens. In the research situation that's very unlikely, it's very unusual, although it does happen. We've become increasingly interested in our department in ethnography, partly because the continual relationship that ethnographic research gives you with often a small group of participants is a bit more like, it's not the same, but it's a bit more like that repetitive, you know, that durable therapeutic relationship. You start to learn the culture you're investigating. But most qualitative research isn't like that. Most of it is still single interviews. And even repeated interviews, which I'm in favour of, you know, two interviews, which I think is a good thing, it's a big move, much better than just the one but still not enough to really judge. So that is a long answer to your question. Well, I can't remember the question actually, but probably it was about . . .

CW: . . . when is it necessary?

SF: Yeah, when is it necessary? So the first thing is while it might be necessary for certain kinds of research question, most of the time the issue isn't whether it is necessary but whether it's possible. And that's the warning, that's the health warning to my students who become very enthusiastic about using the psychoanalytic frame. I'm thinking, for instance, they might want to do something like what Wendy (Hollway) does, that kind of counter-transference work where how what they might feel about the material might be telling them something about it. And we are much more cautious about how confident you can be about interpretations you might make with really little knowledge of a person. And, secondly, there's very little if any facility to make that interpretation in a live way so that the person you're interviewing or you're talking to can come back on you and you can think about what that response was like, which seems to me an absolute *sine qua non* for what goes on in the clinical situation. You say something and the person responds to that, and although what they say doesn't absolutely determine what you think of the validity of what your interpretation has been, it influences it. It's a way of judging it. Do you get a deepening of affect, does something new happen? I mean these are the kind of questions that you might ask and if that happens you might think, I'm on to something. Or does it just get a flat response? Even a flat agreement might make you think, 'it isn't really interesting; what I just said doesn't really do anything, it's not really an interpretation'. It's very rare that you can do that in research. So, in answer to your question about when it is necessary, I think that's not normally what the issue is. The issue is more, given the conditions of research, that it's not actually possible. So we need to tell students and other researchers to be cautious. It doesn't mean that you can't use the psychoanalytic framework for your understanding, the theoretical work, and so on, but be cautious about whether they think they're doing psychoanalytic interpretive work. So I guess I'm saying two contradictory things or partly contradictory, but they're in tension with one another. On the one hand you have to be very careful about what you call an interpretation, and on the other everything you do is interpretive (laughs).

CW: Yes, that's true. And as you were talking about the clinical situation and how that's very different because the client or the patient will contribute, it just made me think that really, maybe what we're saying here is that interpretation is a joint venture. Even though the client or the patient might not be kind of consciously thinking, 'I'm now interpreting'. But the amount of input they have, and the amount of influence they have over what you would then pursue with your interpretations is very large as an input. So is it then a joint interpretation? Or more of a joint interpretation than it would be, if you just read a transcript of an interview and analysed it?

SF: Again there's so much going on in that question. I think the first thing I'd say is that, you know, well, yes of course, of course it's joint in a sense. If you set up a kind of conversational situation in which things move backwards and forwards, in a relatively open way between the researcher and the participant, an active joint interpretation is starting to take place. You're working on a kind of joint narrative, if you like. On the other hand, most qualitative research isn't like that. You do an interview, and then some time later you transcribe, and you sit down and you look at it and you try to make sense of it. Now that, I mean that's not a joint thing. There's nothing joint happening there. The data might be jointly generated, that's fine, and maybe you can be thinking about what the relational context did to the generation of the data, and that might affect your interpretive work. So, there is some link there between what this person did or said to you and how this might affect the way in which you interpret. It's not like there's no connection, but it is still clearly you who is doing that. The other thing I wanted to say though is a bit different. I think rather than thinking about interpretation as something done together, I think it's more that interpretation is always impossible. And that's both a theoretical and a kind of practical thing. You know, it's always impossible. I mean the theoretical side of that, I think, is very heavily influenced by psychoanalysis in my thinking. But also elsewhere, we've done a lot on the Judith Butler stuff, about the limits of what – what does she call it? Basically what she calls the occluded elements of selfhood; particularly in the book *Giving an Account of Oneself*, where what she works on are those impossibilities of knowing both areas of oneself and of the other. And of course that has got a strong psychoanalytical frame in it. She uses Laplanche. Do you know all that work?

CW: Not the Butler book. Not that one.

SF: I really recommend it. It's very strong, very interesting, and what she does, which I think is relevant to this, in that book there's stuff on ethical violence. Again this might interest you because you've got a very strong interest in the ethics of all this work. Ethical violence, it's kind of forcing somebody into a frame, which doesn't fit them. But done without any assumptions that there is a frame that would fit them, a better one. And what she describes very well there, which is a familiar idea, but I just think she does it well, is that the way in which you might recognize another as a human subject, is precisely by recognizing that there's an area of their subject-hood and subjectivity you cannot have access to. And that's precisely what distinguishes them as a separate subject. At that moment where you say, 'I understand you completely', and offer them an interpretation and know what's going on, there's a kind of colonizing act taking place in which they disappear as a separate subject. They become somehow translated into the same terms that you use for understanding yourself and the world. If, by contrast, what you have is a position in which you recognize areas of, not occluded areas, let's call it the unconscious, within your own subject-hood, and recognize that that exists within other subjects as well, then you're left with a position in which the capacity to understand each other is actually marked by what we call epistemic limits. You know, the limit is what we can know about them. Not by our capacity to read them accurately but rather by our capacity to respect that point in which that ends. So when I say, I think interpretation is impossible, actually I mean that quite seriously. It's not just because there are lots and lots of different frames you can put around that, although of course there are lots of discursive possibilities and lots of ways to interpret things. And interpretation changes with social context and changes with historical moment, all these things are completely true. But it's also, you know, on top of that there's a kind of radical impossibility of ever knowing anybody else completely. And it's very important. It's a kind of an ethical act to hold on to that impossibility. Well, I mean, all interpretations have got to be tentative, not just because you say, 'Well, if I was a black woman, I would be reading this differently', you know, from how I do because I'm a white man, or something like that. All of that is true. If I was reading Dora in 1905 rather than 2011, you know, I would read the Dora case differently, yes, that's absolutely the case. But it's more than that. You know it's more than that.

CW: Yes.

SF: And this is why in a way we are quite taken with that whole Lacanian idea of looking not for interpretations, but for interruptions. Something that you do to make things change slightly. Not that it inscribes a certain mode of meaning, announcing the truth of what something means, but rather an act that sort of produces something new.

CW: Yes, yes. It sounds a bit like it's more of a philosophical insight really, about the nature of selfhood. And in fact it reminded me a bit of Sartre as well, his notion of how we make the other into an object, once we try to understand them in this kind of way. So they lose their subject-hood already by us interpreting them in that way.

SF: Yeah, there is some of that influence.

CW: But then it led me on to wondering, as you were talking about that, then why do it at all? You know, why do we analyse interviews and try and make sense of them? You know what, what is that about then? Why do we . . .?

SF: Well, I was really influenced by something a few years ago that we did here. We did an interdisciplinary day called 'After method'. And it was basically a meeting between humanities students and social science students in the college, run by various people; various staff members came to it. It was a very good and interesting day. One thing that happened that day was that Margie Wetherell came, and she presented some material and got everybody to work in small groups to analyse this interview material. And she gave some background, she talked a bit about her mode of discourse analysis, and as ever she was very clever and very charming. And it was really good, all she did, and then as I remember Steve Connor, who is a professor of English, he runs the London Consortium. So he spoke up in the sort of feedback when people talked about what sense they made of it, and lots of things were happening. You could see alternative readings and that was fine. And you could see everybody trying to identify themes in some way and draw them together and categorize them and say, 'This is really what's happening'. And it really struck him what the difference was between the kind of social scientific way of doing this analysis and a literary way. Because he read it, he said, as the kind of beginnings of a radio play. And if he was going to do a literary interpretation about it, it wouldn't be to try and compress it and find the kernel of meaning, you know, the core constructs, or whatever it was. It would be to elaborate it. To imagine what might've happened next. What else might be going on, you know, who else might be in the story, what the person's mother might say about it, and actually expand it. Now, of course, it is a different mode. And whether that's interpretation or something else, I'm not quite sure, but it's quite an interesting epistemological point. Thinking not just methodologically about what constitutes knowledge. I mean, he is probably right and wrong, because not all literary theorists will do that and a lot of them do try to pin things down. But for that mode of literary analysis at least, that kind of romantic mode, you are still creating meaning. But it's being done very explicitly in a mode of the imaginary where some connection is being made between what you find – and in that case on a page maybe in the interview – and what you see, and what you think is possible. So I think it's possible to consider interpretation in lots of different ways. I mean one way is something which might elaborate the possibilities of meaning which you find in situations. Another way, of course, might be just to know that what you're doing is giving you a partial story. And to announce that in a very clear way, that there is this thing going on, and connect it with what's happening with other people. And that might produce some new alternative ways of thinking about things, particularly if there's a kind of received wisdom in there that we are wanting to contest. Therapeutically, I think, it's usually there to move someone along, to give them ideas that something else is possible. I just had another student, Myrnal Gower, who got her PhD a couple of weeks ago. Her topic was adult parenting, what's it like to be a parent of an adult, where the children are in their thirties and forties, that kind of thing. She was interested in that topic for lots of reasons. But the methodology of the qualitative bit of it was to interview people and then to analyse the material, doing that in a narrative analytic framework from five different perspectives.

CW: Right.

SF: So what she did was, first of all she read the whole interview. Then she identified two narratives in each interview. For each of those narratives she would do a reading, which was based on that kind of Gee-type of structuring thing, which is basically reading for meaning. She looked at pronominal use to see what subject was used – 'I, you and he', and that kind of stuff. What could be said from that. She looked at the social assumptions that were present in the material where you could see people draw from received ideas, for example, about what a parent should be, or about independency, continual dependency or whatever. And she looked at the relationship between the interviewee and herself as the interviewer. What she could see coming out from the page when she was reflecting on it later. I mean, I haven't done it coherently, but you can hear that there were five overlapping readings. And, of course, it's very difficult to summarize that at the end. Yet things do float together, something is kind of consistent. When you start with one reading, it semi-determines your other readings. You have got to be careful not to repeat yourself all the time. But, all together, different things arise. It's suggestive, and I'm not sure that one can do much more than that. So, the point I'm trying to make about it is how things change as well. Repeated interviews is something you get very familiar with. I was just reading, actually over lunch, *The Psychologist*. Occasionally I'm astounded that nothing changes (laughs). And how the obvious is sort of stated as completely new. There was a little article in there about reactivity, which means how you prevent your research from being thrown off course by the fact that people react to it. This article could have been written thirty or forty years ago, I'm not sure. But I mean the point is such an obvious one, that we make all the time, you know. You interview me today about my thinking about interpretation. Then I talk to someone else about it tomorrow, and because you've interviewed me, I have different thoughts about it.

CW: Yes.

SF: OK. So, how could you ever know, what I think about . . .

CW: Yes, indeed.

SF: . . . about interpretation because it's got to shift. It should shift because otherwise there's nothing happening.

CW: That reminds me of Hans Cohn. Do you know him? He's an existential therapist who died not so long ago, and his idea of amplification of meaning as the basis for his therapeutic work. So that interpretation is about opening up rather than boiling something down to some underlying structures.

SF: Right.

CW: The idea is to do pretty much what you've just described. To amplify by following routes of thoughts or associations, and allowing the client to open up, which isn't to find out what they're really thinking all along, but to really allow them to pursue a journey of thinking and feeling which perhaps wasn't possible beforehand.

SF: Yeah.

CW: So interpretation is really about kind of expanding outwards, rather than boiling it down to something.

SF: It's very interesting because the group analysts used the same word, which makes it very similar.

CW: OK.

SF: Amplification, but it happens within the group. Each group member can do that kind of thing.

CW: I see.

SF: And I think that's a very useful idea. Actually I think a lot of psychoanalysts would agree, although they probably wouldn't use that terminology. But that's what they do, you know, so the patient sort of speaks and then the analyst says something which is meant to make it easier in some way for the patient to continue to talk (laughs) . . .

CW: Yeah.

SF: . . . to continue to explore something, to take in something new, to allow something to emerge, whatever it is. That sounds to me like a similar process. Of course, if you say, 'You are in love with your mother', that doesn't do the same thing.

CW: It doesn't, no (laughs).

SF: (laughs)

CW: But then again, you could still use this sort of technique of opening up and allowing things to develop outwards while the purpose of this journey is still to bring it back to the root of the metaphorical tree, to see what is there, underlying. And I guess that would be different from saying, you know, you could end up on a different tree?

SF: I think you're probably right.

CW: I think this leads me actually on to the next question, which is probably even more difficult really in a way because it's more personal. What does interpretation mean to you? I mean, is it something you find exciting to do? Or do you see yourself as practising it in any way? Or, you know, what is your relationship with interpretation? What does it mean to you?

SF: (laughs) I'm sure that's the first time I've been asked that. Hmm, interesting question, isn't it? (pause) I mean, I will have to try to think about it from practice up really. So, first of all, there's often a set of dilemmas which I find myself having to work out. Particularly again with PhD students. For example, I had a PhD student who was very committed to accurately representing her research participants. Very identified with them in some way for whatever reason. She was researching what it's like to have an ADHD child. She was doing discursive analysis actually, and it was kind of breaking up the material. So she would look at how certain discourses arose and she was really pulled into wanting to talk about the individual mothers that she was interviewing. She felt very strongly for them, wanted to do something to be of help to them and didn't want to misrepresent them in any way. And there was a kind of tentativeness in that. I mean, I talk about somebody else, I feel the same thing myself, you know, just trying to answer your question. A tentativeness there between feeling as a researcher, you know, you can't know this other person. All you can do is struggle as well as you can, knowing your limits to represent them in a sympathetic way which says what you do honestly believe they are trying to say to the best of your ability, knowing you are going to fail, all that kind of stuff. Which I take also actually to be one of the things that went on in say Standpoint work. Those kind of things in which the researcher articulates the position of others so that their voice gets heard in a particular research terrain. So that's on the one hand. And on the other hand as a researcher, but also just as somebody thinking about the material, you have the right to form your own view of it. And that view is informed by certain knowledge perspectives, which is dangerously close, I suppose, to taking an expert view in which you say, 'Well, because I have read other people's work on this, because I have seen the theoretical frame, because I've read lots of these interviews with lots of other people, I have other people's theory, I've seen what other people say, therefore I might have a better understanding of what this person is talking about than they have themselves'.

So that's the difficulty, that's obviously a power–knowledge nexus. Clearly a very obvious one, which always makes me, you know, personally uncomfortable. Because I do feel both sides of those things. I do think I actually have a right to say, 'You might be wrong in what you said about yourself'. I even have a theoretical position which acknowledges that. It doesn't mean I'm right necessarily, but I might be more right than you are. I might be saying something about you that is in some way more truthful to the feeling that you're representing, or to how you actually understand that experience, even if you described it, and you think in some other words about it. You know, I might understand it better than you and that might be a necessary thing. Because we have certain kinds of privileged access to our own experience but we don't have absolute access to it. I mean that's where I also have a model of the unconscious which I constantly use.

On the other hand, to say I know you better than you do yourself is complete arrogance. You know, how can I? Especially when I've just met you. And I got one interview with you. How can I know all that? How can I arrogate to myself the right to interpret? I'm not sure if I've answered your question, but I mean part of my answer at least is that it leaves me with a quite considerable sense of discomfort. I'm not sure if that's a bad thing, but it does. It's an uncomfortable position to acknowledge both. That you need to do interpretive work, that's what you do, that's what you do anyway, you know, that's what we do obviously. We interpret all the time. And then, on the other hand, to know that that's also part of kind of our nexus. In our department, in which of course we are trying to challenge those power things, we find ourselves in a complicated relationship with this. Again, I mean, I keep talking about my students but that's because pretty much all my empirical work over the last few years and the various things I've been doing, it's been through my students. I had a very good student, who has just got his PhD a couple of weeks ago, Girish Jivaji. He is interested in maths in schools, he's a maths teacher. And interested in the experience of being good at maths, what it means to be good at maths. So he spent time, two years actually, but we used data only from his second year, in a maths class for year eleven, working as a teaching assistant but basically observing and then interviewing, and so on. And in his presentation of his observations in his PhD, he writes up an observation that he might've made on a particular date. He writes separately in italics his understanding of that, and then he has a separate section using the comments facility in Word. He has separate, marginalized comments which comment on what he's noticed about the interpretation, the interpretive grid that he's using in the interpretation that he has made. Of course, it can come over as a bit twee, I think in places it is. You know, it's a bit forced, but actually I don't think he was. He really liked these children, working with these children. He found himself doing interpretative work with them, and also the teacher, observing what the teacher is doing and saying, you know ...

CW: Right.

SF: ... and then he thinks, you know, this teacher seems to be involved in what she's doing. Now, why did she say that, why is it that she decided to teach this function in this way to them? And then he realized actually he's already in something kind of rivalrous between him and the maths teacher as well. And that's all incorporated in the presentation. Difficult to know quite what to do with it once it's done. I mean, other than comment on it, which he does; it's a Foucauldian and Lacanian thesis. But I think, you know, sometimes it's forced but I think it's genuinely principled as well, and it arises out of that same discomfort.

CW: Yes.

SF: Where you say, I want to be like you, and with you, and so on and see myself in you. And at the same time not, you know. I'm in a different structural position. It's a totally familiar situation (laughs).

CW: Yes. So it's kind of a dual process. I mean, with the student it was actually two columns. It was very literal. The way it seems to be happening, also in your mind, would be kind of running alongside your interpretations, there's another little voice that says, 'Yes, but, remember ...'.

SF: Yeah, exactly. That's exactly what to think about it. That's exactly actually what happens on the page in that thesis, so that's quite an interesting one.

CW: Yes, and as you were talking, I was thinking, really, as a client I would really want my therapist to have that dual thought process because if they were simply on the one road thinking, 'Ah, this is what this means. She's saying this because of that', you know, I would feel quite alienated from that person ...

SF: Yes.

CW: … imposing meanings.

SF: Is your book restricted to research, interpretive research?

CW: It is about research but I'm obviously influenced by my experience of therapy in the sorts of questions that I'm asking. When I was not doing therapy work and was just doing qualitative research, a lot of these questions I wouldn't have thought of as being relevant really to the process. So in a way doing the therapy work has made me more aware, you know, as a researcher as well. OK. So just the final question on this personal relationship with interpretation. We've been talking about interpreting participants' talk and data and so on but obviously interpretation is also something we use to understand ourselves better as well. So, the question is really about to what extent you found that having gained so much knowledge, understanding, and practice in applying interpretative frames, does it feel like it's helped you to live your own life? Or do you feel that it's been quite a separate thing from your own life?

SF: (laughs) Yeah, it is pretty difficult, isn't it? Because how can you know the answer to that question? I mean, I dare say it does make a difference in the way I think about myself. I mean, I think in all genuineness, the lesson I've mostly got was, how little it is one knows. Because when people talk about themselves, if you give them the right conditions, they can say very interesting things and important things. But mostly they don't. And partly that's because most of the time people don't have the conditions under which they can really speak. Whether it's conditions of trust, or being taken seriously, you know, or given the language. Whatever it is, certain kinds of cultural capital or whatever it is, if you don't have those, you notice that. But also, so much of what people say about themselves kind of seems so banal, you know. And so when you turn that back on yourself, and I turn that back on myself, actually the same thing is true for me, completely true (laughs). When I want to talk about myself, I would talk about other people; it's just what I've been doing here today. What I learn from outside. But actually being able to reflect is a very complicated, difficult thing. So I think that's a big list.

CW: Right.

SF: Yeah.

CW: Thinking about the thing you said about interruption and the Lacanian idea, I was just thinking how sometimes when we think about our experience and sort of searching to understand, you know, for example, thinking 'Why am I doing this again? Why can't I stop doing this?', wanting answers, as though the answer would change what I do, which it probably wouldn't anyway. So the idea of just saying, 'Hang on, maybe this is a waste of energy searching for this answer. Maybe I should just throw something in there that's completely unrelated, or stop asking the question'?

SF: Yeah. I don't know how it works exactly, you know, it's like the Lacanian short session thing. That whole idea that the client comes to you and starts telling the story they told a million times before and the way you just say, 'I'm not interested. Come back when you've got something interesting to say'. You know, that's incredibly arrogant and very aggressive. It's a very aggressive way of doing work. And I'm not suggesting that researchers should do that. I don't think that researchers in particular have the right to be very aggressive in their questioning somebody. But, I mean, you can ask people, I suppose, to consider things in a different way, in a way they might've not thought before. Knowing that that puts the status of the information they have given you, the knowledge, into doubt.

CW: Yes. Yes.

SF: It has to, all the time.

CW: Yes.

SF: Can I say something else? Actually it's not quite in your question, which was about participants and observing and all that, but a lot of interpretation is actually on text rather than on people. And it's very important, that difference. I mean, the text has already been worked on in some way. And as I said right at the start, in my view that act of creating the text itself is interpretive, certainly selective. Interpretive in a broader sense of deciding what's important and what's not, or what ways to carve up meaning. Once you've then got it, the work you do on it is textual work. It's kind of commentary and that's even more the case when the text is not one that you have produced through your decisions. And a lot of social science work, discourse analytic work is always done on the pre-received text.

CW: Yes. Naturally occurring so called, texts.

SF: Yeah. Which might be anything. It might be the brochure you use for a certain place or a news item, although there isn't a lot of that actually. But they're found, they've not been created by the researcher, although they're still being selected by them.

CW: Yes.

SF: So there are lots of traditions of textual interpretation which are also, I think, really important and interesting to draw on. And I've been particularly interested in classical Jewish texts. Because they are really powerfully performative. They're not just texts people read for pleasure, they kind of direct people's lives. They're religious texts which tell you what you are supposed to do. And when you look at them, what you realize really quickly is they don't do that at all. The texts themselves might be available to all sorts of alternative interpretations. And then when you look again at the traditions, certainly in the Jewish tradition, you find actually lots of alternative interpretations of these texts are made but only some of them become hegemonic. And that's a very interesting process, I think, because it's not just like a literary text on interpreting George Eliot or something like that. These religious texts are extremely powerful, precisely because they often determine the way in which people live their lives. So it's very interesting, when you look at those, I think, to find actually that there're modes of interpretation, even in orthodox traditions, which undercut the dominant ones. And gaining access to those, actually opening out subjugated discourses, you know, subjugated interpretations can be very important.

CW: Yes, and we've seen that now with the Koran. And people really trying to emphasize their reading to justify how things are done.

SF: Yes.

CW: I haven't read it myself but you hear that people claim almost the opposite is being said in the same document.

SF: Absolutely, absolutely. Yes.

CW: But then it makes me think about the ethics. And actually my next question is about ethical issues in interpretation. Just now you were talking about texts that exist in a culture and within history, that can be interpreted differently at different times, and that have really important consequences for people and how they live. But they are kind of disembodied texts, they don't belong to one person. While a lot of what we do in research is about really wanting to study the person through the text. And when we are studying the text, we kind of think that the text is a way to the person, a lot of the time.

SF: Yeah, yeah.

CW: And for me, you know, just thinking about the ethics now, I had such a different response when you're talking about the former type of text. I feel it's completely fine to have lots of different readings. It feels really positive, you know, opening up different discursive positions within that. Because it's a text, it's not a person. But if you said the same thing about somebody's interview or a diary entry or something like that, I would immediately feel, 'Yes, but hang on, but you know, is this really what the person meant, or how would they feel if they heard that?'

SF: But what if they are a novelist and they have written a novel?

CW: Well then I don't know. They might (laughs) . . .

SF: (laughs) There's a tradition in psychoanalysis, a hopeless literary tradition was to read as if it gave you access to the mind of the author. And lots of people still do that.

CW: Yes, yes.

SF: And that's been well and truly deconstructed. I mean that idea that somehow you can do that in any way at all . . . Yeah, so OK, sorry, but I have interrupted you.

CW: We were talking about the ethical kind of dimension of a very pluralistic approach to data and maybe producing very contradictory readings, or different conflicting readings. And within that what is the role of the person who generated this text in the first place that is leading off in all these different directions? Do we have any kind of responsibility to keep going back to them and checking with them that we haven't ended up somewhere where they wouldn't want us to? Who does it belong to in a way? You know, do they still own this text?

SF: So what do you think? (laughs)

CW: (laughs) I find it very difficult. I'm still reluctant to publish any case work with clients. Even if I anonymize it and change the identifying details, I just feel I would be betraying this person if I wrote about them in that way. I find that really, you know, really difficult.

SF: Yeah (pause) I think it's really difficult, isn't it? I mean, there's another difference between clinical work and research in there. In terms of the contract you have with your participant, you've not made a contract to trying to help, in inverted commas, a participant. Whatever their fantasy might be regarding what the research might do for them. So there's a slight difference, I suppose, but it doesn't really get to the heart of way you're saying. I mean I'm really dubious, I suppose, about this assumption about a necessary relationship between the text and the person that's produced it. And yet, I could also see what the problem is with assuming there's no relationship at all. Of course there is. There's a relationship. And it's also true what you say, that the reason why people do this work in research terms is to understand something, somehow, about the person behind it better, you know. So simply writing a radio play, based on what you've got from your participant, although it's something you could do, it would be an interesting and entertaining thing to do, but it's not the same as understanding them better.

CW: Yes. Isn't it?

SF: Yeah there is an issue about that, I guess.

CW: But then we could ask and pick up on something you said earlier about the student who is very highly motivated to study a particular group of people, and perhaps really wants to understand herself better. Because the group of people shares an experience, perhaps, that she herself had. So this motivation, and also the sense of wanting to protect the participant, is perhaps partly about oneself as well then, if the research is quite personal?

SF: Yes (pause) I don't know what I think about what you just said actually, Carla. I'm just trying to think it through a little bit. There are a few different things. One is that the text being produced is a piece of work – this is something we talked about earlier – that happens between the researcher and the participant, if we just think about the interview situation for the moment because it is the easiest one. So it's not a simple product of what the person themselves, the participant, said or what they're like. It's a piece of performance, you know, something that is constructed at that time. And I wouldn't want to go as far as to say, 'Well it's random you know, another time they would produce the complete opposite', or something like that. I don't believe that there's no relationship between that text and the sorts of ways in which they normally think about themselves and account for themselves. There is a relationship between them. And it might be closer, you know, it might be quite a close one at times, when the interviews have really got to something that's of importance to them. Nevertheless, it's not the same thing as having direct access to their experience. You know, it's an account produced in the crucible of a piece of work that's done between two people. So in that sense, trying to understand that has to be separated from trying to understand the person, so called, behind it. And I guess maybe, the way to think about it is that we can only try to understand a text. And that it's a separate piece of work to think about what the relationship might be between understanding that and what might have been going on for the person. So, you're the mother of this ADHD child, say, and you give me an account of what a relief it was to have the diagnosis. At that point you suddenly felt it wasn't your fault. It wasn't your bad mothering. It was something in the child. That discourse becomes the dominant one, which was true for many of my students' participants actually. Diagnosis was relief because it removes blame from them at least for a while. I mean,

I don't actually have to speculate whether that's true or not of you. That's how I understand this text. That's what this text says. It says this speaker in this text is describing that experience. I might actually have to do another piece of work in thinking, 'Well, what brought that about in that moment in the interview?' You know, what was being drawn out? And how strongly would you feel that I've given the context, with all the other things that might have been going on with you? That might be in a separate piece of work. Maybe there's something to be thought about there, in relation to a differentiation between the thing I have in front of me, and the relationship between that thing and this other experience?

CW: Yes. So being an ethical researcher would mean not refraining from doing the interpretation, but it would mean being very clear and explicit in the write-up that you're interpreting this text and really avoiding any slippage in language that would suggest that you're interpreting the person or the person's experience?

SF: Yeah, that's good. Yeah, I think that's a good point. Yeah. It also points to the importance of having the interviewer very present in the text that you are interpreting. I mean, again, it's a banal point but people still don't do it.

CW: Yes. Yes. So that might be one way to try to be ethical . . .

SF: Yes, it helps, it helps. It reminds you that this is a piece of work that was done between the two of you. Rather than it just being the idea that I've just written down what you've said, and what you've said is true.

CW: Yes. My final question is something about your view about the role or use of interpretation in qualitative research in the UK at this point in time. Do you feel there've been changes with that? And what do you think will happen in the future, in terms of where qualitative research is going with interpretation?

SF: Yeah, I don't know.

CW: And where should it be going?

SF: Actually, I have not enough knowledge on that at the moment. My impression is that it has moved forward quite a lot, I think, if we think of the time period of about twenty years. So, I mean basically since *Discourse and Social Psychology* was published twenty-five years ago. The turn to language, the whole discourse thing which swept the whole social sciences anyway, made interpretation, linguistic interpretation, very central. It became a very central idea in all social sciences research. I think that was helpful. It did produce much better thinking about reflexivity, Bourdieu, and so on in social sciences, sociology in particular, all that work, which is relatively recent. You know, it was obviously visible, and in some way there's a return to earlier modes of work in some of this. But nevertheless, it was very, very noticeable. Well, certainly for someone like me. I did my Psychology degree in the 1970s, and a PhD in the early 1980s. You know, this kind of feels like it came afterwards, and it was quite dramatic and enlivening. When I started working here, which was 1979, you couldn't do anything that was qualitative work. You still can't do much in the psychology department (laughs), but in social psychology, discursive work is much broader now than it was, although there's a retrenchment going on. It seems to me that the whole business of top-down versus bottom-up kind of interpretive work which is part of the debate between Margy (Wetherell) and Wendy (Hollway) which we talked about before you turned the tape on, and also which was addressed in a paper I did with Peter Emerson years ago called 'Interpretation and over-interpretation'.

CW: Yes, I have read that.

SF: And that debate I think, I mean a lot of debates look sterile, looking back on them. But it was probably necessary in terms of the timing of it. But I don't think people are that interested in that any more. I mean there's criticism of things that are too top-down. There's also criticism, I think, of the things which pretend to be bottom-up, and yet, you know, there's a theoretical framing going on for them anyway. I suppose all I'm saying is that this whole supposed opposition between surface and depth, between what lies at the discursive level and what lies at the unconscious level, I think people are less worried about that now. And to me, that's quite a good move forward. It has to do with the idea of the constitution of the human subject, you know, as something in motion, where there's constant sort of rolling up past experiences into new ones. And reflecting back on the past ones and changing those through that act of reflection, in contexts which are themselves highly reflexive, such as an interview context or a classroom or whatever it is that we are talking about.

CW: Yeah.

SF: So, it's really a longwinded way of saying that I think interpretation has perhaps become more open-minded. Less worried about the sort of doctrinal approach to the way in which you should do it. And more interested in the sort of over-lapping modes, you know, the bits of meaning that people construct as they go along.

CW: Yeah.

SF: Where will it go? I don't know. I mean I'm very, very pessimistic myself about social psychology. So I don't know where it will go in psychology, which is your primary reference point. All that I can see is social psychology having been pushed out, critical social psychology has been pushed out of psychology departments around the country and in many places around the world as well. And our example here where we formed a separate Department of Psychosocial Studies is just one of them.

CW: Right.

SF: Where social psychology can't really manage in the Department of Psychological Sciences. So I'm kind of pessimistic about it. I think there was a moment, you know around 2000, when it looked like critical social psychology and experimental social psychology might come together, and you might get a new happening. Social psychology, in Britain in particular, might become creative and contribute to the whole post-structuralist turn. And I think that went under the pressure of brain sciences and big equipment and the RAE in this country.

CW: Right.

SF: So, I'm not particularly confident about anything within that field.

CW: Right. And qualitative psychology, do you see that as being a separate sort of umbrella, or is critical social psychology part of qualitative psychology?

SF: No, qualitative psychology doesn't have to be critical.

CW: Right.

SF: I mean it tends to be because people working in the more critical domain are interested in meanings, both personal and social, and they are much more likely to do qualitative work and much less likely to be satisfied with quantitative work. Although, as we know, you can have pretty progressive modes of quantitative work as well, and you can have qualitative work which is just very judgemental kind of case studies.

CW: Yes.

SF: It's not the same thing as saying they go together. I don't know, but I mean look at the ESRC. Its funding priorities are quantitative funding for doctoral students. They think people are being very poorly trained, they're pushing that and people are going to chase the quantitative money again. What can I say? There's a number of tendencies which may be in tension with one another. There's a kind of gross fluidity to some methods which you see in the way Bruno Latour's work has been picked up, John Law's stuff. There's certain kinds of ethnographic work in anthropology, you know turned on British society. There's much self-critical work, people are more amenable to multiple methods and to not feeling they have to get it right. They want to create a method that's going to fit the material they've got and questions they've got. That's one side of it. And then the other side is that there's this push towards orthodoxy, a retrenchment, with heavy funding going into it, and the conservative impact of something being concentrated in only a very small number of places. It moves against all kind of innovative work. Both of these things are happening.

CW: Yes. Yes.

SF: So I'm a bit pessimistic about it.

CW: Yeah.

SF: (laughs)

CW: Sounds like a sad note to end on (laughs). Do you want to say anything else?

SF: Well, it's interesting talking to you. It's one of those examples, isn't it? I would be interested in how you'd interpret it (pause) and I would be interested to see what I'd say about it tomorrow, if you came back to talk to me about it then, as opposed to us having the conversation today.

CW: Yes.

SF: I mean some of these things I've talked to you about, I've repeated elsewhere quite a lot. And some of them have been quite interesting to think about here. And I think that question about the relationship between the text, and those who produce the text, you know, how you think about that epistemologically and ethically in the research process; it poses a really interesting question, worth thinking about it some more.

CW: Yeah. OK, well, thank you very much.

And here are Professor Frosh's recommended readings:

Butler, J. (2005) *Giving an Account of Oneself*. New York: Fordham University Press.

Frosh, S. (2007) Disintegrating qualitative research, *Theory and Psychology*, 17: 635–53.

Frosh, S. and Baraitser, L. (2008) Psychoanalysis and psychosocial studies, *Psychoanalysis, Culture and Society*, 13: 346–65 (plus responses).

II A conversation with Professor Christine Griffin

Christine Griffin and Carla Willig

(CW = Carla Willig; CG = Christine Griffin)

CW: The first question is probably the most difficult one in a way because it's about your definition of interpretation. So, if someone asked you, someone who doesn't know anything about it, somebody from another planet maybe, asks you 'What is interpretation?'

CG: I suppose I'd say, 'Making a sense of various sorts of research material'. So I'm talking about it in the context of research, not generally. Yes, sort of making a meaning or meanings from research material, and the material could be audio, it could be video, it could be field notes.

CW: Right.

CG: It could be online stuff, it could be all sorts of things. And informed by particular theoretical perspectives or theoretical frameworks, questions, like research questions, and also the sort of context, the political and social and cultural context, within which the interpretation and the research is happening.

CW: OK.

CG: I guess. So that's very general.

CW: So is it about bringing something to the material, which isn't already there? Or is the meaning already there?

CG: Probably both. I think it's looking at some material with particular lenses, and it's like doing a reading or bringing out elements of that material. But it's like a sort of conversation maybe or something like that, or an interaction between the interpreter and the material, and the people producing the material. And of course, it's not just necessarily one person doing the interpretation. It can be a team, it could be joint, you know, the team can be all the participants in the research. It doesn't have to be, you know, the researcher as somehow separate.

CW: Right. So it sounds like a very hermeneutic kind of process?

CG: Yeah.

CW: And that would be happening as a process?

CG: Yes, I would see it as a process, and not that there is one interpretation or one reading. But nor are there sort of infinitely, multiple . . .

CW: OK.

CG: ... interpretations, because they're framed also by the biographies of the inter-preters, but also the culture and the context in which they're doing the work.

CW: Right. Yes. And so would you feel that in an interpretation that can be produced as a result of this process of engaging with certain lenses, you know, do you feel that the people who generate the data in the first place, would they need to be in agreement with that or do you think that you could interpret in a way that wouldn't be acceptable or not understood, maybe, by them?

CG: I think it varies in every instance. So there might be some examples where you might very much expect them not to agree. I'm thinking of Mick Billig's interviews with the members of the National Front where he was basically arguing that this is a reflection of a fascist ideology and actually they would probably disagree with that, you know, heavily. So I don't necessarily think there should be sort of hard and fast rules, particularly as a sort of cozy, 'Oh, we should all agree together'. Because actually part of what research is about is being critical, and that doesn't mean negative, but it sometimes means, you know, bringing interpretations to bear which not everybody in a research team might agree with. Never mind other groups.

CW: Right.

CG: And there's also not necessarily one constituency in a research project. So, in a school, you know, there might be teachers, students, different groups of stu-dents, parents. There are some classic cases of ethnographies in schools, where researchers have sort of gone back with their findings ...

CW: Yeah.

CG: ... and all the teachers have disagreed, some of the teachers have disagreed. So you know there's that.

CW: Yes.

CG: And if the funders have disagreed, you can't possibly publish that.

CW: Yes, right.

CG: So it depends on the context I think.

CW: So you are mentioning that the critical dimension of research, not in terms of being negative but in terms of questioning, is that what you (do)?

CG: Yes, I think so. I think it's probably like Foucault's understanding of critique, not to mean some sort of negative demolition job, but as a not taking things for granted and bringing to bear some sort of critical perspective. Something like that.

CW: OK. So that sounds a bit like you might feel that there's never, you never get to the end. So any interpretation could then be interpreted as to, you know, maybe why the parents disagree, or why the researcher came up with what they came up with?

CG: Yes, I don't think that there's sort of a definitive interpretation of a situation. There're always various possible interpretations, and the interpretation I might develop at one moment might well be different ten or twelve or fifteen years down the line of the same material.

CW: Yes.

CG: But those different interpretations are always shaped by the context; they're not just free floating and never ending.

CW: Right. So one could explain perhaps, why this particular interpretation was generated at that point?

CG: Yes. So, for example, I mean an example I gave, which actually isn't a research project, is when I was doing my PhD in the late 1970s in social identity theory and (name of academic) was like the Big Guy, and the first academic conference I ever went to I had a question I wanted to ask him because I was writing my thesis up. So I asked him and as I was asking him, his arm came around my shoulder and I thought, 'Oh my god, what am I going to do?' Here I am in my twenties, he's in his fifties or something, he's a great professor and I want to get the answer from him. But at the same time I want to push him off.

CW: Yeah.

CG: And that happened before feminist work around sexual harassment. So I couldn't think of it as harassment. I thought of it as, 'He's a groper. He's got wandering hands'. So I understood it, as did everybody else in the department as, you know, a foible of his.

CW: Yeah. OK.

CG: You know, he did it with every woman, student and postgrad, post doc. He was never allowed on his own with them. But, you know, by the late 1970s or into the 1980s, I could've understood that with the frame of sexual harassment.

CW: Yeah.

CG: But that discourse hadn't been around to draw on before.

CW: No.

CG: So it's that sort of thing of what can be thought changes. And that's one of the challenges of historical works is to read them in the context in which they were produced.

CW: Yes. And how legitimate is it to interpret something in the light of the later discourse?

CG: Yes, which happens a lot, it happens a lot with the way that feminist work is seen. The feminist work of the 60s, 70s or 80s is often seen through a discursive and political lens of now, which doesn't work, or without recognizing that that process is happening.

CW: This just made me think about therapy because there is a similar process. When people have had experiences of child abuse or something like that, but didn't have the lens or framework to interpret it as that.

CG: Yes.

CW: And then years later in therapy this is made possible.

CG: Yes.

CW: And then there may be distress that perhaps wasn't there in the same way before. Because of the new understanding, and there are ethical issues around that.

CG: Yes, and I think in a way, that bit of the process of interpreting material is a bit like that. It's a process whereby you become increasingly familiar with something, from the point when it was generated in the first place, where you might've been there physically or you might've not been. You keep revisiting it and every time you revisit it, you maybe revisit more of it, or other people's talk, or other information as well. And you sort of refine or I don't know, develop a fuller reading or a different reading over time. Because you keep returning to it.

CW: Yes. We do that throughout our lives, don't we? We reflect. But with research projects, they tend to have an end where we say, 'We're going to stop now'.

CG: Yes. We've got to stop (laughs).

CW: So, do you feel maybe that that in a way is problematic? That a lot of projects have these artificial end dates, where it has to be, you know, completed?

CG: Yeah. Well, I mean, I think that the way we are compelled to do research nowadays is so constrained within academia in the UK, by all sorts of things. By being, you know, the academy being separated somehow, and separated from practitioners, and it's very difficult to do participatory research; it is possible but funders aren't always sympathetic. There's an emphasis on publishing things in certain formats, in certain journals, in certain ways. So there're lots and lots of constraints on what can be done and what counts as research. And if you want to do research, to some degree you've got to sort of compromise with that.

CW: Yeah. So that would limit the interpretations that can be made?

CG: To some degree. But also, I think, the way my orientation to research was formed through being in cultural studies, the Centre of Cultural Contemporary Studies in the early 80s in Birmingham. So that was an interdisciplinary context, but it was also a politically engaged one. So I think that's where I learned to do qualitative research in a way and interpretation. Or I started to learn to do it (laughs). So, to me research is partly always thinking, 'What's going on here?' And also, 'What might it be symptomatic of?' So Stuart Hall and Tony Jefferson, there's been a new edition of *Resistance Rituals*, which is a youth subcultures text from the 70s which came out in 2006. And their editorial talks about this approach, where you would look at a phenomenon in terms of 'what might this be reflecting? What might this phenomenon tell us about people's lives more generally in the context in which they're living?' This they would call a symptomatic reading. And then what they would call a conjunctual analysis, would be, you know, 'why is this happening now?', 'Is there a panic over these phenomena?' And 'what is this panic telling us about how particular groups of people might be seen as a problem' or whatever. And then research, partly I would see it as engaging with those political discourses, through working with people who are maybe looked at as a problem or at risk.

CW: Right.

CG: And look at their perspective on what's going on. And that's partly because a lot of my research has been either on gender and women's experiences, you know, women's lives, or youth or young people's lives. Both of whom are groups that are generally sort of not the ones creating discourse necessarily. Although that's a bit simplistic.

CW: So in terms of the role of theory in interpretation then, what would you say?

CG: Well, I mean, I think, in psychology there have been so many different debates. But I guess one of the main ones is to deal with the sort of realist and a constructivist or constructionist (positions), those sorts of debates about the status of the accounts or the material you might be working with as a researcher or research group. So, in other words, do you take them as some sort of reflection of what is really happening here? Or do you take them as mediated and discursively produced? Well, I mean, you as a researcher are also discursively producing them. So that in psychology, you've got sometimes quite polarized positions where there are just sort of arguments about, 'I am on this side' or 'I am on the other side'. And I probably in my earlier research would have been more realist or critical realist, but that was also because different theoretical frameworks became available over time. So I would probably see my approach as a sort of critical realist and constructivist, I suppose.

CW: Right.

CG: So I wouldn't necessarily take research material as somehow a straightforward reflection of, you know, what is really happening here. But nor is it free-floating away from the conditions in which it was produced. I suppose that's a sort of materialist approach in a way.

CW: Yeah.

CG: So, yeah, I think I would probably approach it that way.

CW: So when theory is brought to data which in some ways as you suggested it has to when interpretation happens, there is some kind of framework, some sort of theoretical lens brought to the data?

CG: Yes, yes. So, for example, at the moment I'm quite interested in neoliberalism as a sort of discourse and a social order, and the way in which that constitutes identity and belonging. And I focus on young people and their social lives and social leisure activities, like drinking or going to music festivals or things like that, which to them are very important, to a lot of young people. So, part of the work of interpretation is to look at what they're saying and what they're doing and where they're doing it and where they're saying it. And look at those practices and the sense they're making of them. But part of it is also to, I suppose, to do another level of interpretation which isn't necessarily reflected in what they're saying, which might be, for example, to argue that because a lot of what they do when they talk about drinking is telling passing out stories, stories about passing out, you know, waking up in A&E, waking up in your own sick and all sorts of things. Blacking out, not being able to remember what happened. And they minimize this and don't represent it as 'passing out' and saying, well, not calling it passing out. So the other level of interpretation would be to say, in a social order that is pressured and in which you are the focus as an individual, and the individual is the biographical project of the self . . .

CW: Yeah.

CG: . . . that Giddens talks about. You can see drinking and passing out through being drunk, and just the chaos of being completely drunk, as a sort of time-out of that. Where that individual literally dies, goes away for a while.

CW: Yeah.

CG: Stops being rational and in control and responsible, and completely loses it with a whole group of other people in the same state. Now that isn't something that people are necessarily going to say to you, that's another sort of interpretation, which is a bit like the conjunctual analysis, I guess. It's trying to say, well, what's going on here, and why might it be happening now?

CW: Yeah.

CG: So, it's that link to context which some, certainly some psychologists, including some I think qualitative psychologists wouldn't want to do; it would be seen as too great a leap.

CW: Right.

CG: Because you can't evidence it. It's not, you know, you can't warrant it, by just finding, you know, the bit that proves it in the data.

CW: So going beyond what's there?

CG: Yes. Yes.

CW: And is that, do you feel that it's for ethical reasons that some people would not want to do that? Or is it more kind of scientific reasons? You know saying this isn't based on evidence?

CG: Yeah. I think probably both. So the reasons that people might say, 'No, I wouldn't want to do that', I completely agree with. It's not that I disagree with them. It might be either because they have a scientific frame and an approach that says, I mean like Jonathan Potter and discursive psychology, you know, 'If it's not in the data, you shouldn't be saying it's there'.

CW: Yeah.

CG: And the other is an ethical one, which is about representing other people's lives, you are reading something into people's accounts or practices that they might disagree with. And those sort of debates about ethics I would frame or would've framed in terms of debates about power in research.

CW: Right.

CG: Which is what feminist debates are about. What is now called 'ethics' used to be couched in terms of power. So, who is able to speak for whom? And that is an issue in research where you're often in a position where you are speaking for people who never themselves write, not even anonymized. And your work might have an impact on debates that might affect them, and they never know about it. So, it's very distanced and it's hard to actually be accountable in the way in which academic research is set up. It doesn't mean it's not worth trying but it makes it very difficult.

CW: Yes. So the ethical issues in a way are about power and whose voice is being heard?

CG: Yes, and accountability, yes, I think so.

CW: Yes. So this recent sort of turn towards psychoanalytic concepts, you know, the psychosocial approach, what do you make of all of that?

CG: Well, I mean, I've certainly followed all of that. I remember Helen Lucey who's here at Bath now has really been involved in that from the start. And also, you know, Wendy Hollway's book. And I guess I found the work really interesting but I don't think I could do it. Because of the way in which, this is just my sense-making, I could be completely missing the point, the sense in which the assumption is that the participants in research are defended. So that your role as a researcher is to penetrate their defences. Whereas I think my model is more of a bringing out meaning or a sort of illumination or 'Verstehen' approach. And it's just not a perspective that I feel I could use . . .

CW: Right.

CG: . . . but sometimes found it very useful.

CW: So, in terms of bringing theory, in this case it's a theory you just don't feel is your thing, you wouldn't want to bring it, but you can see some interesting observations coming out of that?

CG: Yeah. I mean, say I am trying to write something about new forms of femininity at the moment, which I have been trying to write about for at least five years (laughs). And I've drawn quite a lot on Angela McRobbie's work, and some of her work does draw on psychoanalytic theorizing, particularly film studies.

CW: OK.

CG: So she's talking about post-feminism and a sort of post-feminist masquerade, you know, women looking sort of hyper-sexy, hyper-sexual and glamorous, as a way of actually distancing themselves from femininity or normative femininity. Having a sort of knowing, ironic take on it but also producing themselves as sort of ditzy and scatty in order not to risk losing male approval. Now, that's not something that women who dress in that sort of way might necessarily say. But it's an interesting argument. So I would certainly draw on that argument but then look at material from interviews and observations in a project about young people and drinking, and maybe bring aspects of that interpretation to bear. But not necessarily do a whole project using psychosocial methods in the way that the project was set up.

CW: Right.

CG: So I would certainly draw on the ideas.

CW: It makes me think a bit about this distinction between the top-down and bottom-up.

CG: Yes. Yes.

CW: Using theory you're committed to and really believe in and then apply that to data which would be very top-down. Or sort of go from the bottom up drawing from theoretical tools to help you along the way. But kind of more bottom-up.

CG: Yes. I think what I do is almost start from two places. So I start with a growing familiarity with a phenomenon of some kind, it usually has some sort of cultural basis to it, or political/cultural which could be young people drinking, it could be music festivals, it could be all sorts of things. And then a set of theoretical, a body of theory, which I see as useful to explaining why certain things might be happening now. That theory is often on the edges of cultural studies or sociology. It might not be. So then I sort of familiarize myself with both of those two areas, and I tend to write papers that have two bits to them, and then it's trying to bring those two things together. So, to read the sort of interpretation of the research material through the lens of the theory.

CW: Right.

CG: But also to play back the research material to the theory. Because sometimes there are things going on in the research material that aren't in the theory or don't match the theory. So I think what I try to do is both at once, although it would be a lot better if I did one or the other, frankly (laughs). It would be a lot easier.

CW: It would be a lot easier? (laughs)

CG: It would be a lot easier (laughs).

CW: It sounds like the sort of way you're approaching it involves going back to the data a lot?

CG: Yes.

CW: I'm trying to think of the name of an author who wrote about this but I can't remember. Anyway somebody, you might recognize it, this idea of allowing the data to object.

CG: Oh, yes that's a good idea.

CW: That idea that you've got some theoretical concepts that you feel make sense of the data, but you're approaching your data in a way that still allows the data to object and say, 'No, this doesn't fit'.

CG: And that's difficult to do because the theory has a higher status . . .

CW: Yeah.

CG: . . . than people's talk or observations of their lives. And that experience came from the first research I really got involved with after my PhD, which was about young women leaving school. First of all, most of the research about young people is about young men, didn't necessarily fit young women anyway. And secondly, it didn't say anything about sexuality, and that was one of the ways in which they were seen and sort of negotiated their way through school and the labour market and family life. So right from the start, I had experience of sort of clumps, aspects of the phenomena that I was looking at, just not being reflected in the theory or empirical research, until feminist work came along.

CW: Paradoxically, then, I guess, when there is no theory you have the freedom to really allow things to come out and develop new concepts, and then once you've got theories, even if they're really good ones, they become a little bit constraining and maybe harder then to . . .

CG: Yes, that's true actually. Yes (pause) but very difficult for undergraduate and postgraduate students to learn, these sort of processes. It's very difficult to learn (pause) and teach (laughs).

CW: Yes. As you were talking, I was just thinking that really I'm becoming more and more convinced in my own mind that the only way to perhaps teach this, or to practise it oneself, is to just accept that there will always be a tension between sort of allowing the data to object and applying useful, theoretical concepts. And that there's always going to be this kind of struggle that you are describing. Maybe that's it. This is what it is.

CG: Yeah. Yes, I think it is. Yeah.

CW: So maybe that's what interpretation is?

CG: Yeah.

CW: If you do it responsibly, you know, ethically.

CG: Yes, that's right. Yes.

CW: So, I'm interested as well in the terminology, discourse I guess, that we use as researchers, and one thing I'm kind of struck by, and I mention this in the earlier chapters of the book, is that even though we are interpreting, in the way you described . . .

CG: Yes.

CW: . . . in qualitative research we tend to use the word 'analysis'. So in a lot of published work and at conferences people say, 'And my analysis is this'. And very few say, 'My interpretation is this'. We're kind of avoiding the word, even though we are still doing it. And I just wondered, what's the difference there, between analysis and interpretation? Is there a difference, or are they . . .?

CG: Yes. I mean, I think to me analysis is preferable to the word 'findings' or 'results', which is definitely what you have in psychology, sort of traditional psychology journal articles which were based around an experimental model. You'd have, you know, introduction, method, findings or results, and discussion or conclusion. So, to move away from saying, 'These are my findings, and this is what I've found, these are my results'. But the other side of it is that analysis is more (pause) yes what would be analysis? (pause) there's less of a sense that this is an interpretation. It's more like, 'This is the analysis, so it's like this'. Although analysis is still a process, but I get the sense that it's more acceptable within academic research, so I see the problem. I mean, I tend to talk about analysis, but I certainly see it as a process of interpretation. But it is interesting . . .

CW: Yeah, it is.

CG: . . . that it gets called analysis, but the practice is interpretation. But I think, I don't know, I mean my sense is that interpretation is also systematic but at the same time there's an intuitive element to it. And analysis has this sense of being just rational and that anyone could analyse the same bit of material and come out with something similar. Whereas interpretation doesn't have that. And that sense of intuition which I think is part of qualitative, I think it's part of any research actually, but it's certainly more explicit in qualitative work, it scares people shitless, I think.

CW: Yeah.

CG: Because you can't say really what it is. It's a gut feeling, and sometimes, you know, some people find it easier than others. It's very hard to teach it.

CW: Yeah, yeah. It would be interesting to do an experiment and write an article exactly the same, but just replace the word 'analysis' with 'interpretation' . . .

CG: Yes, yes.

CW: . . . submit it to a number of journals . . .

CG: (laughs) Yes.

CW: . . . and see, you know. I would expect the one with interpretation to be less likely to be accepted, perhaps.

CG: Yes, that's a good idea (laughs).

CW: It's a good idea. So, to sort of move on to your own personal relationship with interpretation, could you say a bit about what it means to you? You know, as a person you've spent many years working . . .

CG: Doing it.

CW: ... doing it. So, what does it mean to you to interpret data and what's your relationship with this activity?

CG: (pause) Well, it varies. I mean sometimes it depends and, so say the process of interpretation that might happen in a group which might be, you know, during an interview or talking to people in a particular situation that might end up being recalled and then looked at again later. So (pause) sometimes, more recently, I've been interpreting stuff that maybe other people have done the interview, sometimes not always. And that feels like a more distant experience than if I was there from the start. So, the process of interpretation I think for me starts ...

CW: Right.

CG: ... with talking to people or going to places and asking people questions, so both observing and asking people questions. It's a process of engagement, I think, and it's engagement with people, situations and practices. And I suppose the more traditional sort of interpretation is where, you know, you're sort of faced with papers and stuff that you're reading or listening to and making sense of or finding patterns in. But I think I've experienced it as a process of engagement and the exciting bit for me is seeing something happening or thinking, 'Oh, OK, that's going on there'. I have to feel familiar with particular people's perspectives on the situation they're in. But I can leap to conclusions too fast, so I have to sort of rein myself back and say, 'No, look through this material', you know, or 'Think about it more systematically before you jump to this conclusion'.

CW: Right. Yes.

CG: It might seem terribly interesting and this, that and the other, but really, you know, rein yourself back a bit. And I think also it takes just so bloody long. So at the moment I'm on a six months study leave (because I've been Head of the Department for three years), which I will probably never get again. So I've had time to do the sort of thinking and writing and reading and interpretation actually, that I haven't had for eons, twenty years. I just haven't had this sort of time for a long, long time, and also I think I interpret theory. So if I'm reading something that's theory or data, I'd interpret. I'd bring the same process to bear on it. I think I do interpretative work on theory as well. But, yes, I've never been hugely bothered by that argument, 'Oh, this is subjective, it's just your analysis' or 'It's just your view'. As though that means that it doesn't mean anything. Because I've never really been bothered by that, not because I think I'm right, but rather because I'm often looking at phenomena where not many other people have looked at it in this sort of way. So I'm more thinking, 'Well, at least I and others are saying this', as not many other people are. Maybe. I'm not quite sure about that.

CW: Yeah. Sounds like a lot of what you perhaps enjoy in this process of engaging with material is to allow it to make more and more sense, you know, in a different way?

CG: Yes, yes.

CW: And that's quite exciting, and so sometimes you leap ahead thinking, 'Yes, you know, this is what it means!' And then you rein yourself back in. But again, it sounds like it's a process of making sense, or making a certain kind of sense, making meaning out of something, and finding that satisfying in some way and valuable . . .

CG: Yes, yes.

CW: . . . because it can be shared and something else can happen?

CG: Yes, yes I think so. Yeah.

CW: So how do you know when you are interpreting? And when you're not?

CG: Yes. That's a good question.

CW: Or are you always interpreting, all the time?

CG: Yes, I was just thinking, when I started to say I was interpreting when I read theory. Well, if the process of interpretation is about making meaning for yourself, actually because, on one level interpretation can happen when you're on your own reading something, it happens as a sort of lone practice. But it can happen collectively in a group, you know, online or face-to-face or working over time together on common documents. So it can be a collective process. And it can be an individual process. But it can happen just as much in reading a theoretical piece as it can reading a transcript of an interview or listening to a transcript of an interview. It's just that we think of interpretation as a thing you do to data.

CW: Yeah.

CG: And we think of data as a certain sort of material. But if you think of, you know, reading an entirely theoretical text, I still think I interpret that because I engage with it in a way that makes meaning of it for me in relation to what I want it for.

CW: Yeah.

CG: (There's something I was going to say) something about collective interpretation but I've lost it. But I don't know what the boundaries of interpretation are or what interpretation is different from (laughs).

CW: Yeah.

CG: Is it just reading? Oh, that's what I was going to say, what about the material you might be making sense of? This is something I started to grapple with because I'm interested in young people's uses of social media, which, of course, happen in all sorts of complicated ways and at different sites, and it's visual and textual. How do you make sense of that?

CW: Yeah.

CG: So, you might be interpreting stuff that might be visual or textual or, it might be practices you've observed. That's really difficult actually, ethnographic fieldwork, because there isn't a great tradition of dealing with that material in psychology. So how do you interpret that sort of material? And that's a different issue to the 'What's the boundaries of interpretation?' But, say, if I'm reading a novel, do I interpret it? If I'm reading the paper, or a magazine, or watching the telly, am I interpreting? Sometimes I might, and sometimes I might not be.

CW: And what's the difference between interpreting and simply allowing oneself to react, you know, to be affected by some things?

CG: Yes.

CW: You might read a poem and it just makes you feel very sad.

CG: Yes, yes.

CW: So you've responded to some meaning in there. Is that the same as interpreting it? Do you need to interpret it to be able to feel something? Or . . .

CG: Yes, because if interpretation was entirely a sort of rational process, where you're emotionally distanced from it, although I mean it certainly can be like that, but I think it has to be more than just that. The most useful or exciting form of interpretation is where you're emotionally engaged with it.

CW: Yeah.

CG: As well as, you know, analytically, rationally thinking about it.

CW: Because sometimes when there's an emotional response, I guess, it leads us to ask questions we wouldn't have otherwise asked.

CG: Yes, yes.

CW: So I guess, it could be useful to say, 'Hang on, why do I feel sad when I . . .'

CG: Yes.

CW: '. . . when it doesn't look so bad what's actually being said here'. We sort of ask further questions of the material.

CG: Yes, yes. People are starting to use poetics, poetry, in research. Both is a way of doing research, and talking about research, and expressing aspects . . .

CW: Yes.

CG: . . . different aspects of research, or different aspects of performance. So I mean, I think it's a great idea, but again how does it fit with the research excellence framework and all that stuff?

CW: Actually, my last question is in fact about your view on where things are going in terms of qualitative research, certainly in the UK, in terms of the role of interpretation?

CG: Yes.

CW: Where do you think it is going and what is going to happen?

CG: Well, I don't know, I get a sense that there are quite a lot of new researchers coming through, doing PhDs and different sorts of pieces of work, not all in universities, who are starting to use different methods. And they're partly using the internet, so they're using websites, they're using social networking sites, they're using YouTube, both to develop their projects, to sort of collect material and to find a source of material to interpret and analyse and to disseminate the work in different forms. So I get a sense that there's quite a lot of that going on, quite marginal and much of it sort of Masters and PhD students. So it hasn't had an impact across the board yet. It's come out of a dissatisfaction with traditional ways of doing research and disseminating research. So it will be interesting to see, what happens with that.

CW: Yeah, yeah. And do you think those ways of doing research, for example, using the internet, is that going to have any implications for how interpretation comes into it? Does it allow something to happen that wouldn't have otherwise happened in terms of interpretation?

CG: Well, I don't know because I mean it's such early days. Partly the technology is moving very fast and partly the theory around what's going on is barely keeping up. And it's also so complex to interpret these sorts of things. It's hard enough to interpret what happens offline, but it's more difficult I think to try and understand what's going on online and offline.

CW: Right.

CG: So it's hard to say, really. I imagine there are going to be changes, but it's very hard to see whether they will have an impact on mainstream, traditional psychology and university research, which is getting tighter and tighter and more and more standardized in terms of what counts as research, getting money, who gets the money, where it goes. It might well have more of an impact outside of traditional academia.

CW: Right.

CG: In practice and performance and youth work and community work and also in teaching. It might have a lot of impact on teaching.

CW: Right. So we will have to see what happens?

CG: We will have to see (laughs).

CW: So overall, then, having come to the end of all my questions, do you feel that there's anything that is really important regarding interpretation that hasn't been mentioned so far?

CG: (pause) I think the main thing for psychology is that there's a terrible tendency in psychology to not read outside of psychology, either theory or anything. And I think that's caused all sorts of problems over time. Psychology has sort of disciplinary blinkers. So, I guess, with interpretation as with anything else, the important thing is for psychologists to keep reading and going to conferences and talking to people beyond the discipline.

CW: Right. Yeah.

CG: I think.

CW: Yeah. And that would make the interpretations we produce perhaps less blinkered or less likely to pin something down to one thing?

CG: Yes. And also qualitative psychology is not a huge area, it's not a huge group of people. It's pretty marginal compared to, you know, the stranglehold of cog-neuro, scientific, biological perspectives and experimental research. And people spend a lot of time arguing with one another over miniature points, to do with things nobody outside of psychology has ever heard of. So qualitative researchers in sociology or anthropology have no idea what the hell is going on! So I would always say, you know, pay less attention to debates within qualitative psychology; there are other things to be thinking about that are more important. You know, go to a conference in anthropology or consumer culture or something that may be on the topic you're doing research on, but not in your discipline.

CW: Right.

CG: And then read something else, and it will be more interesting.

CW: (laughs) That's really good advice, actually. Yes, yes, great. Well thank you very much for talking to me. I think we've covered a lot here.

CG: It's really interesting.

CW: Yes, it's really interesting.

And here are Professor Griffin's recommended readings:

Hall, S. and Jefferson, T. (2006) Once more around 'Resistance through Rituals', in S. Hall and T. Jefferson (eds.) *Resistance Through Rituals* (2nd edn). London: Routledge.

Hollway, W. and Jefferson, T. (2000) *Doing Qualitative Research Differently: Free Association, Narrative and the Interview Method*. London: Sage.

Reavey, P. (ed.) (2011) *Visual Methods in Psychology: Using and Interpreting Images in Qualitative Research*. London: Routledge.

III A conversation with Professor Jonathan Smith

Jonathan Smith and Carla Willig

(CW = Carla Willig; JS = Jonathan Smith)

CW: So, first of all, thank you very much for agreeing to have this conversation with me. There are a few questions that I prepared, very general questions. I'll start with the question, what in your view is interpretation? How would you explain it to someone, who is completely unaware, maybe from a culture where this concept doesn't exist? How would you explain what that means to you?

JS: It's interesting 'cos once you get close to these terms, it's, it's very hard to offer clear definitions, they're, they're so thick with nuances and possibilities. So when I think in my own terms of what I mean by interpretation, well there's a general and there's a specific in the sense that: What does it mean *per se*? And what does it mean for, for what I do? And they overlap, they sort of overlap. So I suppose interpretation means making sense of an entity, and trying to understand the meaning of an entity. Now I'm sure you've done this, but I just looked at the OED and it's quite interesting, the thick waveband of readings of what interpretation is, so they're all prefixes of meaning, so *make-out* the meaning of something. *Clarify* the meaning of, *convey, explain, expound* the meaning of. So in a way the dictionary offers that, the very sort of rainbow or range of meanings, which I think are there. It's some sort of combination of those. Make out as in discern, enable to come forth, so in a sense a constructive, in a sense to do with the very discovery of the entity in the first place. Convey, as in express to somebody else. But then explain, explicate. Have an *a priori* that the, thing already exists as something, that you then add something in addition to it. And I would say it's a combination of all of those and I don't normally problematize it or deconstruct it or pose it in that way. But it does, it does have, some sort of Gestalt around those various elements.

CW: So you are saying that even what it is, is already an interpretative act, even to kind of make out what it is. So does that mean really interpretation starts as nothing really there to begin with? Or is there something there that we then pick apart? Or you know how do you sort of understand it in terms of what is the 'it' that we are doing something with when we interpret?

JS: Experience is at the heart of this. The given here is that, I guess as a human science experiential researcher, the thing that I'm trying to interpret is an experience. But given that you can't reconstruct, get at directly at the experience, however hard you try, and you can never recreate exactly one own's experience, it is always an account of experience, a reconstruction, a take on, a meaning of experience. That's partly where this layer of processes, that we broadly call interpretation, come into play. What's emerging here is the model of what we're doing. So, I mean it is me as a researcher, me as a person talking to another person about something that happens. It's not that they have a direct entry to the thing that happened to them either. There are also a series of filters and processes going on for that person that you could say either separate or connect them with the thing that happened. So, we never get at directly, the thing. Rather the closest one can hope to get is some understanding of the understanding the other person has of this thing that it's claimed happened.

CW: Yeah. So the thing we start with, the experience of the phenomenon, it's something that for whatever reason two people are curious about, so you and the participant . . .

JS: Yeah.

CW: . . . have come together because you've decided, that something is worth looking at. You're curious to understand, both them and you, maybe. And then, that's the beginning, that's what you've agreed to start with.

JS: Yeah.

CW: Yeah. So does that mean that interpretation sort of presupposes that people have agreed to make something into an issue, or problem, or something worth even thinking about? You know, because what about all the things we do, that we don't sit down to interpret?

JS: I mean this is where in a sense, there's this dialogue between the broad and the specific. So when I'm talking about the interpretation that I do as a researcher, that's a specific thing, which I'm guessing you may primarily be interested in. But that's sort of connected to and tapping into things that are happening all the time. But they become subsets they're more specified in terms of the particular activity that is happening. So, for this particular project, we are talking about, that is true. Two people have decided that this is worth investing some time and energy in. But there will be a whole continuum or spectrum where there would be a whole series of things that are happening to the person that they will be interpreting all the time anyway. And then there will be a whole series of tacit things that they have interpreted, that they no longer worry about. And there will be a whole series of things that could possibly be and then there would be a whole series of things that it wouldn't be worth or it might be very hard to, because they're so automated, generic that you wouldn't even invest energy in it. So there's a whole series of things that the person is doing on their own. And then this person comes along and says, 'Let's engage in this project talking about this'. So it's gonna be a very rarefied and select part of the whole, the whole nexus.

CW: Yeah. So the term, I mean this is more a question about terminology, but I mean one of the other things I'm saying in the second chapter of the book, is how interesting it is that in qualitative psychology we tend to avoid the word 'interpretation', we prefer 'analysis'. So we might say you know, 'We've analysed the interview'. We don't tend to say 'I've interpreted'. It's becoming a bit more acceptable now, more normal to use the word interpretation within that, but certainly you know fifteen, twenty years ago it would have sounded very strange to say 'I've interpreted my data'. It kind of wouldn't have been really acceptable, almost. And I'm just wondering, whether this difference between meaning-making, which you referred to that happens in everyday life and we don't even recognize we're doing it, half the time, you know it just happens and the research participant will come and have all these meanings already made. But then, when we ask them to reflect in the interview, we are much more consciously and explicitly . . .

JS: Yeah.

CW: . . . doing interpretation with them.

JS: Yeah.

CW: So there's a difference there, isn't there? Between the meaning-making that happens all the time and interpretation in as a sort of, as a research activity?

JS: Yes. But I wouldn't say that the former is not interpretation.

CW: OK.

JS: I mean I, I hear what you're saying, and I have heard you, you've said this before. Whether, I don't know, whether I read about people's discomfort calling or people wouldn't call what they do interpretation. It's never been, I mean it's never been an issue for me. Do you feel that there is some sort of ideological or that there is some valence associated with that? That it was not cool to say, 'What I was doing, was interpretation'.

CW: Yeah. I think I feel what happened was in the early days, this is going back to the 1980s, when I did my PhD and started in this field, you know there was a sense in which interpretation was something either associated with psychoanalysis or psychotherapy or very subjective in some way. And if you wanted to be a psychologist, who is kind of able to stand up and give conference presentations, then even if you're doing qualitative . . .

JS: Yeah.

CW: . . . which was in those days quite hard to do, to be able to get away with. Then if you said 'analysis' it sounds more systematic, more scientific, more objective, than saying 'I've interpreted'. Because using interpretation is sort of acknowledging that you are bringing quite a lot to the text yourself, whether it's theory or personal background.

JS: Yeah.

CW: Whereas analysis kind of implies that a machine could do it. And in fact computer programs do, students often hope that if you're using a programme it will do analysis for you, whereas of course you still need to interpret the categories or themes or whatever. So I have a feeling there, but I found now it's changing.

People are much happier to use that discourse around interpretation. That seems more, more ok now.

JS: And that was irrespective of or not associated with a particular analytical style or an epistemological position? It was more about operating within a more conservative mainstream discipline?

CW: I think so. Because in those days you only really had, you know, discourse analysis was just emerging, and they talked about analysis.

JS: Right.

CW: Not discourse interpretation. And then you had things like grounded theory and they don't really talk about interpretation. They talk about pulling out categories. But nowadays could you be talking about what you're doing as interpretation without feeling that's a stigmatizing?

JS: Yeah. That's interesting. I suppose, I don't, I have to pause, I will have to go back (laughs). I'll have to do the, the concordance analysis of everything I've ever said and haven't said and measure the proportion of 'analysis' to 'interpretation' each year (laughs). I've probably done what you said tacitly without even thinking about it. So, I guess at some level I'm, I may have been aware that there was that sort of issue around. And so maybe tactically just like, you know the compromise of saying in a journal, if you're going to submit a paper to this particular journal you know that you have got to have 'methods' and 'results', because even though you don't see it like that, it's just like that you're not gonna win that particular war on that particular occasion. So probably I would sometimes have just sort of subliminally fed into that particular audience expectation, and say I've done analysis, not interpretation. You remind me of a particular talk that I gave once, where I presented my results, analysis, rhetoric, depiction, construction, etcetera, etcetera. And then I said it's an interpretation, and somebody in the audience, and this was a pretty mainstream set, said: 'Oh, it's just an interpretation'.

CW: Just?

JS: So it's like, so it was alright and, as I recall, he said it with a big smirk that meant, 'now we know what you mean it's just your subjective take, and so I can now dismiss the whole thing you presented'. So yeah I can see, I can see that even though it's always been self-consciously acknowledged as a term within the I (interpretative) part of IPA, so the I is clearly in there, the interpretative part has come more to the fore because of the possible distinction from the descriptive phenomenological positions. So to me it was so self-evidently there, and then it's sort of a surprise that people would actually argue that there wasn't an interpretative component there. And in a way that partly helps clarification because well yeah, there are people who appear to seriously believe there is no interpretation in what they do. And I think that is partly connected to what you are saying anyway. That part of the rhetoric of saying, 'This is entirely descriptive'. It's to talk about it being close to being a real scientist. That people can actually say, I'm not *just* presenting an interpretation. This is a description of what is actually there. You may not be able to see it, it may be an essence that is hard-wired or deeply within somebody or an organism, but it is a description nonetheless. It is not just, it's not just, it is interesting isn't it? Just an interpretation. It's sort of an undercurrent or that it is almost tied up with the package of interpretation, that it is *just* an interpretation. Reminds me of the Temptations song, 'It was just my imagination'.

CW: Yes, that's so interesting, isn't it?

JS: Yeah.

CW: That it flows so easily off the tongue: 'Just an interpretation'.

JS: Yeah.

CW: When in fact you could see it as, you know certainly if you were a client or a patient in the psychoanalytic session, the interpretation is this . . .

JS: Reified.

CW: This big, heavy, significant thing (laughs). You know you wouldn't say: 'It's just an interpretation'. It *is* an interpretation.

JS: What would be the alternative? What would be an equivalent term for this thing that we occasionally find up on the pedestal? So instead of saying 'It's just an interpretation', we might say it's really, it *is* an interpretation?

CW: Yeah, well then you could get into trouble I think, because we could end up then saying it's the 'right' or the 'true' or you know then you're sort of slipping into wanting it to be *the* answer, as opposed to *a* way of making sense of it, for it to be really special, and that's indeed what happens in a psychoanalytical context. The implication is that when you have an interpretation, at least the patient will be led to believe that this is true. They found out the secret.

JS: Yeah.

CW: You know the puzzle is solved. It's not about how about looking at it like this? So it's hard to then, to maybe use the word interpretation with this sort of heavy, serious aspect without then claiming some sort of truth value to what is being said. Maybe that's why it's hard to find . . .

JS: Yes, the word.

CW: . . . which interestingly leads me to a question, which actually isn't the one I've got down here next. But it fits much better, so I'm gonna bring it up now. Which is about theory and this very difficult issue around the role of theory in interpretation and to what extent they are the same thing? If it's a research scenario and one is looking at a text to analyse, then some people would probably feel that interpretation means bringing some theory to bear on it, even if it's maybe not a very established theory. But from a phenomenological point of view, I think one could argue that interpretation can be done without bringing theory in a concrete sense to it. So I wonder, what your thoughts are on that?

JS: Oh, that's very straightforward Carla (laughs).

CW: (laughs)

JS: Yeah. It's, yeah, it's, it's complicated. I think, I think interpretation is personal and *personal is political*, but I think it is. So a computer can't do it. It's not cold. It's hot. It's personal. Now that doesn't mean that it's not, that a person doesn't draw on theory. It doesn't mean that it's not intellectual. It doesn't mean that it's just emotional. But it is personal. So it is sometimes argued, or would be argued that part of hermeneutic phenomenology is saying that you cannot bracket everything out and just let the thing emerge, and you just bear witness to that. Rather one's preconceptions influence that process. Now I think that, that can be read off in a very simplistic way, that I don't think does justice to what either Heidegger or Gadamer meant and actually they are talking about the hermeneutic circle. So one reading of hermeneutic phenomenology, which partly connects to and is useful to people who want to evoke that this is heavily pre-driven by theory is that either one is testing a theory or that you can't imagine investigation that's not heavily, theoretically informed by prejudices and preconceptions. Well my reading of Heidegger and Gadamer is that they're not saying that anyway. And that actually, while this is part of the process, that actually in terms of this circular movement, while these things are there in the beginning, they're both, Heidegger and Gadamer, arguing they can get in the way of actually allowing the thing to shine forth. Which is you know, a Heideggerian and also a Husserlian way of seeing it. So the aim is, in terms of some sort of process, to relate what's new to what was before. It is some sort of dialogue between the two. But importantly part of that process is a recognition that this other thing, the other, is important in its own terms and that that is what interpretation is about: trying to unravel that, make it out, get to grips with it. And the researcher is part of that process, but it may be that the things associated with you could get in the way of or need to be put upfront as part of the negotiation. But also importantly you may not know all of the things that were there pre-existing inside you anyway and in the process of confronting the new, those attitudes might change as well. So there is a complex multifaceted dynamic occurring. So, so how does this relate to theory? Well I suppose partly that, when I am doing an interview with somebody and listening to them, saying to myself 'Aha, that's interesting', yes it's probable that in some way, some psychological theory that I imbibed some decades ago, whatever is rattled ...

CW: Yeah.

JS: ... attuned, raised by this process. But I won't necessarily know what it is. I'm not formally attempting to make that happen. I might worry about it getting in the way of what I'm trying to do and so on. So I think my model of it is, there's all of these things happening and part of the value of seeing it as a circular process, is that it's not, it doesn't stay static. When I think about what the research process is, I think, that what I'm doing at this particular point in the circle is different from what I'm doing at that point and there's a changed emphasis. So I start at home base at the beginning of a research project with worry about engaging in some research. 'Will it be of any interest? These are the things that I'm quite concerned with at the moment and I've got some questions that I think are quite interesting'. And I then move around the hermeneutic circle, leaving my home base and entering the experiential world of the other. And I actually think there's something magical that happens in that encounter, that means actually all the rest of it is backgrounded and that in the 'here and now' there is a real conversation of equals in a Gadamerian sense between me and them. And that there is space for something very new to emerge and part of it is relaxing into and allowing that to happen. And just relinquishing, not worrying about all of this stuff that you had before, because it will still be there in your office when you go back. And you can then look into aspects of what was there beforehand when you return to your home base.

CW: Right.

JS: Does that (answer your question)?

CW: Yeah. What came to my mind as you were talking, is the questions that we ask, you know, we have our provisional agenda and it is obviously for phenomenological methods very flexible . . .

JS: Yeah.

CW: . . . because you will want to adjust that to the participants' frame of meaning and so on. But we usually have a few questions. And I was just thinking as you were talking, whether an example of what you're describing, would be where you might ask a question, which could presuppose some kind of psychological dynamic; for example, if I said to you 'Why did you do that?', I presuppose that people do things for a reason. And I presuppose that there's a level of control or decision-making. So if I say 'Why did you do that?', which isn't a very phenomenological question anyway, but let's say if I said that. And then the participant responded by questioning the question and saying, you know: 'I didn't have a why'. Or 'it happened'. Or 'my body did it' or something like that. It would then be kind of an example of where your provisional frame of theoretical assumptions is tested against the other person who forces you to abandon that.

JS: Yeah.

CW: As long as they feel confident to do that. I mean I guess, if the participant was very scared of you or thinks you're the expert and if you ask: 'Why?' then there must be a reason. They might say something just to please you. So that it depends on the quality of the relationship.

JS: Absolutely. But equally in a way it could be more subtle that. It's not that they challenged, but they didn't answer in that way. That they answered in a completely different way and it may well be that you don't pick up on it at the time, but you realize on reading, spending hours reading afterwards, that that was just the wrong question. And the person can very cleverly subtly, they didn't confront you, they didn't need to, but they talked about something else and you say: 'Well, yeah this has nothing to do with intentional agency; something else is going on here'.

CW: Yeah.

JS: And that's, that's how it is in terms of their account. And you really go with that. So you're monitoring in the interview, and that's absolutely critical. You're right that, the best interviews almost dispense with the schedule and you feel as though, there's something magical happening, sort of elemental happening in the 'here and now', where the two of you are constructing space and something strange happens with time in terms of the way that can happen. And it does mean, let it go. My experience is that if you are confident about this process then it is usually not difficult to do. You may have got some tentative ways of starting. But you're really open to letting them go, and be stretched and so on. It happens in real time in the interview, but then it, it just as importantly happens afterwards.

CW: Yes. Yes.

JS: And reflecting.

CW: So when you come to the text afterwards, the transcript, and you engage with it after the event. So in a different way, because you are by yourself probably and you've got the memory of it. And in fact that does lead on to the ethical issues in a way. Because I was thinking about, in the actual interview you were talking about it as being very collaborative. Because both the researcher and participant change in a way through the interview, they see the world slightly differently, because of their meeting, which is quite similar to some forms of therapy . . .

JS: Yeah.

CW: . . . as well. But then afterwards when we analyse as a researcher, we obviously have more power again then, haven't we? 'Cause we're bringing something to the text, perhaps that is more about us. And I think interpretation in terms of, I can't remember this correctly, but I thought that somewhere you wrote, that you are not necessarily advocating taking stuff back to the participant because it may be that some of the insights are not something the participant would be ready to, to engage with. Or you know it might be not ethical, it might not be appropriate. And the agreement from the participant that your analysis is correct, is not really a validation that it is correct. And so I was just thinking about, you know the ethical aspects of that and I suppose the validity aspects of that.

JS: Yeah.

CW: What do you think?

JS: In a way the validity and ethics I think are closely coupled. So that what I think of as being a valid piece of work, valid, trustworthy, honorable, caring and human, ethical. They sort of run together. Because a piece of work that I would say I'm proud of, that I felt was good in those terms, I could call it valid (certain audiences will call it authentic, caring) would be one where I am telling a story, or I am presenting an analytic interpretative account of this person's experience. It would be littered with, but not overloaded with, things they've said. So they will have a major presence, a stake. There's a selection process, but I'm hoping that there will be enough of the person present, that you will trust that this hasn't been distorted. I mean there is trust here, but there's trust involved in any piece of research. There's material from the person, which is a reminder of the conversation I had with that person that I will be presenting as an interpretation. But it will be interpretation, I'm hoping that the reader can reconstruct or have a sense of the spirit of that process in that my interpretation was one triggered by what was said. That I had an antenna out and that it's closely connected with what the person said. And so I'm not crudely dragging this person kicking and screaming into some other theoretical domain. I *am* saying something that they didn't say. It's not just a description. It may have gone quite a long way in terms of some sort of psychological statement about them. And there will be a paper trail, an audit, that will support it and somebody else could look at it. But, but in the paper it will be clear that I am talking, I'm saying this about this person's experience. They said this and this is my take on it, my making sense of the person's making sense of the experience. A lot of it is about care and cautiousness. So that it would partly be about how it is presented and that it is not presented as some definitive claim of truth.

CW: Right.

JS: There would be a range of ways of doing it. This is one. I think it's grounded and plausible and recurrent and has a stability to it. There's a series of reasons why the person might, there might be some dissonance between researcher and participant in relation to the text produced. That text is clearly informed by where one's coming from and a disciplinary perspective and being systematic and having another audience that one wants to make this available to. And therefore, there could be perturbations in terms of the person's response to, to that. So it's sort of navigating between doing justice to the person's account but at the same time doing something more than merely repeating what the person said. So the spirit of this would be, well I *could* go back for another conversation and I could explain why I've said this and I would hope that the person would understand how I got to that, even though they may say something a bit different.

CW: I mean it sounds to me as though it's a lot to do with this, the idea of how far do you move away from the original account? The distance, because it seems to me that the interpretations you're thinking of and the ones you would be producing, are still very much speaking to the original text. Whereas, perhaps interpretations that are very theory driven and the sorts of things we've seen in social psychology, Kleinian interpretations of interview transcripts, or, as you were talking, I was thinking of maybe someone, who does an interview about their political views let's say and talks about their activities in a Marxist organization, and what they want to achieve and their view on society. And then it gets analysed as being evidence of, I don't know, hostility to the father, because all this anger about the system is really about this person's unresolved issues, you know, with the father, from when they were four years old. So that person will probably, would be quite unhappy and angry about being misunderstood and what they've said wasn't really heard for what it is. It was transformed into something completely different.

JS: Yeah.

CW: And that's probably what you would call a very distant interpretation?

JS: Yeah. And it's not to say that that's not a valid thing to do, it's just not what I do. Now in the scheme of things, the type of interpretations I'm talking about might be described as very gentle. They're not huge, they're not loud, they're not noisy. But the groundedness in this means, well in a way, going right back to what people mean by interpretation, I think that part of the rhetoric here is and part of the reason interpretation might be seen as a dirty word, is that interpretation is this, I think most people, most people's understanding of interpretation within the psychological context is that it is this mythical guru, magical insights from the god-like figure, which are out-with the thing that was said. So the person, the *mere* participant, the humble human said this. 'But actually when I, the special one, do the divination, it's about that. And it's only somebody very special, like me that can do it. So it's, it's heavily loaded, it's magical. I can't show you the connection with what the person said because that's the whole point. I mean they don't know what they're saying. And you have to have had all of my deep experience and training or whatever to be able to see the truth'. Whereas I don't see it like that at all.

CW: Yeah.

JS: The position I am adopting can seem to lose out, not be heard, in terms of all the big noise and clamour and clatter between these big theoretical positions. But that's in a way what it is; it's a very gentle, local process. I really want to differentiate it from a description. But it is an interpretation which is clearly grounded in and responding to what the person said. So I go some steps away from what they said, but not too far away.

CW: And would you say that, if you were to be more loud or more distant in the interpretation, it wouldn't be phenomenological any more? Would it become something different then? Could you have a loud phenomenological interpretation?

JS: I think the way I see that is in terms of Ricoeur's differentiation between a hermeneutics of empathy, and a critical hermeneutics. Where I see IPA sitting is that I don't want people to just go native and just do the empathic. I think that you must start there (with the empathic), or as close to there as possible. But then you can move some way down the critical road. And if you're starting with the empathic, then the way you go down the critical road, will still be tied to the empathic you started with. Rather than if you'd started with the critical because then it becomes something very different. But I think there's quite a lot of scope in terms of going down that critical road. Every step further away you go, the more cautious you are, and the more careful you are about it and what you say about it. But I don't want to be, I don't wanna rule out doing that sort of speculation.

CW: Right.

JS: And I guess I had some experiences like this with students attempting to combine an IPA and a psychodynamic perspective. In fact haven't you examined one or two of these people? And I think it's all up for grabs exactly what that combination could look like. Except that I think it's absolutely critical where your starting point is, 'cos if you start over there at the critical end, you'll never or let's say you are unlikely to get close to here, to the empathic end. So I think the best IPA is doing more than just valorizing and wanting to be the person. At the same time as wanting to be able to get close to the person, it wants to be able to stand outside and say something about them as well. So in the end you are able to say a lot about them because you have been close and then a little bit less close.

CW: Yeah. So in terms of ethics then, would you say that it's, that there're not so many concerns, because you're trying to stay close enough for it to be potentially kind of something that the participant could engage with? But that you would see ethical problems, if one was to take a more distant approach? Or do you think that ethics isn't such a big deal, specifically around interpretation?

JS: If I put myself in the place of somebody doing that other type of interpretation, a hermeneutics of distance, I don't know how I would reconcile that. I don't know what the answer to that is. I personally think I would find it difficult. I'm not wanting to prescribe what can or can't be done. I think it would be important to think about the ethics of it so it is not done too crudely.

CW: Yeah.

JS: But then there is a range of ways of doing things and people can do them. Some people have a greater facility for doing it. So it's a thought experiment about, well I don't know but I think I wouldn't want to rule out that being done. What would make it ethical? I don't know. It would need careful consideration and I'm also recognizing that this is not fool proof. But going back to the type of interpretation I do, I think you know I'm talking about these gems now.[1] So the particular nuggets, the particular interpretations that I think are highly powerful, resonant and so on. And that's what I think a lot of this is about, that one is trying to achieve those. So I think, when I think about most of those that I'm associated with, I do feel that they would be ones, that I would be happy to have a conversation with the person about.

CW: Right. Yeah. And in terms of sort of interpretation, you know as a personal thing, what does it mean to you? And I think when I ask that question, I sort of just really wonder about whether you enjoy it? Does it enrich your life? Is it something that you feel gives you sort of something special? I don't know, what's your relationship with doing this kind of thinking?

JS: That's a sort of variant on the, did you say: 'How did you know when you're interpreting?'

CW: That was, yeah that came up earlier, yeah, I think when we talked about theory and, you know, how do you know you're making meaning? Whereas this is more about, what is it, you know, what's your relationship with interpretation as a person?

JS: 'Cos in a way I was, yeah and I think they're connected. *I interpret, therefore I am.* I actually think that does speak to some of this, because interpreting is such a big part of what being a person is that when I am interpreting, it is a reminder that I am a human being. There's a quote from Duke[2] that describes interpretation or hermeneutics as 'motion'. It involves an agility to move between different positions. There's a motion and in a way that is partly this reminder of being alive when I'm doing the sort of interpretation I'm talking about. So it is this intensive, grounded, careful listening that in the Heideggerian sense, that I need to, that there's something there, but I don't quite know what it is. So the detective has to dig down. So it's sort of a mixture of active and passive, creator and receiver. All of those things are happening and when I'm doing it, it is exhilarating because that is what I do. Whereas when I look at a transcript that's flat, where there isn't enough experience going on, where there's too much talk and there's too much defendedness, there's too much conceptual, I know I'm losing it then. It's like I'm not invigorated, enlivened by it. But if I read this thing and it's sort of, it's multifaceted, it's visceral, it's intuitive, I'm woken up by it and you are like 'wow'. There's something about the construction that holds you, it can be metaphors, or it may not be. But you know you're in the presence of something more powerful than that and there is something sacred about it. So you can read something a number of times and this hermeneutic circle is invoked in that. Ah yes, the person's saying X. But isn't it interesting that over here they're saying Y, and you read through that lens and then there is so much more. Suddenly it's thick with meaning. So it's informed by what's being said over there and it's thick, it's huge, it's big, it's multidimensional, it's alive. And I am alive in response to it. And it's not just that it's from a person who I spoke to. But that actually the thing is moving in real time as well, you know. And there's not a single reading. And you can come back to it and it often happens. I mean it happens quite a lot really and finding, I don't know what your experience is. But I've been asked to do quite a few keynotes recently and it can lead me to wondering what do I have to say that is new? And then getting into a re-visiting. So I go back, and I think well yeah, actually that does, or it's actually that those extracts are right for going down a slightly different interpretative route and connecting with what these people say. That's happening to me quite a lot. So the thing is open and expansive. So it requires a great fluency and agility to keep all of these things in play. And it is, it's not at all static, it's not linear: and going back to Duke saying it is a motion or a movement, one can ask 'What is the motion? What is the sound of the motion?' And it's both a buzz and a hum. So that the motion is both slow and gentle and sort of like, like slow planetary movement, but you also get the sort of buzz and there's a vibrance to it at the same time. And I think that's worth keeping an eye on, or an ear out for. So you don't want to get too carried away, you see this quote here you get excited about it, but you realize the thing goes on and you have to come back to it the next day. And the next day it still must have some resonance. It's not, it's not just a quick and dirty sound bite. So there's buzz and life and vibrance. But there's also order and symmetry. Working out what the process of doing interpretation is and the way all these different elements are working together. I do think that's a project that's, and I don't know what your, we can have another conversation about where you are with the book, but I think it's very early in terms of knowing what is actually happening. Maybe because it was a dirty word. But what is interpretation? What resources is it drawing on? What is, how would you describe that process? Because it's really mysterious what is actually happening. And it's captured in that sort of multi-layered definition as well. Because are we making this thing out? Are we bringing this thing out? Are we conveying it to somebody else? Are we explaining? The fact that the dictionary says that it's all of these things and we use the word interpretation, shows how early we are in terms of our understanding of what it is.

CW: Yes. I think in the literature on counselling and psychotherapy there's more on that and it might be really useful to sort of cross-fertilize.

JS: Yeah.

CW: There's more reflection on the process of what happens when you are sitting with a client, who's talking and you're trying to make sense of that. How much comes from you. And how much comes from them. You know your responses to that. How much is about emotional resonance. How much is about abstract thought.

JS: Yeah. Right.

CW: So a lot more has been done in that discipline, I think to acknowledge these kinds of mysterious processes you're describing.

JS: Yeah.

CW: Which I think as qualitative researchers we could probably benefit from looking at that and sort of drawing from that.

JS: Yeah.

CW: I think that might be worth doing in the future, because currently they are very separate literatures.

JS: Yeah, yeah.

CW: They're completely separate. It's only when I did the counselling training that I realized that there was quite a lot of correspondence going on. But that's not really acknowledged that much.

JS: Is it, is it done well? Do you feel it's multifaceted and resonant and nuanced?

CW: Yeah, I mean again it depends on ...

JS: And some of it, some of it is?

CW: ... the model, you know the different models have different views on that.

JS: Yeah.

CW: But some of the, I think, discussions of process are very sophisticated and very open to acknowledging different layers of whatever activity that goes on. So, I think yeah, again I haven't done that, but thinking about future projects, it would be worth doing a bit more of that, I think. In this book it's more conceptual. It's not so much about the quality of the process. Yeah, perhaps this in fact leads on to the last question, which is always nice when it's quite flowing in terms of the question sort of just making sense at that time ... The last question I had was really about the sort of future directions and where do you think qualitative research is going and within that, you know, what is the role of interpretation? In qualitative research, how will it pan out, do you think? Can you give me any suggestions there?

JS: Well what you just said is very interesting, and I guess what do I think about that? I think, I suppose intuitively I guessed that some of that would be there, so that would be interesting to look at that. Then we are talking about the difficulty of different groups, even when two groups have decided they're going to get into bed together, they don't even know what they are trying to do. In a way I think, I guess there's probably one would hope there was enough self-confidence in it. I'm thinking of qualitative researchers, who acknowledge that they're doing interpretation and are both exhilarated and baffled by it and counselling psychologists and therapists doing their work and feeling confident they're doing something so that they are equal partners. I can see that. There could be useful synergies there. I can see lots of reasons why that conversation could happen, and that could be a very useful, very worthwhile. I've had occasional conversations with some people from the clinical world about these things. I've written a bit with Rudi Dallos about qualitative research and therapy, trying to help clinical psychologists, clinical psychology trainees play to their strengths and see, actually clinical psychologists seeing that what they do as a sort of research and that there would be a way of articulating, formalizing, starting with the thing they do and having a bit more time and space and courage to articulate it as research, as opposed to just practice.

CW: Yeah.

JS: Because trainees are forced to do research and they can become averse to it. But doing therapy is doing research. It's an experiment in the real sense. Doing therapy is doing research. It's doing reflection. It's doing exploration. It's trying to make sense. So actually there would be a lot of value, if we could find a way of finding a bit of space. So I tend to be in my office pouring over manuscripts or whatever. Whereas the therapist is spending most of their time with a client trying to make sense, grapple with. But actually, while there's difference, there's also a lot of overlap. We could gain a lot from that. So, that could be, could be a really powerful way forward. Now turning to think about where IPA is going in the future, I think we will see a clearer confidence about doing the interpretative part. I think there is now more discussion and articulateness about interpretation and the quality of interpretation and a conviction about doing it, as opposed to doing the sort of rather bland, descriptive, analysis that is you know not going very far. So I'm hoping and expecting there to be more of that. So it will be more of a corpus of work that is higher quality IPA, because it is more interpretative. And then in terms of the future of qualitative research more generally, I'm looking forward to the synthesis, which I, I mean it's some way off, but you know qualitative psychology is like the infant kicking and screaming or whatever, that psychology is so late in terms of getting into qualitative research. We're at the stage of these groups, trying to work out, trying to define themselves, often in opposition to each other and throwing stones at each other. What do I mean by this idea of synthesis? You know although at one level epistemologically it seems that IPA is far away from discourse analysis. In many ways the sort of work that other people are doing that I respect most is careful micro CA/DA work, because it's done so meticulously. And sometimes when I'm doing a piece of analysis or interpretation in IPA, I'm thinking of rhetoric and language, the way the person's working with that and I don't think of myself as being that different from a discourse analyst. And it would be really exciting to try and bring these things together in a way that would work. At the moment it's so politicized about where we are and that there was a temporal sequence in which these positions got instantiated and IPA, and indeed phenomenology, came along rather late into the way most people think about qualitative psychology. And you know there's a danger of all these projections, that for example IPA is essentialist and individualist, but it's not, it's social constructionist. There are entities, discourses pre-existing, there is a social order that strongly influences the person and it's the symbiosis between the individual trying to make sense of what's happening to them and the resources they have to do that. And it will be good to see more interpretation, which is trying to combine a more individual and a more societal or social. So any IPA analysis that forgets the social and any discourse analysis that forgets the individual experience, to me is still partial. And that's OK, but you know it would be good to see more of the, the connection between them. When's that gonna happen? I mean I wouldn't put any time scale on that because there are so many pressures on people and so many obstacles for qualitative psychologists still to overcome. But that would be a way forward, I think.

CW: So that would mean rather than you know a student or academic saying, 'I'm going to do an IPA study on XYZ', it would be about saying, 'I want to understand what is going on when somebody is experiencing this'. And that understanding would include various aspects: the language they use, the quality of experience, the embodiment side of things, maybe even some biographical information about you know psychodynamics, and kind of putting all of that together to understand what is going on?

JS: Yeah.

CW: And not having to call it just one particular type of thing?

JS: Yeah.

CW: So that would be a sort of a pluralist, we mentioned earlier the idea of, you know this new idea of pluralism.

JS: Yeah.

CW: Which is a bit of a catch-phrase, but I'm wondering whether in a way it acknowledges that maybe we can bring things together. To gain a fuller understanding, rather than all splitting off in different camps and doing something very specific.

JS: Yeah, it all depends on how it's done.

CW: Yeah.

JS: I'm talking about something much more akin to a synthesis.

CW: Yes. It happens together.

JS: Yeah, and happens together and happening at the same time. I'm talking about the lens being stretched, and it's going to be difficult and there will be different elements happening. But that they will be happening more concurrently as opposed to separately.

CW: I mean, again there're probably lots of different ways of doing it, but the way I'm thinking of it now, would be almost a bit like an integrative psychotherapist, who would say: 'OK, I'm sitting with this client, who's bringing you know these issues and I'm not going to approach this from any specific theoretical model. I'm just going to listen and mainly start off in a person centered way to just allow some meaning to emerge, and then if it sounds like now the language the client is using is really noticeable. You know, perhaps she keeps repeating the same thing. I would pick up on that'.

JS: Yeah.

CW: And then over time you draw on different models to shed light on different aspects.

JS: Right.

CW: And in the end your understanding of the client's problems or experience would've been informed by many models.

JS: Yeah.

CW: And in a way I see the pluralist, if it's done in that way in research, to be similar that one would approach the transcript, kind of going through it with different perspectives on it. Either one after another or at the same time or moving between, just depending on the material, really. But there's a reading produced, which would pay attention to all of these aspects, a fuller reading.

JS: Yeah.

CW: Which obviously means the researcher has to be skilled in all the different methods, to some extent, or we would have to work in groups more.

JS: Yeah.

CW: Then of course it would raise epistemological questions as well. You'd have to make sure it's not contradicting.

JS: Yeah, yeah.

CW: In tension too much, but that would need to be addressed.

JS: Yeah, yeah.

CW: It would be much more challenging for the researcher and again when we're thinking about students, perhaps you know it would be asking quite a lot for that to happen and it probably couldn't be done from the beginning.

JS: Yeah, yeah.

CW: It would be a higher level of work.

JS: Calling it integrative is more in line with what I think both you and I are thinking. 'Cos the term pluralist clearly sounds good. But it can mean lots of different things, can't it? For example it can mean respecting other ways of thinking but the different ways of thinking staying separate or working in parallel rather than coming together as a new Gestalt.

CW: 'Integrative qualitative research' could be a nice way of bringing it together and then one could also kind of draw on psychotherapy, as a precedent of sort of what can be done in this way.

JS: Yes.

CW: Do you have anything else that you would like to add? We've had a very full and extensive discussion, really. There were lots of new ideas coming out. But is there anything you feel still needs to be said before we finish?

JS: Just give me a minute to reflect. This does indeed sound like a really exciting project. And of course we are talking about something new because of the text. Because I'm sure there will be a lot of value, there will be people who have thought, people who have thought about, reflected a lot about what is going on when they're doing interpretation in therapy. The extra bit here is that you've got this text that you live with for longer, and you therefore analyse in a way and at a level at a pace that is different from that. It's connected to it, but different. So it is the case that here's something very powerful that happens in the interview, that's obviously close to therapeutic experience, but then there is this thing that you are confronted with afterwards a, this reconstruction or a transformation of it as a set of words. That's what I spend more of my time looking at – these pages recapturing the words that people have said. That's the difference between qualitative research and therapy and that indeed suggests another series of useful conversations to be had with hermeneuticists, historians, people who are struggling with theological texts, literary texts, and so on. And indeed experiential qualitative psychology occupies quite a distinctive position in relation to the other things we have been talking about. To simplify things for a moment for clarity. Therapists are working with a person; people in the humanities are working with a text. Experiential qualitative psychologists are working with a text but there is a person who generated that text and whom one's analysis is also directed at, whose experience, as represented in the text, one is trying to make sense of.

CW: But then if you think about supervision, what comes to mind is that although it's true that with a client it's sort of in the moment you're doing it, there and then, and you might be, the interpretation process is very much about the relationship with the person. It's very much about what goes on between you. But then when you go away afterwards and you write your client notes, which is transforming it into another kind of text . . .

JS: Yeah.

CW: . . . where you already interpret more than you did in the session, because you're thinking about it again. Then you have your supervision and you read again what you've written. You tell your supervisor. Then they ask you about aspects of what you've written, which you hadn't considered. So now the interpretation is created between you and the supervisor, which then when you go back to the client, you then sometimes revisit stuff that they said. And to clarify, so there is something happening outside the encounter, which is a bit like research and as you've said it is a bit like research. But you're not working with a text in the same way we would do in research. You're working more with your memories of what was said and done.

JS: Yeah.

CW: So it's interesting; both the differences and similarities are very interesting.

JS: I acknowledge what you're saying and I can see that. And I'm sure an experienced, skilful therapist remembers a lot about what was actually said. But what I'm so, what I'm so struck by is with the work that I do, is you know the importance of literally what was said. That is partly the connection with the DA, because that's what I'm sometimes aware of that I think strangely what often connects a good piece of CA or DA and IPA, is this really close textual analysis. So just looking at one sentence and the way it unfolds. And that is a deeply textual activity.

CW: Yes.

JS: So I think people who you know spend all their time looking at texts and who are from other disciplines, should have a lot to say to this as well. Yeah, and then in terms of what else needs to be heard I mean I sort of touched on this, but it's, the sense in which interpretation, doing good qualitative research is always about combining things. It's not a singular thing. It is multifaceted and breaks polarities. So that's what I think I am doing when I am doing good interpretation. There's something about combining the active and the passive. There's something about both the assertive and abeyant. So that when I'm with the person, I'm moving between claiming who I am, in the sense that I'm not just some empty vessel, that there's a person here that wants to hear what you are saying. But at the same time being abeyant and holding back. But then I'm hearing things myself and so I'm then exhilarated and I'll say something. So I'm in a constant move like a dance or a circle. There's a move between broadly the active and the passive, the assertive and the abeyant. And then in addition it's working at different levels or with different domains. So there is a cerebral and an intuitive, affective and embodied. It's all of those different things are happening at the same time. And then there is more still. In terms of moving between parts and wholes, so that the person is saying this particular thing now, but it's embedded in a sentence. And I'm listening to what they said earlier on and so on. And then in terms of then the account that one writes up, there's a presence of the participant and of the researcher. And is it what they said or what I said? It's always about navigating, in crude terms it's both art and science, in that it's both creative and going for metaphors and depth of texture from the individual and it's scientific in terms of being systematic and plotting it out. I don't buy that in the sense that I think all of this actually is a science. I say that not because it is intrinsically important to me but because mainstream psychology wants to see itself as doing science. Well I don't have any problems seeing everything we're doing as being science. But there's an artistic science and scientistic science and both are involved in interpretation. The main thing is that it is, it's very elaborate, it's very multi-layered, it's always both/and, not either/or, it's sort of navigating in the middle of all of these things. I think that's what it's like. That's part of what makes it complicated. But it really is like that. And attempts to rationalize it, streamline it, categorize it, usually miss the very thing that's there, which is that it's in between, it's in the mix. I sort of alluded to that earlier, but that's what I think the process is like really.

CW: Well ok, fantastic, thank you very much.

And here are Professor Smith's recommended readings:

Schleiermacher, F. (1998) *Hermeneutics and Criticism and other Writings* (A. Bowie, trans.). Cambridge: Cambridge University Press. A classic and very readable collection.

Smith, J.A., Flowers, P. and Larkin. M (2009) *Interpretative Phenomenological Analysis: Theory, Method and Research.* London: Sage. This is a comprehensive guide to interpretative phenomenological analysis and includes extensive coverage of interpretation theory alongside worked examples of it in practice.

Vandervelde, P. (2005) *The Task of the Interpreter.* Pittsburgh, PA: Pittsburgh University Press. A recent book that has useful material on various theoretical positions in relation to interpretation.

Notes

1. See Smith, J.A. (2011) 'We could be diving for pearls': the value of the gem in experiential qualitative psychology, *Qualitative Methods in Psychology Bulletin*, 12: 6–15.
2. Duke, J. (1977) Translater's introduction, in F. Schleiermacher, *Hermeneutics: The Handwritten Manuscripts* (H. Kimmerle, ed.; J. Duke and J. Forstman, trans.). Missoula, MT: Scholars Press.

References

Ainsworth, M.D.S. (1967) *Infancy in Uganda: Infant Care and the Growth of Attachment*. Baltimore, MD: Johns Hopkins University Press.

Alvesson, M. and Skoldberg, K. (2002) *Reflexive Methodology*. London: Sage.

Austin, J.L. (1975) *How to Do Things with Words*. Cambridge, MA: Harvard University Press.

Barker, M., Hagger-Johnson, G., Hegarty, P., Hutchison, C. and Riggs, D. (2007) Responses from the Lesbian & Gay Psychology Section to Crossley's 'Making sense of "barebacking"', *British Journal of Social Psychology*, 46: 667–77.

Bengry-Howell, A. (2005) *Performative motorcar display: The cultural construction of young working class masculine identities*, Unpublished PhD thesis, University of Birmingham.

Berger, P.L. and Luckman, T. (1967) *The Social Construction of Reality: A Treatise in the Sociology of Knowledge*. London: Allen Lane.

Besemeres, M. (2006) Language and emotional experience: the voice of translingual memoir, in A. Pavlenko (ed.) *Bilingual Minds: Emotional Experience, Expression and Representation*. Clevedon: Multilingual Matters Ltd.

Bowlby, J. (1988) *A Secure Base: Clinical Applications of Attachment Theory*. London: Routledge.

Boyatzis, R.E. (1998) *Transforming Qualitative Information: Thematic Analysis and Code Development*. London: Sage.

Braun, V. and Clarke, V. (2006) Using thematic analysis in psychology, *Qualitative Research in Psychology*, 3: 77–101.

Brinkmann, S. and Kvale, S. (2008) Ethics in qualitative psychological research, in C. Willig and W. Stainton Rogers (eds.) *The SAGE Handbook of Qualitative Research*. London: Sage.

Bucholtz, M. (2000) The politics of transcription, *Journal of Pragmatics*, 32: 1439–65.

Calle, S. (2007) *Take Care of Yourself*. Arles, France: Actes Sud.

Celsi, R.L., Rose, R.L. and Leigh, T.W. (1993) An exploration of high-risk leisure consumption through skydiving, *Journal of Consumer Research*, 20: 1–23.

Chamberlain, K. (2000) Methodolatry and qualitative health research, *Journal of Health Psychology*, 5(3): 285–96.

Charmaz, K. (2006) *Constructing Grounded Theory: A Practical Guide Through Qualitative Research*. London: Sage.

Clarke, J. (1992) Cancer, heart disease and AIDS: what do the media tell us about these diseases?, *Health Communication*, 4(2): 105–20.

Clayman, S.E. (1992) Footing in the achievement of neutrality: the case of news-interview discourse, in P. Drew and J. Heritage (eds.) *Talk at Work: Interaction in Institutional Settings*. Cambridge: Cambridge University Press.

Cohen, M.Z. and Omery, A. (1994) Schools of phenomenology, in J.M. Morse (ed.) *Critical Issues in Qualitative Research*. Thousand Oaks, CA: Sage.

Cohn, H.W. (2005) Interpretation: explanation or understanding?, in E. van Deurzen and C. Arnold-Baker (eds.) *Existential Perspectives on Human Issues: A Handbook for Therapeutic Practice*. Basingstoke: Palgrave Macmillan.

Colaizzi, P. (1978) Psychological research as the phenomenologist views it, in R. Valle and M. King (eds.) *Existential-phenomenological Alternatives for Psychology*. New York: Oxford University Press.

Cornish, F. and Gillespie, A. (2009) A pragmatist approach to the problem of knowledge in health psychology, *Journal of Health Psychology*, 14(6): 800–9.

Crossley, M. (2000) *Introducing Narrative Psychology*. Buckingham: Open University Press.

Crossley, M. (2001) Sexual practices, community health prevention and issues of empowerment, *Journal of Community and Applied Social Psychology*, 11: 111–23.

Crossley, M. (2004) Making sense of 'barebacking': gay men's narratives, unsafe sex and 'resistance habitus', *British Journal of Social Psychology*, 43(2): 225–44.

Csikszentmihalyi, M. (1975) *Beyond Boredom and Anxiety*. San Francisco, CA: Jossey-Bass.

Curt, B. (1994) *Textuality and Tectonics: Troubling Social and Psychological Science*. Buckingham: Open University Press.

Cushman, P. (1995) *Constructing the Self, Constructing America: A Cultural History of Psychotherapy*. Cambridge, MA: Da Capo Press.

Deber, R.B., Kraetschmer, N., Urowitz, S. and Sharpe, N. (2005) Patient, consumer, client or customer: what do people want to be called?, *Health Expectations*, 8: 345–51.

Denscombe, M. (2003) *The Good Research Guide*. Buckingham: Open University Press.

Denzin, N. (1997) *Interpretive Ethnography*. London: Sage.

Duke, J. (1977) Translator's introduction, in F. Schleiermacher, *Hermeneutics: The Handwritten Manuscripts* (H. Kimmerle, ed.; J. Duke and J. Forstman, trans.). Missoula, MT: Scholars Press.

Dury, R. (ed.) (2004) Introduction, in *Strange Case of Dr Jekyll and Mr Hyde*. Edinburgh: Edinburgh University Press.

Eatough, V. and Smith, J.A. (2008) Interpretative phenomenological analysis, in C. Willig and W. Stainton Rogers (eds.) *The SAGE Handbook of Qualitative Research*. London: Sage.

Edgar, D. (2011) Whose bible is it anyway?, *The Guardian Review*, 19 March, pp. 2–4.

Edwards, D. (2004) Discursive psychology, in K. Fitch and R. Sanders (eds.) *Handbook of Language and Social Interaction*. Mahwah, NJ: Lawrence Erlbaum.

Edwards, D. and Potter, J. (1992) *Discursive Psychology*. London: Sage.

Ehrenreich, B. (2009) *Smile or Die: How Positive Thinking Fooled America and the World*. London: Granta Publications.

Eiser, J.R. (1984) Addiction as attribution: cognitive processes in giving up smoking, in J.R. Eiser (ed.) *Social Psychology and Behavioural Medicine*. Chichester: Wiley.

Emerson, P. and Frosh, S. (2004) *Critical Narrative Analysis in Psychology*. London: Palgrave.

Fingarette, H. (1963) *The Self in Transformation: Psychoanalysis, Philosophy, and the Life of the Spirit*. New York: Harper & Row.

Finlay, L. (2009) Debating phenomenological research methods, *Phenomenology and Practice*, 3(1): 6–25.

Fleischman, S. (1999) 'I am ..., I have ..., I suffer from ...': a linguist reflects on the language of illness and disease, *Journal of Medical Humanities*, 20(1): 3–32.

Flowers, P. and Langdridge, D. (2007) Offending the other: deconstructing narratives of deviance and pathology, *British Journal of Social Psychology*, 46: 679–90.

Forrester, M.A. (1996) *Psychology of Language: A Critical Introduction*. London: Sage.

Forshaw, M.J. (2007) Free qualitative research from the shackles of method, *The Psychologist*, 20(8): 478–9.

Frank, A.W. (1995) *The Wounded Storyteller: Body, Illness and Ethics*. Chicago, IL: University of Chicago Press.

French, C.C. and Santomauro, J. (2007) Something wicked this way comes: causes and interpretations of sleep paralysis, in S. Della Sala (ed.) *Tall Tales about the Mind and Brain: Separating Fact from Fiction*. Oxford: Oxford University Press.

Freud, S. (1957) 'Wild' psychoanalysis, in J. Strachey (ed. and trans.) *The Standard Edition of the Complete Psychological Works of Sigmund Freud*, Vol. XI. London: Hogarth Press (original work published 1910).

Freud, S. (1976) *The Interpretation of Dreams*. Harmondsworth: Penguin.

Frosh, S. (1997) *For and Against Psychoanalysis*. London: Routledge.

Frosh, S. (2007) Disintegrating qualitative research, *Theory and Psychology*, 17(5): 635–53.

Frosh, S. (2010) *Psychoanalysis Outside the Clinic: Interventions in Psychosocial Studies*. Basingstoke: Palgrave Macmillan.

Frosh, S. and Emerson, P.D. (2005) Interpretation and over-interpretation: disputing the meaning of texts, *Qualitative Research*, 5(3): 307–24.

Frosh, S. and Young, L.S. (2008) Psychoanalytic approaches to qualitative psychology, in C. Willig and W. Stainton Rogers (eds.) *The SAGE Handbook of Qualitative Research*. London: Sage.

Frosh, S., Phoenix, A. and Pattman, R. (2003) Taking a stand: using psychoanalysis to explore the positioning of subjects in discourse, *British Journal of Social Psychology*, 42: 39–53.

Frost, N. (2009a) 'Do you know what I mean?': the use of a pluralistic narrative analysis approach in the interpretation of an interview, *Qualitative Research*, 9(1): 9–29.

Frost, N. (2009b) Pluralism in qualitative research: a report on the work of the PQR project, *Social Psychological Review*, 11(1): 32–8.

Fulder-Heyd, Y. (2011) *Women's experiences of psychological homelessness and identity management*, Unpublished DPsych thesis, City University London.

Gadamer, H.-G. (1991) *Truth and Method* (2nd revised edn., J. Weinsheimer and D.G. Marshall, trans.). New York: Crossroad.

Galántai, D. (2002) Literal meaning in translation, *Perspectives*, 10(3): 167–92.

Gee, J.P. (1991) A linguistic approach to narrative, *Journal of Narrative and Life History*, 1(1): 15–39.

Gellner, E. (1985) *The Psychoanalytic Movement*. London: Paladin.

Gergen, K.J. (1973) Social psychology as history, *Journal of Personality and Social Psychology*, 26(2): 309–20.

Gergen, K.J. (1989) Social psychology and the wrong revolution, *European Journal of Social Psychology*, 19: 463–84.

Gergen, K.J. (1999) *An Invitation to Social Construction*. London: Sage.

Gillies, V. and Willig, C. (1997) 'You get the nicotine and that in your blood': constructions of addiction and control in women's accounts of cigarette smoking, *Journal of Community and Applied Social Psychology*, 7: 285–301.

Gillies, V., Harden. A., Johnson, K., Reavey, P., Strange, V. and Willig, C. (2005) Painting pictures of embodied experience: the use of non-verbal data production for the study of embodiment, *Qualitative Research in Psychology*, 2: 199–212.

Gilligan, C. (1982) *In a Different Voice*. Cambridge, MA: Harvard University Press.

Giorgi, A. (1992) Description vs. interpretation: competing alternative strategies for qualitative research, *Journal of Phenomenological Psychology*, 23: 119–35.

Giorgi, A. (2008) Difficulties encountered in the application of the phenomenological method in the social sciences, *Indo-Pacific Journal of Phenomenology*, 8(1): 1–9.

Giorgi, A.P. and Giorgi, B. (2008) Phenomenological psychology, in C. Willig and W. Stainton-Rogers (eds.) *The SAGE Handbook of Qualitative Research in Psychology*. London: Sage.

Glaser, B.G. (1992) *Emergence vs. Forcing: Basics of Grounded Theory Analysis*. Mill Valley, CA: Sociology Press.

Glaser, B.G. and Strauss, A.L. (1967) *The Discovery of Grounded Theory: Strategies for Qualitative Research*. New York: Aldine.

Goffman, E. (1981) Footing, in *Forms of Talk*. Philadelphia, PA: University of Pennsylvania Press.

Gough, B. (2004) Psychoanalysis as a resource for understanding emotional ruptures in the text: the case of defensive masculinities, *British Journal of Social Psychology*, 43: 245–67.

Grant, J. and Crawley, J. (2002) *Transference and Projection*. Buckingham: Open University Press.

Griffin, C. and Bengry-Howell, A. (2008) Ethnography, in C. Willig and W. Stainton-Rogers (eds.) *The SAGE Handbook of Qualitative Research in Psychology*. London: Sage.

Gubrium, J. and Holstein, J. (2000) Analysing interpretive practice, in N. Denzin and Y. Lincoln (eds.) *Handbook of Qualitative Research*. London: Sage.

Hammersley, M. (2010) Reproducing or constructing? Some questions about transcription in social research, *Qualitative Research*, 10(5): 553–69.

Haraway, D.J. (1988) Situated knowledges: the science question in feminism and the privilege of partial perspective, *Feminist Studies*, 14(3): 575–97.

Harcourt, D. and Frith, H. (2008) Women's experiences of an altered appearance during chemotherapy, *Journal of Health Psychology*, 13(5): 597–606.

Heidegger, M. (1962) *Being and Time* (E. Macquarrie and J. Robinson, trans.). Oxford: Blackwell (original work published 1927).

Heidegger, M. (1993) Letter on humanism, in D.F. Krell (ed.) *Basic Writings* (2nd revised and expanded edn). New York: HarperCollins.

Hollway, W. and Jefferson, T. (2000) *Doing Qualitative Research Differently: Free Association, Narrative and the Interview Method*. London: Sage.

Hollway, W. and Jefferson, T. (2005) Panic and perjury: a psychosocial exploration of agency, *British Journal of Social Psychology*, 44(2): 147–63.

Holstein, J.A. and Gubrium, J.F. (2000) Interpretive action and social practice, in N.K. Denzin and Y.S. Lincoln (eds.) *Handbook of Qualitative Research* (2nd edn). London: Sage.

Horton-Salway, M. (2001) Narrative identities and the management of personal accountability in talk about ME, *Journal of Health Psychology*, 6(2): 247–59.

Jacobs, M. (1998) *The Presenting Past: The Core of Psychodynamic Counselling and Therapy* (2nd edn). Buckingham: Open University Press.

Kagan, C., Burton, M. and Siddiquee, A. (2008) Action research, in C. Willig and W. Stainton-Rogers (eds.) *The SAGE Handbook of Qualitative Research in Psychology*. London: Sage.

Kendall, G. and Wickham, G. (1999) *Using Foucault's Method*. London: Sage.

Kirk, J. and Miller, M. (1986) *Reliability and Validity in Qualitative Research*. London: Sage.

Kvale, S. (1996) *InterViews: An Introduction to Qualitative Research Interviewing*. London: Sage.

Kvale, S. (2003) The psychoanalytic interview as inspiration for qualitative research, *Social Psychological Review*, 5(2): 20–42.

Labov, W. (1972) The transformation of experience in narrative syntax, in W. Labov (ed.) *Language in the Inner City: Studies in the Black English Vernacular*. Philadelphia, PA: University of Pennsylvania Press.

Langdridge, D. (2007) *Phenomenological Psychology: Theory, Research and Method*. Harlow: Pearson.

Laplanche, J. and Pontalis, J.-B. (1983) *The Language of Psycho-Analysis*. London: Hogarth Press.

Larkin, M., Watts, S. and Clifton, E. (2006) Giving voice and making sense in interpretative phenomenological analysis, *Qualitative Research in Psychology*, 3: 102–20.

Latour, B. (2000) When things strike back: a possible contribution of 'science studies' to the social sciences, *British Journal of Sociology*, 50: 107–23.

Le Breton, D. (2000) Playing symbolically with death and extreme sports, *Body and Society*, 6(1): 1–11.

Lincoln, Y. and Guba, E. (1985) *Naturalistic Inquiry*. New York: Sage.

Lloyd, C., King, R., Bassett, H., Sandland, S. and Savige, G. (2001) Patient, client or consumer? A survey of preferred terms, *Australasian Psychiatry*, 9: 321–4.

Lomas, P. (1987) *The Limits of Interpretation: What's Wrong With Psychoanalysis?* London: Penguin.

Lopez, K.A. and Willis, D.G. (2004) Descriptive versus interpretive phenomenology: their contributions to nursing knowledge, *Qualitative Health Research*, 14(5): 726–35.

Lowe, R. (1985) *Basic Uummarmiut Eskimo Grammar*. Inuvik, Canada: Committee for Original Peoples Entitlement.

Lupton, D. (1994) *Medicine as Culture: Illness, Disease and the Body in Western Societies*. London: Sage.

Lyons, E. and Coyle, A. (eds.) (2007) *Analysing Qualitative Data in Psychology*. London: Sage.

Madill, A., Jordan, A. and Shirley, C. (2000) Objectivity and reliability in qualitative analysis: realist, contextualist and radical constructionist epistemologies, *British Journal of Psychology*, 91: 1–20.

Marsh, P., Rosser, E. and Harré, R. (1978) *The Rules of Disorder*. London: Routledge.

McLeod, J. (2001) *Qualitative Research in Counselling and Psychotherapy*. London: Sage.

Mishler, E. (2003) Representing discourse: the rhetoric of transcription, in Y. Lincoln and N. Denzin (eds.) *Turning Points in Qualitative Research*. Oxford: Altamira Press.

Mitchell, J. (2000) *Mad Men and Medusas*. London: Allen Lane.

Moghaddam, F.M. (1999) Reflexive positioning: culture and private discourse, in R. Harré and L. van Langenhove (eds.) *Positioning Theory*. Oxford: Blackwell.

Morrow, S.L. (2005) Quality and trustworthiness in qualitative research in counselling psychology, *Journal of Counseling Psychology*, 52: 250–60.

Mosher, C.E. and Danoff-Burg, S. (2009) Cancer patients versus cancer survivors, *Journal of Language and Social Psychology*, 28(1): 72–84.

Mulhall, S. (1996) *Heidegger and Being and Time*. London: Routledge.

Murray, M. (2003) Narrative psychology, in J.A. Smith (ed.) *Qualitative Psychology: A Practical Guide to Research*. London: Sage.

Nair, B.R. (1998) Patient, client or customer?, *Medical Journal of Australia*, 169: 593.

Oliver, D.G., Serovich, J.M. and Mason, T. (2005) Constraints and opportunities with interview transcription: towards reflection in qualitative research, *Social Forces*, 84(2): 1273–89.

Ortega y Gasset, J. (2000) The misery and splendour of translation, in L. Venuti (ed.) *The Translation Studies Reader*. London: Routledge (original work published 1937).

Packer, M. and Addison, R. (eds.) (1989) *Entering the Circle: Hermeneutic Investigation in Psychology*. Albany, NY: State University of New York Press.

Parker, I. (1992) *Discourse Dynamics: Critical Analysis for Social and Individual Psychology*. London: Routledge.

Parker, I. (2005a) *Qualitative Psychology: Introducing Radical Research*. Maidenhead: Open University Press.

Parker, I. (2005b) Lacanian discourse analysis in psychology: seven theoretical elements, *Theory and Psychology*, 15: 163–82.

Polkinghorne, D.E. (2005) Language and meaning: data collection in qualitative research, *Journal of Counseling Psychology*, 52(2): 137–45.

Pomerantz, A. (1986) Extreme case formulations: a new way of legitimating claims, in G. Button, P. Drew and J. Heritage (eds.) *Human Studies*, 9: 219–30 (Special Issue: Interaction and Language Use).

Popper, K. (1945) *The Open Society and its Enemies*. London: Routledge & Kegan Paul.

Porter, R. (1997) *The Greatest Benefit to Mankind: A Medical History of Humanity from Antiquity to the Present*. London: HarperCollins.

Punch, K. (1998) *Introduction to Social Research*. London: Sage.

Radley, A. (1994) *Making Sense of Illness: The Social Psychology of Health and Disease*. London: Sage.

Radley, A. and Taylor, D. (2003) Images of recovery: a photo-elicitation study on the hospital ward, *Qualitative Health Research*, 13: 77–99.

Raine, C. (2005) I remember my mother dying, *The Times Literary Supplement*, 25 November, p. 5.

Reason, P. and Bradbury, H. (2001) Introduction: inquiry and participation in search of a world worthy of human aspiration, in P. Reason and H. Bradbury (eds.) *Handbook of Action Research: Participative Inquiry and Practice*. London: Sage.

Reavey, P. (ed.) (2011) *Visual Methods in Psychology: Using and Interpreting Images in Qualitative Research*. London: Routledge.

Reavey, P. and Johnson, K. (2008) Visual approaches: using and interpreting images, in C. Willig and W. Stainton Rogers (eds.) *The SAGE Handbook of Qualitative Research*. London: Sage.

Reicher, S. (2000) Against methodolatry: some comments on Elliott, Fischer, and Rennie, *British Journal of Clinical Psychology*, 39: 1–6.

Reid, J., Ewan, C. and Lowy, E. (1991) Pilgrimage of pain: the illness experience of women with repetitive strain injury and the search for credibility, *Social Science and Medicine*, 32: 601–12.

Rennie, D.L. (2004) Anglo-North American qualitative counselling and psychotherapy research, *Psychotherapy Research*, 14: 37–55.

Ricoeur, P. (1970) *Freud and Philosophy: An Essay on Interpretation* (D. Savage, trans.). New Haven, CT: Yale University Press.

Ricoeur, P. (1991) The task of hermeneutics, in *From Text to Action: Essays in Hermeneutics*, Vol. 2 (K. Blamey and J.B. Thompson, trans.). Evanston, IL: Northwestern University Press.

Ricoeur, P. (1996) On interpretation, in R. Kearney and M. Rainwater (eds.) *The Continental Philosophy Reader*. London: Routledge (original work published 1983).

Ross, J.W. (1989) The militarization of disease: do we really want a war on AIDS?, *Soundings*, 72(1): 39–58.

Ross, J. (2010) Was that infinity or affinity? Applying insights from translation studies to qualitative research transcription, *Forum: Qualitative Social Research*, 11(2): 1–13 (article 2).

Ryan, G.W. and Bernard, H.R. (2000) Data management and analysis methods, in N.K. Denzin and Y.S. Lincoln (eds) *Handbook of Qualitative Research* (2nd edn). London: Sage.

Santomauro, J. and French, C.C. (2009) Terror in the night, *The Psychologist*, 22(8): 672–5.

Sartre, J.-P. (2003) *Being and Nothingness: An Essay on Phenomenological Ontology*. London: Routledge.

Schmidt, L.K. (2006) *Understanding Hermeneutics*. Stocksfield: Acumen.

Seale, C. (2001) Sporting cancer: struggle language in news reports of people with cancer, *Sociology of Health and Illness*, 23(3): 308–29.

Shorter, E. (1992) *From Paralysis to Fatigue: A History of Psychosomatic Illness in the Modern Era*. Oxford: Maxwell Macmillan International.

Simmonds, J.G. (2006a) The oceanic feeling and a sea change: historical challenges to reductionist attitudes to religion and spirit from within psychoanalysis, *Psychoanalytic Psychology*, 23(1): 128–42.

Simmonds, J.G. (2006b) Freud and the American physician's religious experience, *Mental Health, Religion and Culture*, 9(4): 401–5.

Smith, B. and Sparkes, A.C. (2002) Men, sport, spinal cord injury, and the construction of coherence: narrative practice in action, *Qualitative Research*, 2: 143–71.

Smith, B. and Sparkes, A.C. (2006) Narrative inquiry in psychology: exploring the tensions within, *Qualitative Research in Psychology*, 3: 169–92.

Smith, J.A. (2004) Reflecting on the development of interpretative phenomenological analysis and its contribution to qualitative research in psychology, *Qualitative Research in Psychology*, 1: 39–54.

Smith, J.A. (2007) Hermeneutics, human sciences and health: linking theory and practice, *International Journal of Qualitative Studies on Health and Well-being*, 2: 3–11.

Smith, J.A. and Osborne, M. (2003) Interpretative phenomenological analysis, in J.A. Smith (ed.) *Qualitative Psychology: A Practical Guide to Research Methods*. London: Sage.

Smith, J.A., Flowers, P. and Larkin, M. (2009) *Interpretative Phenomenological Analysis: Theory, Method and Research*. London: Sage.

Sontag, S. (1991) *Illness As Metaphor: AIDS and its Metaphors*. London: Penguin Books.

Sontag, S. (1994) Against interpretation, in *Against Interpretation and Other Essays*. London: Vintage/Random House (original work published 1966).

Spears, R. (2005) Commentary – where did Vince's van go?, *British Journal of Social Psychology*, 44(2): 165–8.

Spinelli, E. (1994) *Demystifying Therapy*. London: Constable.

Spinelli, E. (2001) *The Mirror and the Hammer: Challenges to Therapeutic Orthodoxy.* London: Continuum.

Spinelli, E. (2007) *Practising Existential Psychotherapy: The Relational World.* London: Sage.

Spivak, G.C. (1988) Can the subaltern speak?, in C. Nelson and L. Grossberg (eds.) *Marxism and the Interpretation of Culture.* Urbana, IL: University of Illinois Press.

Spivak, G. (1992) The politics of translation, in M. Barrett and A. Philips (eds.) *Destabilizing Theory: Contemporary Feminist Debates.* Cambridge: Polity Press.

Stacey, J. (1997) *Teratologies: A Cultural Study of Cancer.* London: Routledge.

Stevenson, R.L. (2004) *The Strange Case of Dr Jekyll and Mr Hyde* (R. Dury, ed.). Edinburgh: Edinburgh University Press.

Stewart, D.C. and Sullivan, T.J. (1982) Illness behaviour and the sick role in chronic disease, *Social Science and Medicine*, 16: 1397–1404.

Stibbe, A. (1997) Fighting, warfare and the discourse of cancer, *South African Journal of Linguistics*, 15(2): 65–70.

Strauss, A.L. and Corbin, J. (1990) *Basics of Qualitative Research: Grounded Theory Procedures and Techniques.* London: Sage.

Strauss, A.L. and Corbin, J. (1998) *Basics of Qualitative Research: Grounded Theory Procedures and Techniques* (2nd edn). London: Sage.

Sullivan, P. (2008) Our emotional connection to truth: moving beyond a functional view of language in discourse analysis, *Journal for the Theory of Social Behaviour*, 38(2): 193–207.

Sullivan, P. (2010) The self–self relationship in qualitative psychology, *Qualitative Methods in Psychology Bulletin*, 9: 12–16.

Summerscale, K. (2008) *The Suspicions of Mr Whicher.* London: Bloomsbury.

Temple, B. and Edwards, R. (2002) Interpreters/translators and cross-language research: reflexivity and border crossings, *International Journal of Qualitative Methods*, 1(2): 1–12.

Temple, B. and Koterba, K. (2009) The same but different – researching language and culture in the lives of Polish people in England, *Forum: Qualitative Social Research*, 10(1) (article 31).

Teo, T. (2008) From speculation to epistemological violence in psychology: a critical-hermeneutic reconstruction, *Theory and Psychology*, 18(1): 47–67.

Teo, T. (2010) What is epistemological violence in the empirical social sciences?, *Social and Personality Psychology Compass*, 4/5: 295–303.

Tilley, S. and Powick, K. (2002) Distanced data: transcribing other people's research tapes, *Canadian Journal of Education*, 27(2/3): 291–310.

Vance, L.M. (2011) *A brief history of the King James Bible.* Available at: http://www.av1611.org/kjv/kjvhist.html (accessed 2 March 2011).

Van Manen, M. (1990) *Researching Lived Experience: Human Science for an Action Sensitive Pedagogy.* Albany, NY: State University of New York Press.

Van Rijn-van Tongeren, G. (1997) *Metaphors in Medical Texts.* Amsterdam: Rodopi.

Venuti, L. (1995) *The Translator's Invisibility: A History of Translation.* London: Routledge.

Venuti, L. (1998) *The Scandals of Translation: Towards an Ethics of Difference.* London: Routledge.

Weir, P. (2010) The gout myth, *The Guardian* (Health section), 6 July, pp. 14–15.

Wetherell, M. (2001) Debates in discourse research, in M. Wetherell, S. Taylor and S.J. Yates (eds.) *Discourse Theory and Practice: A Reader.* London: Sage.

Wetherell, M. (2003) Paranoia, ambivalence and discursive practices: concepts of position and positioning in psychoanalysis and discursive psychology, in R. Harré and F. Moghaddam (eds.) *The Self and Others: Positioning Individuals and Groups in Personal, Political and Cultural Contexts.* New York: Praeger/Greenwood Publishers.

Wetherell, M. (2005) Commentary – unconscious conflict or everyday accountability?, *British Journal of Social Psychology*, 44(2): 169–73.

Whorf, B. (1956) *Language, Thought and Reality.* Cambridge, MA: MIT Press.

Wiggins, S. and Potter, J. (2008) Discursive psychology, in C. Willig and W. Stainton Rogers (eds.) *The SAGE Handbook of Qualitative Research.* London: Sage.

Wikipedia (undated) *Authorized King James Version.* Available at: http://en.wikipedia.org/wiki/Authorized_King_James_Version (accessed 2 March 2011).

Williams, E.N. and Morrow, S.L. (2009) Achieving trustworthiness in qualitative research: a pan-paradigmatic perspective, *Psychotherapy Research*, 19(4/5): 576–82.

Williams Camus, J.T. (2009) Metaphors of cancer in scientific popularization articles in the British press, *Discourse Studies*, 11(4): 465–95.

Willig, C. (2000) A discourse-dynamic approach to the study of subjectivity in health psychology, *Theory and Psychology*, 10(4): 547–70.

Willig, C. (2004) Discourse analysis and health psychology, in M. Murray (ed.) *Critical Health Psychology.* Basingstoke: Palgrave Macmillan.

Willig, C. (2005) *A phenomenological investigation of the experience of taking part in extreme sport*, Unpublished MA thesis, Regent's College London.

Willig, C. (2007a) Qualitative research – the need for method, *The Psychologist (Letters)*, 20(10): 597.

Willig, C. (2007b) Reflections on the use of the phenomenological method, *Qualitative Research in Psychology*, 4: 1–17.

Willig, C. (2008a) *Introducing Qualitative Research in Psychology* (2nd edn). Maidenhead: McGraw-Hill/Open University Press.

Willig, C. (2008b) A phenomenological investigation of the experience of taking part in extreme sport, *Journal of Health Psychology*, 13(5): 690–702.

Willig, C. (2009a) Reflections on 'interpretation', inspired by Sophie Calle's 'Take care of yourself', *Qualitative Methods in Psychology Newsletter*, 7 (May): 12–14.

Willig, C. (2009b) 'Unlike a rock, a tree, a horse or an angel ...': reflections on the struggle for meaning during the process of cancer diagnosis, *Journal of Health Psychology*, 14(2): 181–9.

Willig, C. (2011) Cancer diagnosis as discursive capture: phenomenological repercussions of being positioned within dominant constructions of cancer, *Social Science and Medicine*, 73(6): 897–903.

Willig, C. (2012) Perspectives on the epistemological bases for qualitative research, in H. Cooper (ed.) *The Handbook of Research Methods in Psychology*. Washington, DC: American Psychological Association.

Willig, C. and Stainton Rogers, W. (eds.) (2008a) *The SAGE Handbook of Qualitative Research in Psychology*. London: Sage.

Willig, C. and Stainton-Rogers, W. (2008b) Introduction, in C. Willig and W. Stainton-Rogers (eds.) *The SAGE Handbook of Qualitative Research in Psychology*. London: Sage.

Wortman, C.B. and Dunkel-Schetter, C. (1979) Interpersonal relationships and cancer: a theoretical analysis, *Journal of Social Issues*, 35(1): 120–55.

Index

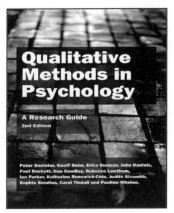

QUALITATIVE METHODS IN PSYCHOLOGY
A Research Guide
Second Edition

Peter Banister

9780335243051 (Paperback)
October 2011

eBook also available

Qualitative Methods in Psychology: A Research Guide, the *Second Edition,*
provides advanced undergraduate and postgraduate psychology students with
an accessible introduction to qualitative methods. It combines a solid grounding
in the theory behind research methods, as well as serving as a practical guide to
conducting qualitative investigations and a critical assessment of these methods.

Key features:

- Covers the BPS syllabus for Qualitative Methods
- Shows readers how to evaluate methods critically
- Includes new chapters on phenomenology, psychosocial analysis,
  narrative inquiry, future directions for qualitative research, emerging forms
  of representation, and problems in qualitative research

www.openup.co.uk

OPEN UNIVERSITY PRESS
McGraw - Hill Education

QUALITATIVE RESEARCH METHODS IN PSYCHOLOGY
Combining Core Approaches

Nollaig Frost

9780335241514 (Paperback)
June 2011

eBook also available

Qualitative Research Methods in Psychology: From Core to Combined Approaches provides research students with practical guidance and thoughtful debate on carrying out qualitative research in psychology. The book is written in a clear and accessible manner designed to support students from the beginning of their research experience at undergraduate level through to postgraduate research and beyond.

Key features:

- Includes case studies and group projects
- Provides problem-based questions
- Incorporates reference lists

www.openup.co.uk

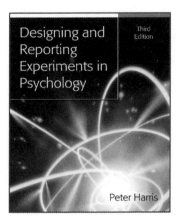

DESIGNING AND REPORTING EXPERIMENTS IN PSYCHOLOGY
Third Edition

Peter Harris

9780335221783 (Paperback)
2008

eBook also available

This book will help undergraduate psychology students to write practical reports of experimental and other quantitative studies in psychology. It is designed to help with every stage of the report writing process including what to put in each section and recommendations for formatting and style. It also discusses how to design a study, including how to use and report relevant statistics. As such, the book acts both as an introduction and reference source to be used throughout an undergraduate course.

Key features:

- Provides new pedagogy website icons
- Includes a completely revised section on how to find and cite references
- Gives advice on the ethics of conducting research on the Internet

www.openup.co.uk

OPEN UNIVERSITY PRESS
McGraw - Hill Education

**INTRODUCING QUALITATIVE RESEARCH
IN PSYCHOLOGY**
Second Edition

Carla Willig

9780335221158 (Paperback)
2008

eBook also available

Introducing Qualitative Research in Psychology is a vital resource for students new to qualitative psychology. It offers a clear introduction to the topic by taking six different approaches to qualitative methods and explaining when each one should be used, the procedures and techniques involved, and any limitations associated with such research.

Key features:

- Contains more interactive exercises and tasks
- Includes three qualitative research reports with annotations highlighting key issues for novice researchers
- Examines appropriate ways of writing up research

www.openup.co.uk

OPEN UNIVERSITY PRESS
McGraw - Hill Education